# Nation Building in South Africa

NATIONAL LOTTERIES COMMISSION
LOTTO FUNDED

First published by the Institute for Preservation and Development in 2023
P.O. Box 4154
The Reeds
Pretoria
0158
South Africa

PRINT ISBN       978-0-7961-2055-7
EBOOK ISBN       978-0-7961-2055-4

This book has been reviewed by independent external reviewers.

Set in Stempel Garamond 10.5/14pt

# Nation Building in South Africa

Internal Migration of the African People
and the Transformation of their Ethnicity,
Languages, Surnames, Culture and
Intangible Cultural Heritage

Edited by Sehlare Makgetlaneng

INSTITUTE FOR PRESERVATION AND DEVELOPMENT
PRETORIA

# Contents

# Acknowledgements

This book is based on the research funded by the National Lotteries Commission of South Africa. We are greatly indebted to it for its grant for the publication of this book project. We register our sincere appreciation for its support to us as chapter contributors. This support enabled us to produce and provide knowledge vital to the understanding of how the process of migration of the African people of South Africa transformed their ethnicity, languages, surnames, culture and intangible cultural heritage and how their view primarily in terms of ethnic, linguistic, cultural and intangible cultural heritage diversity or differences is a misunderstanding if not a distortion of their ethnic, linguistic, cultural and intangible cultural heritage commonality. We sincerely thank colleagues for having made serious efforts in producing and providing evidence in their chapters that African people of South Africa share a common history of ethnicity, languages, surnames, culture and intangible cultural heritage that disputes a popular, hegemonic and dominant view that over-emphasise that they are different in terms of ethnicity, languages, surnames, culture and intangible cultural heritage. The celebrated thesis of ethnic, linguistic, cultural and intangible cultural heritage diversity is the sophisticated version of the policy of dividing Africans so as to continue ruling them economically and financially in their African country in which they are the decisive majority of its national population.

# About the Contributors

**Sehlare Makgetlaneng** is Extraordinary Professor, School of Government Studies, North-West University and Research Associate, School of Social Sciences, University of Limpopo. His research interests include political governance in Africa's development, race-class and internal-external dialectical and organic relationship in African and global affairs and politics, and key issues, processes and developments in African and global affairs and how they affect South Africa, Southern Africa, Africa and the globe. His recent publications include his books, The African Renaissance Project of Thabo Mbeki: Its South African Roots and Targets (2022), and Kwame Nkrumah and the Pan-African Ideal: Debates and Contestations (2021).

**Monicca Thulisile Bhuda,** an indigenous knowledge systems scholar, children's book author, award winning academic and cultural expert, coordinates a course and lectures on culture and heritage studies at the University of Mpumalanga. She has Honours, Masters and PhD in Indigenous Knowledge Systems. Her PhD research focused on Ndebele mathematics as a means of cultural identity. Her research interests include decolonisation of education, African indigenous research methodologies, traditional medicine, traditional customary laws and leadership, promotion of indigenous languages, indigenous knowledge preservation, protection, management and dissemination.

**Theodore Nkadimeng Mahosi** is a Senior Lecturer in the Department of Humanities, Creative Arts and Education, Faculty of Educational Sciences, Walter Sisulu University, Mthatha Campus, Eastern Cape Province, South Africa. His areas of specialisation include Afrocentricity, research methodology, traditional leadership matters and African history. He is a member of the South African National Geographic Names Council, the Limpopo Province Geographic Names Committee and the Limpopo Province Archives and Records Services Council. He is included in the Data Base for Investigative Committee to Resolve Traditional Leadership Disputes in the Limpopo Province. He served as a member of the Kgatla Limpopo Provincial Commission on Traditional Leadership Disputes and Claims (2012-2017).

**Rachidi Molapo,** writer and researcher with extensive experience, served as a lecturer and researcher at the University of Cape Town, the University of Western Cape and the University of Venda. He is an independent scholar with research interests on exile, the countryside, gender, history and the land question.

**Busile Cynthia Ndhlovu,** a PhD candidate in African Languages, Department of Humanities, at the University of Johannesburg, is a member of the African Language Association of Southern Africa. A lecturer and Honours Co-ordinator for Siswati at the University of Mpumalanga, School of Social Sciences, Faculty of Economics, Development and Business Sciences. Her research interests include African languages: Applied linguistic, literature and Literary theories, Indigenous Knowledge System, language history dynamics (Nguni language-cluster), Gender Based Violence and related social issues. Her recent published works include book chapters on the African Transformation Agenda to Promote Inclusive Education. Her journal article on the Indigenous Knowledge System is scheduled to be published in 2023.

# Introduction
## Specific Objectives, Relevance and Service of the Book to South Africa

*Sehlare Makgetlaneng*

We introduce this book by providing information about its purpose and specific objectives. Central to its purpose are its relevance and service to South Africa in its policy efforts to achieve its nation building agenda objectives through the theoretical and practical call for national integration of its African people and their fellow South Africans in their struggle to resolve the national question.

This book interrogates the popular, hegemonic and dominant view of ethnic, linguistic and cultural diversity in the case of the African people of South Africa. It uses the process of their migration within their country in executing this task. This process affected issues, processes and developments of their ethnicity, languages, surnames and culture as Africans of particular ethnic groups moved from some parts of South Africa to its other parts where they settled permanently. This movement of the African people internally within South Africa has profound transformative impact on their ethnicity, languages, surnames, culture and intangible cultural heritage such as the traditional leadership. Not only ethnicity and culture of Africans who left their original locations for other locations in other provinces were transformed, their languages and surnames were also transformed. Some key factors characterising their intangible cultural heritage such as the traditional leadership were also transformed in the sense that some traditional leaders became leaders of Africans whose ethnicity and languages are not that of those who became their leaders.

The process of internal migration of the African people within their country and how it transformed their ethnicity, languages, surnames, culture and intangible cultural heritage is pivotal to the production and provision of scholarly interrogation of the popular, hegemonic and dominant view of ethnic, linguistic and cultural diversity of the African people.

This book attempts to produce and provide evidence that African people of South Africa share a common history of ethnicity, languages, surnames, culture and intangible cultural heritage that disputes this popular, hegemonic and dominant view of their ethnic, linguistic and cultural diversity. Central to this view is that they are ethnically, linguistically and culturally diverse or different. Rather than recognising the fact that they have continued living together in social relations of common history of ethnicity, languages, surnames and culture, this view has been successful in forging and sustaining the narrative of ethnic, linguistic and cultural differences which is popularly, hegemonically and dominantly celebrated in the name of ethnic, linguistic and cultural diversity. The celebrated thesis of ethnic, linguistic, cultural and intangible cultural heritage diversity in the case of the African people is the sophisticated version of the policy of dividing Africans so as to continue ruling them economically and financially in an African country in which they are the decisive majority of its national population.

Has the celebrated thesis of ethnic, linguistic, cultural and intangible cultural heritage diversity which has become more popular, hegemonic and dominant contributed towards the ethnification of the African people of South Africa even by some of its African scholars to the point that it is used to discriminate against other Africans on the basis of ethnicity since the end of a settler colonial and racist rule in 1994? Has it contributed towards an increase in a number of South Africans who are ethnic-centric in their view of themselves as Africans and in their view of their fellow Africans of their country since 1994? Is the increased intensity of ethnic identity and identity view of South Africans the consequence of this ethnic, linguistic, cultural and intangible cultural heritage diversity thesis?

What should be our political, economic and ideological

position on ethnicity and ethnic groups? Should the fact that the colonial state and capital or the social forces of colonialism and racism used ethnicity in advancing their agenda and interests be central to our position on ethnicity? Did they not use any means necessary in advancing their agenda and interests? What about state and capital in neo-colonial African countries in which state houses are occupied by Africans who use ethnicity in advancing their agenda and interests? Are African enemies of African people and their regions and continent not use any means necessary in advancing their agenda and interests?

Despite the fact that African languages have no word for ethnicity and no expression for ethnic group, the issue of ethnicity should be taken into account seriously on political, economic and ideological fronts of the struggle for the resolution of the national question through the nation building project in South Africa. This theoretical and practical task is necessary to achieve the equality of the material conditions and rights or what the African National Congress (ANC) refers to as a better life for all. Pointing out that that "history has stripped Africa's people of the dignity of building their nations on their own indigenous values, institutions, and heritage" and that the "modern African state is the product of Europe, not Africa," Francis Mading Deng maintains that:

> To attempt at this late date to return to ancestral identities and resources as bases for building the modern African nation would risk the collapse of many countries. At the same time, to disregard ethnic realities would be to build on loose sand, also a high-risk exercise.[1]

He then raises the question as to whether it is "possible to consolidate the framework of the modern African state while giving recognition and maximum utility to the component elements of ethnicities, cultures, and aspirations for self-determination."[2] He answers this question when he points out that ethnicity is

> more than skin color or physical characteristics, more than language, song, and dance. It is the embodiment of values, institutions, and patterns of behavior, a composite whole representing a people's historical experience, aspirations,

and world view. Deprive a people of their ethnicity, their culture, and you deprive them of their sense of direction or purpose.[3]

Pointing out that analysts have "tended to have two views of the role of ethnicity" in African conflicts. While some "see ethnicity as a source of conflict; others see it as a tool used by political entrepreneurs to promote their ambitions" and that in "reality, it is both."[4] The point is that:

Ethnicity, especially when combined with territorial identity, is a reality that exists independently of political maneuvers. To argue that ethnic groups are unwitting tools of political manipulation is to underestimate a fundamental reality. On the other hand, ethnicity is clearly a source for political manipulation and entrepreneurship.[5]

Central to Deng's position is that as "long as the Africans avoid confronting the issue of ethnicity and fail to develop norms and means for managing diversity within the framework of unity, peace and stability will continue to elude the pluralistic state."[6]

Deng's has no solution to the problem he created. The solution is not a lack of national identity. National identity is the product of the theorical and practical demonstration of the political leadership conducive for the achievement of the national integration through the service to the country and its people in the strategic area of sustainable development. For political leaders to achieve national integration on the basis of the qualitative improvement of the material conditions and rights of the citizens, leaders should "legitimately exercise power and authority over the control and management of the country's affairs in the interest of the people and in accordance with the principles of justice, equity, accountability and transparency."[7]

Claude Ake maintains the position that hostility to expressions of ethnic identity is misguided in that ethnicity is not a problem. Central to his position is that:

It is not clear that ethnicity by itself generates conflict or that it is inherently threatening. One may prefer one's kinfolk or one's community without being antagonistic to others. It is odd that those who consider ethnicity as a manipulative instrument are also the ones who regard it as a problem. If ethnicity is manufactured at will and manipulated to serve any number of selfish purposes, then it is only an 'object,' the case for calling it a cause of the numerous problems regularly attributed to it would not be sustainable. Conflicts arising from the construction of ethnicity to conceal exploitation by building solidarity across class lines, conflicts arising from appeal to ethnic support in the face of vanishing political legitimacy and from the manipulation of ethnicity to divide colonized people, are not ethnic problems but problems of a particular political dynamics which just happens to be pinned on ethnicity. By the same token, solutions to these problems must address the political dynamics in question, not ethnicity.[8]

Ake continues in his respectful answer to his question, what is the problem of ethnicity in Africa? His answer is respectful in that he is known as a scholar who does not abuse those he disagrees with on issues, processes, developments, social orders or systems, institutions and organisations. Throughout his life as a scholar, he addressed himself to issues, not to individuals raising and either maintaining or defending them or criticising or rejecting them. He was a truly human being considerate of his fellow human beings. His passing away was a great loss not only to Nigeria, West Africa, Africa, the South but also to the world as a whole in the struggle for the equality of the material conditions and rights. In answering his questions, he maintains that:

> If the current state of scholarship on ethnicity and development is any guide, it is apparently a problem for development; ethnicity supposedly epitomizes backwardness and constrains the development of Africa. This presupposition is misleading, however, for it is development rather than the people and their culture which has to be problematized. Development has to begin by taking people and their culture as they are, not as they might be, and proceeding from there to define the problems and strategies for development. Otherwise, the problematic of development becomes a tautology. The people are not and

cannot be a problem just by being what they are, even if part of what they are is ethnic consciousness. Our treatment of ethnicity and ethnic consciousness reflects this tendency to problematize the people and their culture, an error that continues to push Africa into confusion.

In all but a few African countries there is an obsession with ethnicity and its problems. Even if this interest is hostile, it nonetheless underlines the fact that it is a most significant element of the African reality. It that is the case, we do violence to the African reality by failing to explore the possibilities of ethnicity. In failing to follow the contours and its rhythm, for that would be part of starting with the way we are instead of discarding if for what we might be. The point of course is not to romanticize the past and be captive to it but to recognize what is on the ground and strive to engineer a more efficient, less traumatic, and less self-destructive social transformation.[9]

Ake concludes:

To the question, 'Is there a problem of ethnicity in Africa?,' I am inclined to answer that there is no such problem, that is, in the sense that ethnicity is inherently a problem. We see ethnic conflict too ubiquitously – in ethnic misrepresentations of survival strategies, in emancipatory projects and strategies of power. We confuse our abuse of ethnicity with its inherent abusiveness. Most importantly, we tend to forget that even though ethnicity might be constructed it is also a living presence, an important part of what many Africans are. Surely, part of what we are as people who must find themselves, most likely in the desperate act of inventing a cultural identity to assert a humanity and set ourselves on the path of becoming a going concern. How we are fabricated, cultural identity and all, cannot be a problem except in the context of some notion of how we might be. Even then, what can be appropriately problematized is not the way we are but the process of 'becoming.' It cannot be desirable for Africa to return to the past or to stagnate in a present which promises no future. Africa must move on. But this forward movement has to be in the direction of self-development and self-fulfillment, not self-denial and alienation. It must begin with the crystallization of our identity and build on what we are, ethnic and all. For those who do not know who they are cannot really know where they are going.[10]

We gave Ake extensive platform for him to share with us his position on ethnicity given our position that the issue of ethnicity should be taken into account on political, economic and ideological fronts of the struggle for the resolution of the national question through the nation building project in South Africa. This is necessary to achieve the equality of the material conditions and rights or what the ANC refers to as a better life for all.

The division of South Africa into ethnic groups, like into racial groups, is not in itself the problem. It cannot be solved because it is not the problem. The reality is that even in its socialist and communist eras it will continue being divided into ethnic and racial groups. There are no ethnic and racial divisions in the country to be solved. It is its division into social classes which is the problem of antagonistic interests not only of different interests which should be solved by ending the existence of social classes through the establishment of a classless society.[11]

Its primary target being the popular, hegemonic and dominant ethnic, linguistic, cultural and intangible cultural heritage diversity view of the African people of South Africa, this book serves as an intellectual and scholarly farewell to their tribalisation. It renders this service by making serious efforts to be of vital importance for the South African nation building agenda. It is of theoretical and practical creative use in forging unity and solidarity among Africans of various ethnic, linguistic and cultural groups. It serves to contribute towards the achievement of social solidarity in an environment where ethnicity is often associated with conflicts and tensions among Africans whose ethnicity, languages and culture are not the same and are emphasised if not over-emphasised in the name of ethnic, linguistic, cultural and intangible cultural heritage diversity or differences. The achievement of this social solidarity will be a substantial and welcome addition to South Africa's policy efforts to achieve objectives of its nation building project and best and effectively contribute towards Southern African regional integration and African continental integration. The achievement of national integration through nation building by any country is indispensable to its theoretical and practical contribution towards regional integration and continental integration. South Africa is the ethnic, linguistic and cultural microcosm of the majority parts of Southern Africa. Its African ethnic groups and their languages, surnames, culture and intangible cultural heritage are socio-political and historical formations in Botswana, Eswatini, Lesotho, Malawi, Mozambique, Namibia, Tanzania, Zambia and Zimbabwe. This socio-historical relationship should be its proud national asset or theoretical and practical weapon in its contribution towards the achievement of Southern African regional integration for its to walk together with its Southern African Development Community partners in their contribution towards the achievement of African continental integration.

As the editor of this book volume, we are conscious of the unevenness of the length of its chapters. This was due to reasons beyond our control as the editor. Topics researched and the data collected; and the socio-historical periodisation of its chapters are some of the key reasons behind their unevenness. The specific objectives of this book volume are to:

- interrogate the popular, hegemonic and dominant view of ethnic, linguistic and cultural diversity in the case of the African people of South Africa;
- identify migration of African people within South Africa and its transformation of their ethnicity, languages, surnames, culture and intangible cultural heritage;
- explore the views of scholars and experts of socio-historical interlinkages among African ethnic groups, their languages, surnames, culture and intangible cultural heritage; and
- identify how best and most effective migration of African people within South Africa and its transformation of their ethnicity, languages, surnames, culture and intangible cultural heritage can be used in serving the nation building project and the cause for national integration in South Africa.

The relevance and service of this book to South Africa are to:

- help in forging and sustaining the national network of alliances, friendships and commonality of interests and common patterns of cooperation among African people of South Africa of various ethnic, linguistic and cultural groups;
- use the past of the African people as guide for the future as a means to generate invaluable ideas serving as the driving force of action by which to establish the truly South African community as a basis of social life;
- help in finding and detecting the dangers inherent in the popular and hegemonic view of ethnic, linguistic and cultural diversity in the case of African people of South Africa in the cause to resolve the national question in South Africa, and
- set the stage for dialogue, debate and deliberations on the popular and hegemonic view of ethnic, linguistic and cultural diversity in the case of the African people of South Africa as a means to seek a theoretical and practical basis for a concerted action by state and non-state actors in their efforts to resolve the national question in South Africa.

Briefly, the relevance and service of the book to South Africa is to serve it in its efforts to achieve its nation building agenda objectives through the theoretical and practical call for national integration of its African people and their fellow South Africans in their struggle to resolve the national question.

The resolution of the national question in South Africa cannot be achieved without its African intellectuals playing a leading role in using their leadership of political parties, and civil society organisations, their individual knowledge and skills within the state, capital and civil society organisations as a proud collective national asset towards this progressive goal or objective. They are better placed more than intellectuals of all other racial groups in the country in using their strength and resources to ensure that the national leadership and institutions work towards the achievement of this national goal and organise the South African people in defeating their internal and external enemies. As producers of knowledge, creators of leaders and establishers of institutions, they are more than intellectuals of all other racial groups organically rooted in the African languages spoken internally in the country and are in a better position to best and most effectively mobilise socio-political, ideological and organisational resources necessary for the resolution of the national question. They are linguistically, culturally and in other life aspects more interlinked with the African working class than intellectuals of all other South African racial groups. The African working class is central to the national social fabric more than the working class of all other racial groups. It is the social class at the heart of the national socio-economic life in the most fundamental way. All these factors charactering the African people make them indispensable to the successful nation building project and the resolution of the national question in the country.

Theory emerges out of practice and in turn serves practice as state and non-state actors confront problems for their resolution. The development of theoretical positions that interrogate the popular, hegemonic and dominant view of ethnic, linguistic and cultural diversity in the case of the African people of South Africa as required by the need of identifying how best and most effective their migration within their country and its transformation of their ethnicity, languages, surnames, culture and intangible cultural heritage can be used in serving the cause for its nation building is not purely or exclusively an academic task. It is a task specified by practice as state and non-state actors confront challenges or problems faced in forging and sustaining the national network of alliances, friendships and commonality of interests and common patterns of cooperation among South Africans, especially Africans who it is emphasised and over-emphasised that they belong to different ethnic, linguistic and cultural groups.

In our opposition to the tribalisation of the African people of South Africa, we register our sincere appreciation of the Daily Maverick's position that the popular, hegemonic and dominant diversity perspective raises the question as to whether there is "one thing that we can all relate to, that makes" we South Africans South Africans. Congratulating the Springboks for having fought on "with its fibre of their very being" in their World Cup quarterfinal victory, it articulated its position on this issue when it pointed out that:

In a country of such huge diversity, 12 official languages, a melting point of different cultures and histories, it is an art to pinpoint what exactly defines "being South African" … that one thing that we can all relate to, that makes us "us."[12]

# Chapter One
## The Socio-Historical Relationship among Bapedi, Batswana and Basotho: Issues of Ethnicity, Languages, Surnames, Culture and Intangible Cultural Heritage

*Sehlare Makgetlaneng*

### The Purpose of the Chapter

This chapter provides analysis of the socio-historical relationship among Bapedi, Batswana and Basotho as the process of their ethnic, linguistic, cultural and intangible cultural heritage commonality. Their surnames are an integral part of their commonality in this relationship. This commonality is of strategic importance to the resolution of the national question through nation building project.

### Ethnicity, Language, Surnames, Culture and Intangible Cultural Heritage of Bapedi, Batswana Basotho: The Position of Paul S. Landau

In his book on the popular politics in the history of South Africa from 1400 to 1948, Paul S. Landau rejects popular, dominant and hegemonic socio-historical vocabulary used for "Bantu-Sotho speaking people" and adopts a new lexicon of naming them and their places. He identified the existence of a political process he refers to as "one of overlapping movement and the persistence and transmutation of authority-building practices[1] that propelled political actions in the early and mid-colonisation period. In providing history of African people before they were transformed into tribes by Europeans, he prefers a centralising role that amalgamated people of various progeny into an association governed from a location he refers to as "prestige place association" or "prestige place." This is moshate or ka difokeng in Sotho. Pointing out that "prestige place" or "prestige place association" signifies "political hegemony and power,"[2] he maintains that all prestige places and their descendants established themselves on a similar principle that used "twin court" to attach outsiders and accord junior houses recognition within the "prestige place" in "the idiom of brotherhood."[3] Genealogies were evaded to bring residents who are not related into the ranked descent line. In his words:

> Collateral lines of men split off, and others formed new alliances in their own interests; sometimes they achieved their aims with a military posture, sometimes without one…. Genealogies might merge by consensus and cover the tracks of amalgamations.[4]

As "strangers" or immigrants are welcomed and accommodated into a new social formation through "a political tradition" and its capability "nurtured"[5] for this task, they became its members enjoying rights enjoyed by the established community members.

Landau rejects identity categories such as Bakwena and Batlhaping. His reason is that the "ethnic or tribal approach results only in a fog of particularity."[6] He uses, in their place, their totemic or place identities. In the case of Bakwena, he uses" the crocodile people" or kwena, "crocodile." In the case of Batlhaping, he uses "people of the fish place" tlhapi, "fish."

Language is of vital importance in his view of Africans. He pays a particular attention to what he regards as "analogous morphemes" that signify senior-junior court relationship, which served as the basis of solving problems emerging out of the inclusion of outsiders into royal authority.[7] The recognition of the senior-junior court relationship is important in that it helps to account for the constant movement from the senior traditional leadership. It is a product of splits and conflicts of social forces leading to relocation from and entry into already established or settled areas under a leadership of a senior leader.[8] His view of language as of vital importance in his view of Africans is challenged by his notion of "Bantu-Sotho speaking people." Given the fact that there are other Africans who are not Sothos who speak Sotho, it is appropriate to speak of Sotho referring to those who became Sothos. The point is that Sotho people speak also other languages which are not Sotho. The fact that people are Sotho-speaking does not necessarily mean that they are Sotho.

**The Linguistic Commonality of Bapedi, Batswana and Basotho**
The over-emphasise of ethnic, linguistic and cultural diversity of the African people and its use in promoting the negation of their ethnic, linguistic and cultural commonality is responsible for the popular, hegemonic and dominant position that Sepedi or Northern Sotho, Setswana or Western Sotho and Sesotho or Southern Sotho are diverse or different languages. This is contrary to the reality that are common not diverse or different. This position was promoted and used by the forces of settler colonialism in their struggle to divide African people in general and the Sotho group in particular for the strategic purpose of ruling them. This reality is supported by P. Eric Louw when he maintains that:

> The Afrikaner nationalism built on and systematized the colonial British divide-and-rule policy. Since whites constitute a minority of South Africa's population, the most effective way to rule was to prevent the 75% black-African population from cohering into a unified group. A key means of achieving this was an active state-sponsored encouragement of African tribalism in South Africa. The central feature of apartheid was the creation of tribal political 'homelands' (originally called 'Bantustans'), each tied to a separate black 'nation' with its their own language. The 'nations' and 'national languages' engineered into existence in this way were: ... Bophuthatswana (Tswana); Lebowa (North Sotho); Qwa Qwa (South Sotho).[9]

Pointing out that African "national languages and the homelands have more to do with the geo-political divide-and-rule needs of apartheid than with linguistic criteria," he concludes that the Sotho language-cluster is one of the two African language-clusters.[10] Another language cluster is the Nguni language consisting of Ndebele, Shangaan-Tsonga, Swati, Venda, Xhosa and Zulu.

It is correct to refer to Setswana as Western Sotho as an integral part of Sotho language-cluster in the same way other two members of Sotho language-cluster are referred to and Batswana as Western Sothos, Bapedi as North Sothos and Basotho as Southern Sothos are referred to. South Africa has two main African language-clusters. By maintaining that they are not Sothos, a considerable number of Batswana have excluded and continue excluding themselves from the Sotho group of which they are an integral member. As the result of this socio-historical development, words shared by Sotho language-cluster are incorrectly regarded as Tswana words only. The notion of the Sotho-Tswana people[11] is challenged by some scholars who use it. One of these scholars is Martin Legassick. They are basically the Sotho people. He supported this position when he pointed out that people who are referred to as Sotho-Tswana are Sotho or that Sotho is the generic term for the Sothos.[12] While using the notion of the Sotho-Tswana people,[13] at the same time, he rejects it by maintaining the correct position that people who are referred to as the Sotho-Tswana are Sotho as they are generically called.

### The Ethnic, Linguistic, Cultural and Intangible Cultural Heritage Commonality of Bapedi, Batswana and Basotho: The Position of Thato Mabolaeng Maryanne Monyakane

Monyakane in his 2016 doctorate thesis provides the ethnic, linguistic, cultural and intangible cultural commonality of the Sotho group. On the issues of migration and language, he maintains that as people moved to find their separate territorial spaces for settlement, the geographical distance played a key role in the way the language is used and its variations are developed. He concludes that despite this geographical distance, these language variations are not original. The consequence is that they are "similar" and of "one origin."

Monyakane's position is supported by the commonality of surnames of the Sotho group. Surnames of Bapedi, Batswana and Basotho are common. They share surnames such as Mokwena, Mokoena, Mokuena, Mogale, Mohale, Mashishi, or Masisi. While names such as Lekoko, Nkwane, Sehlare, Shopeng, Temane, are first names of Bapedi, they are surnames of Batswana. Shopeng is spelt Shuping among Batswana. Lekoko and Shuping are surnames of traditional leaders among Batswana. Shopeng as first name among Bapedi is originally from the surname, Shuping among Batswana. Ba ga Shuping upon arrival in Bopedi where they permanently settled, their surname was slightly transformed into Shopeng by Sepedi. As originally Bakgatla ba ga Mmakau, a section of Batswana, upon arrival in Bopedi where they permanently settled, Sepedi transformed their ethnicity from Batswana into Bapedi. They are still referred to as Bakgatla ba Mmakau in Bopedi.

Surnames, among others, such as Diale and Kau which originally were only those of Batswana whose bearers upon arrival in Bopedi were not transformed by Sepedi. It is only their ethnicity as Batswana which was transformed into Bapedi upon their arrival in Bopedi where they permanently settled. Despite being called Bapedi, they still refer to themselves and are still referred to as Bakgatla among Bapedi.

On the issue of intangible cultural heritage, he maintains that there are common patterns of cooperation and alliances characterised by traditional leaders to acquire power and authority in their vicinity. In the case of those who exercise power and authority as senior traditional leadership, he maintains that:

> A central chiefdom cooperates with other chiefdoms through a formal agreement to unite in governance. The leader of the central chiefdom acts as a coordinator and senior chief.

Monyakane is referring to the king or the queen. While kings and queens occupy their positions on the basis of birth and are recognised by the South African state, their agreement with other traditional leaders of the same ethnic group and people under their leadership is critical for their continued legitimacy and credibility of their leadership. This is despite the fact that the institution of traditional leadership is recognised by the national constitution. Kgoshi ke kgoshi ka sechaba not because of the state and government.

Legitimacy and credibility are critical in the continued content and operations of the institution of traditional leadership and those who lead it. Without them it will be difficult to have the requisite cooperation between the king or the queen and other traditional leaders and between them and members of communities under their leadership. On this required working relationship between leaders and the led, Monyakane maintains that on issues of "governance and land," Sothos have "political systems" that "indicate the same origin." They operate as "clans, chiefdoms, groups or as a nation, to allocate resources" particularly those which are natural. Their "coming together as collectives of communities is the natural effect of a booming population looking for amicable means to share resource as a Sotho society." This commonality within the Sotho group applies to the case of the Nguni group consisting of the Ndebele, Shangaan-Tsonga, Swati, Xhosa, Venda and the Zulu. According to him, "the boundaries" created among African people of South Africa into "Nguni and Sotho" are "artificial" and should be brought to an end to enable them to truly "reclaim their shared heritage of culture and identity." Briefly, he provided evidence of ethnic, linguistic, cultural and intangible cultural commonality not only of Bapedi, Batswana and Basotho, but also of other African people of South Africa.

What is regarded as their ethnic, linguistic, cultural and intangible cultural diversity or differences is a misunderstanding of their transformation of their ethnicity, languages, surnames, culture and intangible cultural heritage as a result of their internal migration within South Africa. This can best be understood if we come to grips with the reality that there was a time when Southern Africa was a borderless social formation in which Africans where under the leadership of traditional leaders. It is for this reason that traditional leaders are referred to by the African people as the owners of the soil or beng ba mabu in Sepedi. It is for this reason that Landau maintains that popular politics of South Africa is an integral part of the Southern African regional history and the history of its people should be viewed dialectically and organically as a process which is interlinked. His position is that, firstly, the "nationalist understanding of popular politics as the twentieth-century movement to transcend tribes and chiefs unwittingly accepts an imperialist and ultimately apartheid vision of Africans' history." Secondly, the history of political organisations, and "not just resistance, may indeed be traced to South Africa's past." Thirdly, the history of South Africa "over the centuries should not be abstracted from the history of Lesotho, Botswana, even

Zimbabwe (nor Swaziland and Mozambique." Fourthly, Lesotho was "a mass political movement in the heartland of the country before it became a bordered labor reserve and "nation-state." Fifthly, "Europeans dispossessed those in their way and combated, translated, and redirected Africans' claims" through wars which led, among others to migrations. The history of African people of South Africa included "great turmoil, wars and migrations."

Migrations transformed not only ethnicity, languages, surnames, culture and intangible cultural heritage of the African people as they move from their original places to other locations upon which they permanently settled among other African people. Issues "of great turmoil" and "wars" as characterised the history of the African people also affected their intangible cultural heritage such as traditional leadership. They also transformed their names as they contributed towards some Africans particularly traditional leaders acquiring new names and leaving their original names. This development characterised Sekhukhune 1 in his leadership of Bapedi in the struggle against imperialism and colonialism and his efforts to defeat Mampuru 11 to be the king of Bapedi. His extraordinary achievements and leadership roles during conflicts and wars with the Boers.

## The Handling of Traditional Leadership Disputes and Claims by the Commission and Courts as a Means to Restore Bapedi Kingship to its Rightful Lineage as an Intangible Cultural Heritage: The Case between Sekhukhune and Mampuru Royal Families

The Commission on Traditional Leadership Disputes and Claims (the Nhlapo Commission) under the leadership of Thandabantu Nhlapo as its chairperson was appointed by President Thabo Mbeki in 2004 to investigate and decide all kingship disputes and claims by considering and applying "customary law and the customs of the relevant traditional community as they were when the events occurred." It was announced to the public through the Government Gazette published on 22 October 20004. Its mandate was to restore senior traditional leadership among African ethnic groups to its rightful bearers. The rightful king of Bapedi was one of disputes to be decided and claim to be resolved. The Commission provides a historical background of Bapedi as follows:

The Bapedi community originates from Bakgatla ba Makau,

a Batswana clan, which resided near the Vaal river during the sixteenth century. They were led by Tabane who had five sons namely, Diale, Kgwadi, Kgetsi, Matsibolo and Mosia.

Diale was the heir and successor to Tabane. Diale had a wife, Mmathobela. According to legend the child cried whilst in her womb. The community wanted to kill both mother and child, as they perceived this incident to be a bad omen.

Diale left with his wife and followers. He eventually settled at Fateng, close to the present Fort Weeber.

The Bakgatla who left with Diale were later to constitute the core of Bapedi.

Thobela, the son of Diale, founded the Bapedi traditional community round about 1650. He settled at Mohlake, at the foot of Leolo Mountain. His royal palace was at Tšate.

The Commission concluded that the "kingship of Bapedi resorts under the lineage of Sekhukhune." The issue is the question as to whether it did justice to its mandate to restore the kingship of Bapedi to its rightful bearer. It acknowledged that Kgagudi Kenneth Sekhukhune was appointed as "the acting paramount chief" or king of Bapedi. He was appointed to serve as acting king so as to ensure that the future king was to be borne by bakgomana ba moshate (royal councillors) and the community. A senior wife was married by the community for this purpose. She is the mother of Sekwati Sekhukhune. The key issue was and remains that it is not so much that Rhyne Thulare and his son, Victor Thulare should have been recognised as the legitimate kings of Bapedi in succession. It is whether the Commission was correct in deciding that the "kingship of Bapedi resorts under the lineage of Sekhukhune" not that of Mampuru. It is for this reason that Bapedi Mamone Marota challenged its decision and the rulings of the North Gauteng High Court, Pretoria and the Supreme Court of Appeal based on this decision.

The Constitutional Court of South Africa in Bapedi Marota Mamone v Commission of Traditional Leadership Disputes and Claims and Others heard on 26 August 2014 and judgement delivered on 15 December 2014 in its majority judgement points out that:

The applicant persisted in the argument that the Commission

had ignored relevant that was placed before it and that the impugned decision was irrational. To substantiate the argument, the applicant contended:

While the High Court and the Supreme Court of Appeal have accepted and in fact ruled that Sekhukhune 1 legitimately usurped the kingship from Mampuru 11, because it was not "unusual at that time for kinship to be obtained by might and bloodshed," both the High Court and the Supreme Court of Appeal have nonetheless failed to locate any justification of this critical finding in the Commission's report. No reasons or specific examples of pertinent cases were provided by the Commission's report. No reasons or specific examples of pertinent cases were provided by the Commission in its report to substantiate its statement and to justify its deviation from the normal rules of customary succession by birth when it adopted the premise that "it was not unusual at the time for kingship to obtained by might and bloodshed. Applicant contended before the Supreme Court of Appeal (and also contends with respect before this Court) that no historical records show that the principal of usurpation of kinship was a custom among the Bapedi nation.

The applicant is correct. The reason why the Constitutional Court disagreed with the applicant on this key issue central to its mandate is because its task was not to find out whether its decision is correct or incorrect. It was to find whether its decision or determination was rational or irrational. The fact that Sekhukhune "usurped" the kingship from Mampuru "by might and bloodshed) was illegitimate. It is against African popular principle that molato ga o bole or that time does not change truth. The position that it was not "unusual at that time for kinship to be obtained by might and bloodshed" is irrational, incorrect and ahistorical. The applicant is correct that "no historical records show that the principle of usurpation of kinship was a custom among the Bapedi nation." The applicant is also correct that "the Commission failed in its report to substantiate its statement and to justify its deviation from the normal rules of customary succession by birth." The Constitutional Court incorrectly justified its decision by pointing out that:

> In essence the complaint captured in the statement above is that the Commission failed to apply the customary law rule of succession in reaching its decision. It will be recalled that we are concerned here with the decision to the effect that the kingship of the Bapedi traditional community presently resorts under the lineage of Kgoši Sekhukhune. It will also be remembered that in making this decision, the Commission had to consider events that occurred before 1 September 1927 which was the cut-off date for claims and disputes investigated by the Commission.

The 1st of September 1927 as cut-off date for traditional leadership disputes and claims investigated by the Nhlapo Commission is injustice to its mandate to resolve disputes and claims on the sensitive issue of the kingship of Bapedi as their intangible cultural heritage. It is contrary to the culture of the African people expressed in the Sepedi proverb, molato ga o bole or that time does not change the truth. This culture is also their law. According to Mogobe Ramose, a South African philosopher, one of the key scholars to have consistently popularised African philosophy, especially ubuntu philosophy internationally, "an injustice that endures in the historic memory of the injured is never erased merely because of the passage of time." Pointing out that African law is "flexible, unformalised, reasonable and linked to morality," that its flexibility "speaks to the idea that it is law without a center" in that "ubuntu philosophy holds that being is one continuous wholeness rather than a finite whole," he maintains that, culturally and legally, African understanding of "justice as the restoration of equilibrium means that law as a continually lived experience cannot reach a point of finality." Accordingly, "prescription is unknown in African law." The fact that "an injustice that endures in the historic memory of the injured is never erased merely because of the passage of time" can best be understood if we come to grips with the reality that the "African believes that time cannot change the truth" and that just as "the truth must be taken into consideration each time it becomes known, so must no obstacle be placed in the way of the search for it and its discovery."

The saying that truth does not have cut-off date is another

culture of Africans disputing the issue of cut-off date in resolving disputes and claims among themselves. This saying is another culture of Bapedi and other Africans ethnic groups disputing the issue of cut-off date in resolving traditional leadership disputes and claims and other disputes and claims within Bapedi in particular and among African people in general. The fact that cut-off date for kingship disputes and claims was set by Thabo Mbeki as the president of South Africa and five African members of the Constitutional Court saw nothing wrong with it and also their false argument supporting injustice raise fundamental questions. This injustice perpetrated by the Constitutional Court through its judges is based on a false argument in its majority judgement that the Nhlapo Commission was "required to establish the relevant customary law as it was when the events that gave rise to the dispute or claim occurred and to apply" the Traditional Leadership and Governance Framework Act 41 of 2003 in accordance with section 25(3) as the "relevant law," that the fact that Mampuru "lost the kingship in 1861 when Kgosi Sekhukhukhe 1 challenged and drove him out of the kingdom," that the fact that Sekhukhune usurped the kingship "through might and bloodshed" and that "customary law" that "existed at the time" recognised "the validity of this usurpation." This is totally incorrect. In addition, the legislation does not change the truth and customary law of succession to traditional leadership. It justified this injustice when it further ruled that "the decisions of specialist bodies must be treated with appropriate respect." This means incorrectly and unjustly that the decisions "must treated with appropriate respect" because they are made by "specialist bodies." The Constitutional Court should have ruled correctly and justly that the Nhlapo Commission should not have deviated from its ruling based on "the evidence before it" which it "considered" that "Kgosi Mampuru 11 was the rightful heir to the kingship in terms of the Bapedi customary law of succession at the time" with false arguments. Bapedi Marota Mamone were correct that the Commission acted irrationally and failed to take facts into account." However, the Constitutional Court ruled irrationally by ignoring these facts.

Justice Christopher Nyaole Jafta as "the dissent would have set aside the Commission's decision on the basis that it failed to consider relevant facts and was not rationally connected to the information before it and that it did not apply the relevant law that existed at the time, as it was obliged to do so by the Framework Act." His minority judgement, supported by Justice Baaitse Elizabeth "Bess" Nkabinde, that the Commission did not apply the relevant customary law that existed at the time as it was obliged to do so by the legislation was correct, just and rational. The majority judgement is incorrect, unjust and irrational. It is based on the political reality that Sekhukhune led Bapedi in the struggle against imperialism and colonialism. He is well-known and remembered for this role in the history of Bapedi. This is the basis of the Commission in its decision in favour of his descendants.

The Commission released its report on 15 January 2008. It ruled in favour of the Sekhukhune lineage against Bapedi Marota Mamone. It ruled that, despite the fact that Mampuru was the rightful heir, it "was not unusual for the kingship to be obtained through might and bloodshed and therefore the usurpation of the kingship by Sekhukhune" when he "challenged and drove Mampuru 11" was "in line with the common practice of that time." Accordingly, for the Commission, Sekhukhune, illegitimate heir, had legitimately became king. Mampuru did not win the kingship after he killed Sekhukhune. This is because he fled the kingdom and was executed for having killed Sekhukhune. The consequence is that Sekhukhune's descendants are incorrectly and unjustly recognised as Bapedi kings by the country which does not recognise governments which came into existence through "might and bloodshed."

Bapedi Marota Mamone instituted review proceedings on 26 August 2008 in the North Gauteng High Court in Pretoria. It asked it to set aside the Commission's decision by maintaining that it firstly ignored relevant facts and evidence placed before it and that in its report it did not mention Mampuru's inauguration. Secondly, it pointed out that its decision was irrational and not connected to the information placed before it and ignored reasons given by it. It pointed out that while it ruled that Sekhukhune's usurpation of kingship "by might and bloodshed" and that given the fact that it argued that as it "was in line with the common practice at that time," this was legitimate. Central to its problem on this issue was that it applied its argument inconsistently. It did not apply this argument in the case of Mampuru who returned and killed Sekhukhune. Therefore, according to it, its conclusion was irrational and bias.

The ruling of the Commission that Mampuru's killing of Sekhukhune did not take place in the context of a kingship contest and that immediately upon killing him and leaving the kingdom, after which he was captured and then executed and the ruling of the North Gauteng High Court in Pretoria was the criminal act does not hold water. The solution to this problem was to marry a woman to serve as a candle wife to bear an heir and successor for a deceased Mampuru who as a rightful heir was killed without having heir. This is how Africans continue solving this problem.

The Court concluded by explaining its role in review proceedings. It pointed out that it was only to test the Commission's decision for rationality not to re-take the decision or determine whether it agrees with the Commission and that owes its finding's expert a measure of deference. The Supreme Court of Appeal in dismissing the appeal by Bapedi Marota Mamone in its ruling on 28 March 2014 held that Mampuru's killing of Sekhukhune and subsequent flight from the kingdom were totally inconsistent with an intention to assume and exercise kingship power and that was "sheer murder." It was for these reasons that it dismissed the applicant's application with costs. Charles Mbikiwa's position on 25 August 2014 that if the Supreme Court of Appeal were to set aside the Nhlapo Commission's decision, it would probably not have an opportunity to re-determine the kingship. The reason is that the Framework Act was amended in 2009, curtailing the Commission's powers. Instead of determining the kingship, the Commission can only "make recommendations" to the President, who is free to depart from them as per its sections 25(2) (a) and 26 (2) to (4). This was already too late. In addition, it made it clear that it was not its task to either set aside or not set aside the decision of the Nhlapo Commission.

The rulings of the North Gauteng High Court, Pretoria, the Supreme Court of Appeal and the Constitutional Court based on the decision of the Nhlapo Commission are miscarriage of justice. They avoided to consider and apply the Bapedi customary law of succession in deciding the lineage in which the Bapedi kingship resorts. They contradicted themselves on key issues. They acknowledged that Mampuru was the rightful and legitimate heir to Sekwati 1 and that Sekhukhune challenged him for the kingship. Mampuru declined the challenge and fled the kingdom and that this was the demonstration of cowardice on his part and not the determination to be a king. Sekhukhune took over the kingdom through "might and bloodshed." Mampuru returned and killed Sekhukhune. This was his opposition to being regarded as a coward and not determined to be a king.

Realising that the issue of Sekhukhune having usurped kingship through might and bloodshed is not reliable and convincing, they argued incorrectly that Mampuru was a coward and not determined to be a king and that this was supported by the fact that he fled the kingdom. Why it is only Mampuru's killing of Sekhukhune regarded as "sheer murder?" Why did the Supreme Court of Appeal not apply this to the case of Sekhukhune and his supporters who engaged in what basically constituted "sheer murder?"

In the case between Kgagudi Kenneth Sekhukhune and Rhyne Thulare, the Constitutional Court subsequently bestowed the kingship to Victor Thulare. This was despite the fact that Rhyne Thulare was never inaugurated as a king. Kgagudi Kenneth Sekhukhune was never removed from kingship by sechaba or the nation and bakgoma and bakgomana. If its ruling in favour of Victor Thulare was the case of restorative justice, it should have applied to Mampuru. As we pointed out in this work, their argument legitimising the way Sekhukhune usurped kingship is contrary to the Bapedi customary law of succession to bogoši. This law is expressed, among others, through Bapedi sayings that bogoši bo a tswalelwa and bogoši ga bo timele go ya ga bo bjona. This means that bogoši is not contested through blood and might but determined through lineage and suitability. Central to this requirement is birth. It was never available for contestation by any person. It always had a suitable and rightful person to occupy its seat. In the specific case of Bapedi in this question, it was Mampuru not Sekhukhune who was born for it. Given this principle, it is the lineage of Mampuru not of Sekhukhune in which Bapedi kingship resorts.

Mafori Charles Ramushu, in his work based on works by experts on Bapedi kingship and extensive fieldwork research interviews with African elders and experts on it for his Master of Arts in History at the University of Limpopo, provides conclusive and irrefutable evidence that Bapedi kingship resorts under the lineage of Mampuru not of Sekhukhune. He also disputes the Sekhukhune royal family's claims. Providing causes of conflicts and tensions between Mampuru and Sekhukhune and key reasons why Mampuru declined Sekhukhune's challenge to decide who should be Sekwati 1's successor through might and bloodshed and why he left the kingdom, he maintains, based on facts, that Mampuru left to get allies to defeat Sekhukhune and the forces of imperialism and colonialism and to make Bopedi more powerful through common patterns of cooperation and alliances with other traditional leaders. He also maintains that central to what the forces of imperialism and colonialism wanted to do was to divide or fragment Bopedi in order to be able to govern and control it.

One of Mampuru's staunch allies was Nyabela, the Ndebele regent king of Ndzundza who materially supported and protected him. The Boers tried to bribe the Nzundza with 200 head of cattle in their attempt to capture him. Upon being asked to surrender him by the Boers, he told them that he had swallowed him and if they wanted him, they would better take out a knife and cut his stomach open it and then take him out. How much the Zuid-Afrikaansche Republiek (ZAR) or South African Republic and the Boers feared Nyabela and Ndzundza fighters was made clear in no uncertain words in the 18 July 1883 edition of the Volkstem, the ZAR official newspaper, when it noted that:

> The tribe of Mapoch was regarded by other tribes within and without the Republic as the most powerful in the country ... If [Nyabela] had succeeded in withstanding the Boer forces, it would probably have meant the end of the Transvaal Republic. An alliance of all hostile tribes would probably have followed, which would have made habitation of the country by whites difficult, if not impossible.

Ivor Powell points out: "With Sekhukhune dead and Mampuru, who had always been bitterly opposed to white settlement, in a position to consolidate the Pedi monarchy against them, the Boers set about hunting Mampuru down." It was for these reasons that Commandant General Piet Joubert, commandeering about 2,000 fighters, was "authorized" by ZAR to "use whatever means might prove necessary to apprehend Mampuru" and to "prevent the Nzundza from ever consolidating their power again." They besieged the caves, confining the Ndzundza and their allies to their mountain fortress and ensuring that they were subjected

to starvation, after nine months, with little water and foot left, .
cut off from all supplies, starving and ill, they were forced to
surrender. The ZAR fighters used dynamite to destroy "many of
the Nzundza's storage areas" and other measures to defeat them
and force to surrender and surrender Mampuru to the Boers they
stripped naked hanged him in public at the Pretoria Central Prison
on 22 November 1883. Nyabela was arrested and sentenced to
death. Other Ndzundza were imprisoned with him in Pretoria
Central Prison, renamed Kgoshi Mampuru Prison. Following the
intervention of Britian on the basis that he was its subject, the
punishment was later commuted to life imprisonment for fifteen
years with hard labour (in chains)." He was released in 1899 after
serving fifteen years. He passed away four years later after his
release in 1903.

The Nzundza were severely punished by ZAR. Its parliament
declared that they owed the Boers five years' forced labour. They
served as indentured labourers for Boer farmers for five years.
Their royal house was razed and cattle seized. Powell maintains
that "all the lands of the Nzundza – some 36 000 hectares - were
confiscated and divided mainly among the Boers who had fought
Nyabela." The consequence was that they had no land to return
to. They remained on Boer farms as labour tenants. These severe
measures visited upon them was to ensure that they were not
to regain their power to challenge the ZAR again like they did
previously.

Mampuru's descendants continue being denied justice they
deserve in the post-settler colonial era of their country. Ephraim
Mampuru Makgoba as judge of the North Gauteng High Court,
Pretoria in his ruling on the case brought before the court by
the Mampuru royal family provided key reasons why it should
have ruled in favour of the Mampuru family. These reasons are
submissions by these families and its own findings. The court
raised rhetorical issues:

> The factual issue to be determined is whether by virtue
> of forcefully driving Mampuru 11 away Sekhukhune 1
> legitimately usurped kingship. Furthermore, whether
> by killing Sekhukhune 1 Mampuru 11 did in fact assume
> kingship, and if so, did he do that legitimately.

The court provided submissions of two families and its findings as follows:

> The version of the Mampuru royal family that maternity not paternity is the overriding consideration in determining succession to bogoši is correct, as this is the case in many African communities. Therefore the contention by the Sekhukhune royal family that Mampuru 11 could not be king because he was not fathered by Sekwati cannot hold water.

The court cancelled these submissions and its own findings with its incorrect and ahistorical ruling which is contrary to customary succession law to a traditional leadership of Bapedi in particular and Africans in general as follows:

> However in the present case the determination of the lineage of kingship was not necessary based on birth but on the fact that it was not unusual for the kingship to be obtained through might and bloodshed, hence it found Sekhukhune 1 legitimately usurped kingship by forcefully driving Mampuru 11 away. Mampuru 11 fled with his followers without kingship.

It is this incorrect position that the Nhlapo Commission used in unjustly and unfairly denying the Mampuru royal family the kingship of Bapedi. The North Gauteng High Court, Pretoria, the Supreme Court of Appeal and the Constitution Court in their rulings that their task was to find out whether its decision was rational or irrational not whether it was correct or incorrect became participants in this incorrect, bias, unjust and unfair decision.

This decision is political. In his ruling, Judge Makgoba pointed out that over "the years imperialism, colonization and repressive laws of the past are some of the main causes" of distortion of the institution of tradition leadership. Sekhukhune led Bapedi in the struggle against imperialism, colonialism and repressive laws. His descendants are beneficiaries of his role. This is done at the expense of descendants of Mampuru 11. This is not the correct handling of the succession disputes and claims particularly on the basis of African customary laws. Bapedi kingship disputes and claims were handled on the basis of "might and bloodshed" or wars, victories and defeats not on the basis of birth, correctness and truth.

Sekhukhune was a king of Bapedi at the same time Cetshwayo ka Mpande was a king of the Zulus. They led Bapedi and the Zulus in the struggle against imperialism and settler colonialism. They and Bapedi and the Zulu people under their leadership were viewed by Britain as a main threat to its programme of action to take over the whole of South Africa as its colony. Theophilus Shepstone, the Secretary for Native Affairs in Natal, wrote a furious letter to Lord Carnarvon, the British Secretary of State for the Colonies in London in which he maintained that Cetshwayo must go and that unless his leadership of the Zulu people was brought to an end there was no hope for Britian to make progress in seizing the whole of South Africa as its colony. He wrote that:

Cetewayo [sic] is the secret hope of every ... independent chief hundreds of miles from him, who feels the desire that his colour shall prevail....The sooner the root of the evil ... which I consider to be the Zulu power and military organisation, is dealt with, the easier our task will be.

Sekhukhune and Cetshwayo worked closely together and supported each other materially in the struggle against imperialism and colonialism. Mangosuthu Buthelezi correctly pointed out that it "was unusual" in the nineteenth century Britain for "any newspaper to write about African leaders." The London Times gave the measure of respect for Sekhukhune for his determination and bravery, "even if" it was "grudgingly given" in its lengthy editorial dedicated to him:

We hear this morning from Durban of the death of one of the bravest of our former enemies, the Chief Sekhukhune. He with his son and fourteen followers, has been killed... The news carries us some years back to the time when the name of Sekhukhune was a name of dread, first to the Dutch and then to the English Colonists of the Transvaal and Natal... It was, indeed to a great extent the danger caused by the neighbourhood for this formidable chief that led to the annexation of the Transvaal by England. When war was declared against the Zulu king, operation went on simultaneously against Sekhukhune and early in

1879 his stronghold was attacked... Obstacles stood in the way of these operations, and when after Ulundi, Sir Garnet Wolseley entered the Transvaal, he endeavoured to humiliate the Chief.

But Sekhukhune was safe, as he imagined, in an impregnable mountain fortress, and scornfully rejected the terms offered by the British General. It became necessary to attack him in force. A combined movement of columns, containing 2, 000 English and 10, 000 Swazis and other native troops was planned and carried out with great skill, and on the 28th November, 1879, the kraal was taken by assault. Still the Chief and great number of his men held the 'koppie' and from the caves and cracks in the rock they poured an incessant fire upon their assailants. At last the Summit was gained, and after a desperate and sanguinary struggle, the enemy was subdued. Sekhukhune however, like Cetshwayo, succeeded in escaping and was only captured a few days later. He was treated for a time as a State prisoner and his land was settled somewhat after the Zulu manner.

On the tragedy and injustice faced by Bapedi and the Zulus and their struggle against them, Buthelezi maintains that they

share a painful history of tragedy and injustice. Our kings were imprisoned and our land was taken. We both have waged an enduring struggle for the restoration of our kingdoms. Even now we share a struggle, for we continue to battle the oppression of our people.

Britain opened the way for the whole of South Africa to be its colony by, firstly, defeating the Zulus and Bapedi, and secondly, the Boers in the 1899-1902 Anglo-Boer War. Upon its seizure of the Orange Free State (OFS) and Transvaal from the Boers and the establishment of its colonial state with the central authority over the whole of South Africa, the country became its colony as the Union of South Africa on 31 May 1910. The settler colonial state articulated this development as follows:

The country as a single entity came into being as the Union

of South Africa on May 31, 1910, when the two British colonies of the Cape of Good Hope and Natal, and the two conquered Republics of the OFS and Transvaal (now the four provinces of South Africa) were joined in a legislative union, or unitary state, under a single government.

### Conclusions and Recommendations
This chapter has produced and provided evidence of ethic, linguistic, cultural and intangible cultural heritage commonality among Bapedi, Batswana and Basotho as central in their socio-historical relationship. Their surnames are an integral part of this relationship. This commonality is of strategic importance to the resolution of the national question through nation building project. This commonality among them does not mean that state and non-state actors should not strenuously ensure the correct handling of contradictions within and among them and within the society in resolving the national question through nation building project.

The correct handling of disputes and claims of traditional leadership disputes and claims is of vital importance in managing reconcilable reconcile contradictions among members of the society. This is the case given the fact that in resolving conflicts very often other conflicts emerge out of the resolved conflicts. The state should have measures in place to resolve conflicts which emerge out of the resolved conflicts. The South African state in its efforts to handle Bapedi kingship disputes and claims between Sekhukhune and Mampuru royal families through the Nhlapo Commission was incorrect, unjust and unfair. The state in its efforts through the North Gauteng High Court, Pretoria, the Supreme Court of Appeal and the Constitutional Court to handle these disputes and claims was also incorrect, unjust and unfair.

The decision on these disputes and claims is based not on a customary succession law to a traditional leadership characterised by the primacy of birth, correctness and truth. It was based on politics, "might and bloodshed" or wars, victories over a rightful heir to kingship and his descendants by illegitimate heir and his descendants and defeats suffered by legitimate heir and his descendants. The consequence is historical injustice to Mampuru and his descendants. It is historical judicial tragedy that this national historical injustice was ratified by the North Gauteng

High Court, Pretoria, the Supreme Court of Appeal and the Constitutional Court. Sekhukhune's leadership of Bapedi in the struggle against imperialism and colonialism legitimised his being illegitimate heir and leader and his descendants being beneficiaries for his role. This is not the solution to the dispute and claim.

What should be done in solving this problem? Three South Africans help to answer this important question. As Kate O'Regan, former justice of the Constitutional Court, maintains that the majority ruling of the Constitutional Court in favour of the Sekhukhune family against the Mampuru family is "the controversial appointment," it should be revisited as a matter of justice and fairness for it to be resolved in the best interest of South Africa in its correct handling of traditional leadership disputes and claims. This is supported by Pius Langa, former Chief Justice, when in a lecture in memory of Bram Fischer, maintained that:

> Disagreements sharpen our understanding of key issues in the handling of contradictions in the society. A judgement of a court sets the law in stone and in the process silences other voices as wrong. A dissent keeps those voices alive. The voice may be faint, but it is there for future generations to hear.

In other words, as Ramose maintains, "an injustice that endures in the historic memory of the injured is never erased merely because of the passage of time." Molato ga o bole. Time does not change the truth. South Africa cannot proudly declare the principle of the African solutions to African problems while through its state and judicial branch of government it does not resolve this problem.

# Chapter Two
## The Socio-Historical Relationship between Balobedu and Vhavenda: Issues of Ethnicity, Languages, Surnames, Culture and Intangible Cultural Heritage

*Theodore Nkadimeng Mahosi*

**Introduction: Towards a discussion of the socio-historical relationship between Vhavenḓa and Balobedu**

This study was borne out of concern about the popular and hegemonic Eurocentric discourse that holds that Africans of South African exist within a diversity of identities that are underpinned by the culture and the 'ethnic,' linguistic, cultural and intangible cultural heritage. Importantly, their socio-historical origin dictates that they share a history of origin that is closely tied to their socio-historical process of migration into the different borders of this country. This chapter argues that it is equally irresponsible to ignore the reality that Africans share a common history that is cloaked or hidden in the colonially created identity of 'ethnicity,' 'ethnic' groups and 'tribes.'[1] This historical factor is embedded in South Africa's political landscape of racism, segregation, oppression and suppression, wherein the white authorities elevated 'ethnicity' by using languages, surnames, culture and intangible cultural heritage in the name of the separate development for Africans. Ironically, although white people hailed equally from different origins, cultures and languages, they depicted themselves as the same, unique, and more senior and civilised than Africans. Upon being colonised, Africans became segregated into ghettoes, separated on the basis of 'tribal identity' in the homelands; a feature of apartheid social engineering.[1] This chapter stands to defeat the generalised Eurocentric emphasis on this inherent diversity, which they used as a pretext for misrepresentation and misinformation about Africans.[1] However, the author intends to dilute this Eurocentric and hegemonic 'cast-in-stone' claim that the said diversity is 'inherent' in the 'ethnic,' linguistic, culture and intangible cultural heritage and surnames of the Africans of South Africa. Essentially, the frequent mistake is to emphasise 'ethnic' differences at the expense of structural similarities, whereas obvious differences in cultural characteristics should not lead to an assumption that such cultures automatically represent different 'ethnic' or 'tribal' groups.[2] This chapter bemoans the manner in which the origin, history, and African tenets of traditionalism, customs and norms were reinterpreted, used, misused, abused, and misrepresented at the altar of colonial and Eurocentric expediency to glorify the colonial policy transactions of racism, thereby demeaning the African values of *vhuthu/botho/Ubuntu* and *African-ness*.

It suffices to say that a self-justificatory discourse has advanced the proliferation of fragmentation and distinctiveness, which in essence is not far from the Eurocentric and colonial view about Africans. Therefore, it is essential to take cognisance of the role and impact of migration within and across the artificial colonial and apartheid boundaries: a source for interrogation in this study and a challenge to this self-justificatory discourse from an Afrocentric standpoint. Mandla Darnece Mathebula supports the preceding statement by saying that the problem with the history of the Africans of South Africa is that most research fails to scientifically link them with other groups outside the borders of South Africa except in limiting history to recent times.[3] In this chapter, the author specifically focuses on the socio-historical relationship between the Balobedu and Vhavenḓa. Seeing that this chapter deals with "an enquiry towards understanding social human problems."[4] it fits within the realm of a qualitative research methodology underpinned by an Afrocentric approach.

## A bird's-eye view of Africans of South Africa: Vhangona-Bakone-AbaNguni

The history of the southward migration of Africans into South(ern) Africa, reportedly from the Great Lakes Region of the continent, reveals similar fashions of movement.[5] Within the borders of South Africa, this socio-historical movement was characterised by internecine warfare among Africans themselves, during the unique era of their own socio-political development. However, later Africans became victims of forced removals that gave rise to 'ethnic' reserves and later the apartheid policy formation of the homelands. The hegemonic Eurocentric discourse based the creation of the 'ethnic' homelands on a claim about the diversity of linguistic, ethnic, culture and intangible cultural heritage among Africans. Reminiscent of this, and to drive the point home, the chapter refers to selected quotations from some sources that "Apartheid ... attributed to ... racial groups *a separate sense of nationhood and a political mission* to maintain this identity in separate group areas. At the same time, it set up a system of *divide and rule, which fostered and concealed white domination.*[6]

John Donely Fage similarly maintains that: "The whole of South African history is subject to similar distortion ... few if any have heard of the impressive Iron-Age sites associated with the Bantu speakers in Southern Africa such as Zimbabwe or Mapungubwe."[7] According to David Welsh, the consequence of this socio-historical development is that "when white South Africans overcame their political divisions, it was invariably *at the expense of black rights by denying them access to land* on the basis of segregation."[8]

This chapter invokes these three quotations as an attempt

to capture the essence of the political developments that are enclosed therein. The impact of the political developments included the migrations of Africans within South Africa's borders. Accompanying these migrations were forced removals and the imposition of segregated settlements on Africans, who were segregated along 'ethnic,' linguistic and cultural lines, while their common ethnic, linguistic, culture and intangible cultural heritage was ignored. This political development resulted from the 'ethnic' policy of apartheid, which gave birth to homelands, and obliterated the pre-colonial socio-political and economic development of Africans at the stroke of a pen. Having said this, the process was inimical to the inherent political, socio-historical, economic and cultural rights of Africans. Overtime, the focus was on the socio-political development of Africans in the disciplines of history, political studies, anthropology and archaeology from the eye of the coloniser. Regardless of this, Peter Delius, Tim Maggs and Alex Schoeman attest to the experiences of Africans in the Iron Age through to early farming, which thus vindicates the fact that they went through a period of socio-economic development.[9] However, these disciplines downplayed this significant era of evidence of the socio-economic and political dynamism of Africans in order to present the European chapter of transformation from a colonial lens, while in the main they promoted cultural diversity and suppressed their holistic commonality. The author contends that this was a Eurocentric and hegemonic deviation from the shared common history of ethnicity, languages, surnames, culture and intangible cultural heritage of the African people. The pretext was that Africans are ethnically, linguistically and culturally different or diverse as is their intangible cultural heritage. It is for these reasons that it is of critical importance to discuss and explain their ethnic, linguistic, culture and intangible cultural heritage commonality.

Vele Chrisopher Neluvhalani researched the socio-historical link among the Banguni-Bakone-Ba(Vha)ngona of South Africa by looking at their origin and cultural and historical perspective.[10] It is on account of this that, regarding the Vhavenḓa of Kal(r)anga/Shona/Rozvi, he asserts that:

non-such Autochthones migrated into South Africa in waves across the Limpopo River, as if the writers, as government agents, were there to witness the drama of (the) Africans cross the Vhembe (Limpopo) River and dubbed them migrants whereas they crossed it daily except when in (sic) full during January and February only since Creation. The river was never an impediment ever since Creation. The mutual interrelationship amongst the same people cannot be gainsaid, as supported by the dynastical commonality of their languages, culture and religion found to be in practice long before the arrival of Europeans.[11]

Neluvhalani's assertion rings true regarding the free movement of Africans within Southern Africa before the colonial era. The search for seasonal favourable conditions influenced the nomadic life of the people of this particular region in which favourable conditions created an environment of abundance in animals for hunting, or commodities to be gathered. However, such an assertion should not obscure periods when and where skirmishes arose in the quest for territorial protection and competition among Africans themselves. During that time, population density and distribution were not as profound and as complex as we see today, as people settled on land sparsely and unevenly because they preferred well-watered areas such as forest margins, valleys, riversides, lakeshores and coastal plains.[12] This statement shows that such people relied on fishing, hunting and gathering, which they complemented with pastoralism and grazing for their livestock, to support their socio-economic lives: evidence of adoption of and adaptation to lifestyle and dynamism. This caused competition for favourable land, the competition that usually brews violent skirmishes, conquest and subjugation, as well as forced migration. The creation of such an environment assists the process of socio-political development in any area and at any given point in time. Equally, Neluvhalani's assertion about a free movement across the Vhembe River, not as a boundary, needs to be understood in the context of the economic interaction that attests to the era of socio-economic development during the Iron-Age that gave rise to the kingdoms of Monomotapa/Munhumutapa/Munomutapa, Mapungubwe, Dyambeu/Dyambewu and Changameri/Changamire, on both sides of the river.[13]

In this regard, John Illife postulates that by AD 400, early Iron Age cultivators speaking Bantu languages were scattered around much of eastern and southern Africa in an uneven pattern.[14] The sparse and uneven style of occupation of the geographical space related to the background of the size of populations during the same period, which were relatively small compared to the realities of the population of our time. The author refers to archaeological evidence of societies that built circular huts as homesteads, that domesticated animals and dug storage pits as well as graves for burial purposes.[15] Such evidence is socio-culturally characteristic of the people of the Soutpansberg area of Limpopo Province (then known as the far northern Transvaal). Essentially, the VaShona/VhaShona fall into the category of people whose origin is within these proximities, but who by virtue of their dynastic advantage were still numerically dominant by AD 1000. Such effects later became predominant on the southern bank of the Vhembe (Limpopo) River, at Mapungubwe and later Great Zimbabwe to the north, after the abandoning of the former, and within the Rozvi/Lozwi state of Changamire where the Balobedu came from. Reportedly, it was the subordinate dynasty of the Changamire of the Rozvi, known as the destroyers, which conquered Vhavenda (Vhangona) south of the Vhembe (Limpopo) River in the Southpansberg mountain range area.[16] Before this era of southward migration, the Changamire Dombo dynasty of the kingdom of Munhumutapa controlled the south-eastern part of southern Africa, under the VaRozwi/VaRozvi (VhaLozwi in Tshivenda) kingdom, the former Vakaranga/Vhakalanga empire that existed from 1684 to 1695, whose influence spread over much of the region, including South Africa.[17] The above statement(s) by Illife attest to a shift from nomadism or a migratory life to stability, settlement and permanence, with some complex changes taking place in today's Zimbabwe, the Zambezi Valleys and the plateau of the Vhembe, where a higher degree of political organisation developed, testimony of a dynamic life.[18]

Significantly, this dynamic life may also be related to Neluvhalani's assertion that Africans, apparently VaRoziv/VaKaranga, crossed the Vhembe River daily, "except when in (sic) full during January and February, and that the river was never an impediment ever since Creation." This paints a picture of a people whose lives only revolved around socio-economic factors, as if they were stateless. In contrast, the region's first states were born out of interaction among hunters, gatherers, pastoralists and cultivators, and evidence of pastoral trade that laid a foundation for a values-based social organisation, culture and ideology.[19] The mention of the emergence of these kingdoms supports the centrality of the mutual socio-political development and the dynamic commonality of the people of the region. This bird's-eye view of the people leads towards a discussion on "the socio-historical relationship between Vhavenḓa/Vhangona and Vhasenzi/Masingo[20] vis-à-vis Balobedu." This mutual interrelationship needs to support their dynastic commonality in origin or the common history of migration, cultural/'ethnic' affinity, linguistic affiliation, names/surnames, culture, religion and intangible cultural heritage, which was their lifeblood long before the arrival of Europeans on these shores.

### Vhangona-Vhavenḓa-Vhasenzi/Masingo and Balobedu: A historical context

The experiences of the Southern African region of a proliferation of stonewalled ruins such as at Mapungubwe in the north-western part of the Limpopo Province, which bear common names as attested by renowned archaeologists, is testimony of a common culture among the Vhangona-Vhavenḓa-Vhasenzi/Masingo and Balobedu. Evidence from the Great Zimbabwe Ruins in the southeastern part of Zimbabwe (dzimbabwe (sing.)/madzimbabwe (pl.)) in Chishona and Tshingona/Tshivenḓa), which word originates from the Chishona word dzimba/dzamabwe, meaning 'stone building,' is evidence of the Stone

Age.[21] The commonality of stone buildings also occurs around the Mbelengwa or Berengwa Mountains (in Tshivenḓa or Chishona, respectively); more testimony of the unique cultural connection between Africans within Southern Africa, where in Dzata in Venḓa confirms this archaeological-historical commonality: Vhangona-Vhavenda are the autochthones with the most ancient settlements, then, now and always. These Africans in Southern Africa (Lukungurubwe in Tshingona), in Botswana (Lehurutse in Setswana) and Vhulozwi (in Tshinvenḓa) and Vurozvi (in Chishona) attest to shared historical connection among the three cultural groups since time immemorial.[22]

As a case in point, Neluvhalani and Mphaya Henry Nemudzivhadi mention the Basotho as the Bakone collectively, and advance that they are composed of the Bapedi, Batswana and Basotho. These authors further make a comparative reference of both of the Vhangona/Vhavenḓa, Vhasenzi/Masingo and the Balobedu of VuRozvi/VuKaranga/VhuKalanga/VuRonga origin north of the Vhembe (Limpopo) River, which is now the border between South Africa and Zimbabwe.[23] In corroboration with the preceding statement, Shillington posits that further north towards the middle Vhembe (Limpopo) Valley lay the kingdoms of Balobedu and Vhavenḓa, with both their origins stemming from the Mashona of Zimbabwe.[24] This statement confirms a socio-historical relationship between the Vhangona/Vhavenḓa and Balobedu. Vhasenzi and Vhalemba reportedly lost their TshiKalanga/ChiKaranga affinities through intermarriage with and became assimilated into Tshingona/Tshivenḓa culture and language after having settled in Venḓa, along the Soutpansberg Montain Range (which is referred to as Dzwaini in Tshivenḓa), most of which is presently known as the Vhembe District Municipality.[25] According to Lufuno Jean-Pierre Mulaudzi, the nucleus of the people forming the distinctive element in the present Tshivenḓ-speaking group had its home probably somewhere in the current Malawi, Zambia and Zimbabwe. He attests that the region is socio-historically and culturally associated with the VaRozvi/VhaLozwi/VaKaranga/VhaKalanga, before their southward migration, during which period they incorporated members of other groups. In addition, during their migrations, they periodically settled amongst the Vhashona/Vashona-speaking peoples of today's Zimbabwe and absorbed a certain proportion of VaShona blood and culture through assimilation, acculturation and enculturation. This includes the African value essence of customs, beliefs and worldview, which transcends a cultural and linguistic relation with people of the Limpopo in modern Zimbabwe.[26]

Hugh Arthur Stayt maintains that it is important to distinguish the social organisation and beliefs of Vhavenḓa as being incomparable to any other communities in South Africa. The author further avers that because Vhavenḓa legend and customs are in close proximity to the culture that is within the ruins of Great Zimbabwe, there emerged links between the older forms of the Tshivenḓa language and those of present-day Zimbabwe.[27] Regardless of this, this chapter would argue that the silent or 'Judas Iscariot' 'ethno'-socio-historical objective(s) of such authors as Gerald Paul Lestrade and Stayt must not be lost, since they researched as agents of the 'ethnicisation' project that was steeped in the hegemonic Eurocentric 'ethnic' diversity claim.[28] One must not lose sight of the fact that in the face of Stayt's assertions, the Vhavenḓa had experienced cross-influences from their Bapedi neighbours, which cannot be ignored by the author or the reader. In support of this, Hanisch posits that it is an accepted fact that the Tshivenḓa language, over and above the strong linguistic resemblance that it has with ChiShona, also strongly resembles Sesotho.[29] Such evidence of cross-influences further confirms the socio-historical connection between the Vhavenḓa and Vhasenzi vis-à-vis the Balobedu.

Historical evidence shows that in the nineteenth century a subordinate dynasty of Vhasenzi/Masingo established itself among Vhavenḓa people south of the Limpopo (Vhembe) River, and asserted political power around the Soutpansberg area.[30] Other sources on Vhavenḓa history posit that the aboriginal Vhavenḓa people who settled in the Venḓa area far earlier than any other group are the Vhangona.[31] Flowing from this, historical evidence describes Vhangona as Vhavenḓa proper, who the Vhasenzi/Masingo of the dynasty of Dimbanyika/Vele-la-Mbeu/ Thohoyandou/Ramabulana found, conquered and subjected under themselves.[32] A critical look at the statement about the historical establishment of the kingdom of Dombo of a subordinate dynasty among the Vhavenḓa of VaRozvi/Changamire is more evidence that the Vhasenzi/ Masingo are the ones who conquered and subjected the Vhangona. They also assimilated them into themselves. Therefore, the preceding contentions would logically mean that the Vhasenzi/Masingo have historical, if not agnatic links with the VaRozvi dynasty of the northern part of Southern Africa. Neluvhalani mentions that the Vhangona/Bakone of Vhakwevho and the Balobedu/Vhalovhedzi of Bakgwebo adopted the wild pig (nguluvhe, in Tshivenḓa or kolobe in Khelobedu, the Balobedu language) as their totem, but that European orthographic influence, gave rise to a different nomenclature of Vhangona and Bakone.[33] The commonality of both groups using the wild pig as totem further confirms an agnatic link between the Balobedu and the Vhangona/Vhavenḓa. This further supports an assertion by Shillington that the origins of the kingdoms of Balobedu and Vhavenḓa stemmed from the Vhalozwi/Varozvi of Zambia.[34] It follows that all Vhakwebo (Bakgwebo), who are Vhavenḓa, use nguluvhe/kolobe (wild pig) as a praise name or totem, are part of the Balobedu sib, and vice versa. Earlier evidence on both the Vhasenzi/Masingo and Balobedu attests to the fact that they share agnatic links with the main Vhalozwi/Varozvi/Vhakalanga/ Vakaranga/Vashona group of Malawi, Zambia and Zimbabwe. However, during their southward migration the Vhasenzi/Masingo came across the Vhalemba at Mount Mberengwa/Mbelengwa in the southern part of Zimbabwe, who they conquered, subjugated and assimilated with themselves during their southward migration before they crossed the Vhembe River.[35] Furthermore, on their arrival south of the Vhembe River at the foot of the Soutpansberg Mountain, the Vhasenzi/Masingo conquered the Vhangona/ Vhavenḓa and established themselves as a kingdom under

Dambanyika/Ḍimbanyika.[36] In support of the existence of an agnatic link between Vhangona/Vhavenḍa-Vhasenzi/Masingo and Balobedu/Vhalovhedzi, Mathole Motshekga, an advisor of the Balobedu royal family, and an expert in indigenous knowledge systems, maintained that "Balobedu are Bakwebo, born of those who regard the wild pig as taboo, are Vhalozwi/Balozwi/VaRozvi who hail from Monomotapa/Munhumutapa; they also taboo a khwebo, a dove."[37]

In corroboration of Motshekga's statement, Hermann Otto Mönnig postulates that the Balobedu (Vhalovhedzi) are culturally closer to the Vhavenḍa[38] than to the Bapedi (which name Neluvhalani[39] asserts is a corruption of a Tshivenda name of Vhambedzi); the Batau (who exist as and are referred to as the Vhadau, among the Vhavenḍa) and the Bakone/Bangona. The Batau (Vhadau) and Bakone (Vhangona) call themselves the Balobedu and show significant differences in relation to the Bapedi, especially regarding initiation customs and their social structure.[40] Neluvhalani shares similar historical evidence in the preceding paragraphs about the relationship among the Vhangona/AbaNguni/Bakone on the one hand, and refers to the same by other sources, as it is above, regarding the relationship between the Vhasenzi and Balobedu/Vhalovhedzi, on the other. In reference to this, there is mention of their agnatic link *vis-à-vis* the VaRozvi/Vhalozwi of Malawi and Zambia as well the Vhakalanga/VaKaranga. To concretise this, Neluvhalani refers to the Balobedu (Vhalovhedzi) as the Kolobe/Nguluvhe who belong to the Vhakwevho (Bakgwebo) sub-group of Vhangona/Vhavenḍa, a derivation from the totem kolobe/nguluvhe.[41] Besides the fact that the Vhangona are regarded as the aboriginal inhabitants and the real Vhavenḍa of the area to the far northern part of Limpopo Province, the link between the Vhasenzi and Balobedu depicts a very credible socio-historical relationship among these linguistic-cultural groups, as corroborated by Stayt, Mphaya Henry Nemudzivhadi, Mönnig, Neluvhani and Nkadmineng Mahosi.[42]

However, as the apartheid policy evolved, the Balobedu found themselves classified as the North-Eastern Basotho of the then Transvaal, more so because they had later settled around Modjadjiskloof (former Duiwelskloof) and Tzaneen.[43] This is another piece of evidence of the undermining the socio-cultural and historical link between the Balobedu and Bakone (Vhangona/Vhangoni) *vis-à-vis* the Vhavenḓa/Vhangona. The fact that there is reference to the Balobedu as the Bakone and Vhalovhedzi and the Vhavenḓa as the Vhangona is a vindication of the predominance of Bapedi linguistic acculturation or enculturation, according to Andre Chris Myburgh, on the Vhalovhedzi and Vhangona.[44]

The fact that the Balobedu were ironically classified as the North-Eastern Basotho of the then Transvaal, thereby placing them in the Bapedi fold, is a travesty of socio-politico-cultural justice and infringed on their rights to enjoy the historical significance of commonality with the Vhavenḓa.[45] Equally, this sounds like socio-political-cultural hypocrisy because colonial/apartheid rule placed the Balobedu, Batau (Vhadau) and Bakone under the cultural dominance of the Bapedi in the quest for artificial cultural homogeneity, regardless of their stark differences with the latter. It is therefore understandable why there is evidence of corruption of the names Vhalovhedzi to Balobedu, Vhadau to Batau and Vhangona to Bakone, respectively, a vindication of the influence of the predominance of Bapedi social intercourse, linguistic acculturation or enculturation on the Balobedu of Varozvi.[46]

In contrast, the socio-political objective of the apartheid policy in either integrating some people with others or even separating some was racially, 'ethnically' and 'tribally' motivated to promote diversity. This also denigrates the most abiding principle of the system of thought of African values of morality, of *vhuthubotho*, which refers to solidarity as an organising element of African morality and moral equilibrium.[47] Therefore, it would be naïve to pretend that the colonial/apartheid and hegemonic promotion of cultural diversity has not inflicted painful and longstanding damage on the African thought and systems of *vhuthubotho* among Africans of South Africa. Apartheid used an 'ethnicised' version of 'custom' to enforce a dual political identity; a racial identity that united beneficiaries on an 'ethnic' identity that fragmented victims; which victims are Africans.[48]

Earlier in the chapter, its author mentions how the white authorities used the apartheid policy to divide the AmaXhosa into two socio-cultural groups in the Transkei and the Ciskei, regardless of common socio-cultural affiliations. Thereafter, the apartheid government imposed 'homeland independence' on the Transkei and the Ciskei. In the same manner, it divided the Balobedu into two socio-culturally and artificially diverse and 'distinct' groups of southern Transvaal BaRozwi and Eastern Transvaal BaRozwi, regardless of the fact that both of them were "bana ba *tšie*khalaka" (children of the locust of the VhaKalanga/VaKaranga).[49] Similarly, it is important to indicate that, in Tshivenḓa, there is a proverbial-cultural reference to the phrase "bana ba tšiekhalaka," which in Tshivenḓa reads "vhana vha *nzie*tshikalanga" (*nzie* (locust), and carries a common meaning as in Khelobedu.[50] It is important to note that in each case the relation of the children is linked to the Tshikalanga/ChiKaranga, which is a sib of the TshiLozwi/ChiRozi, which was confirmed above as a common origin of both the Vhavenḓa and Balobedu. Therefore, the reference of the children of the Tshikalanga helps one to understand it refers to both Vhavenḓa and Balobedu, as the children/grandchildren/great-grandchildren of the VhaKalanga. It is the contention of the author of this chapter that this further proves another essence of socio-linguistic-cultural commonality that is inherent in the phrase "bana ba *tšie*khalaka" in the case of the Balobedu phrase, and the Tshivenḓa phrase "vhana vha *nzie*tshikalanga." It is important to understand that regardless of the different periods during which both migrated southward many centuries ago, the colonial and apartheid policies failed to dilute the foundation of the linguistic-cultural commonality of the Balobedu and Vhavenḓa.

Flowing from the above, Moyahabo Rosina Mohale mentions that when the Balobedu arrived in South Africa, they settled in the Soutpansberg area (also called Tswaing in Khelobedu, and Dzwaini in Tshivenḓa), near the Phiphiḓi Waterfalls, northwest of the town of Ṱhohoyanḓou, under the leadership of Makhaphele. After his followers were buried, Makhaphele later died at Phiphiḓi[51] The Vhavenḓa revere the Phiphiḓi Waterfalls as a sacred place where the Vhavenḓa periodically perform royal rituals.[52] Although Makhaphele, a Molobedu, did not live to see the continuation of the journey to the present settlement of Balobedu, at Bolobedu or Ga-Modjadji/Mojaji, the fact that his followers buried him at the sacred place of Vhavenḓa, the Phiphiḓi Waterfalls, speaks volumes about the agnatic link to the Vhavenḓa. This also bears a significant reference to his socio-historical commonality as a Molobedu from VhuLozwi/VuRozvi/BoLozwi *vis-à-vis* the origin of the Vhavenḓa and Vhasenzi. Therefore, it is no coincidence that Makhaphele not only initially settled in Venḓa, but that his followers laid him to rest at a sacred place of and amongst the Vhavenḓa. In addition, after the death of Makhaphele, his son Mohale, a grandson of the Mamabolos (who are also dikolobe/dzinguluvhe) and are related to the Nengwekhulus (the prefix Ne- means owner of, -ngwe- means tiger, and the suffix -khulu means, great/big), succeeded him. He established his settlement and royal cross at Bolobedu.[53] Both the Mamabolos and the Nengwekhulus claim their origin from and relatedness to the Ramabulana dynasty of Makhado, the grandson of Ṱhohoyanḓou of the Vele-ḽa-Mbeu of Ḓambanyika/ Ḓimbanyika.[54] This statement further consolidates their deep-seated agnatic link and further helps to cement their relationship, which the author of this chapter believes logically defines their royal closeness and socio-historical commonality.

## In the name of political organisation

Mohale advances that the Balobedu queen communicates with people via her male councillors and village leaders and *magoshi*. In the same protocol of the VhaLozwi/VaRozwi, Vhavenḓa and Vhasenzi, the ruler communicates with his subjects through the male councillors, who are *mantona* (in Khelobedu) or *dzinduna/ magota* (in Tshivenḓa). It is for this reason that traditionally, and within the Balobedu and Vhavenḓa, it is customary to talk of a council of elders as well as checks and balances.[55] It suffices to say that when Queen Modjadji died, Makobo succeeded her as queen of Balobedu, and ascended to the throne on 16 April 2003, during which time the then Vhavenḓa king, Tony Peter Ramabulana Mphephu, officially inaugurated her. In addition to this, after the death of Queen Makobo, her brother Mpapatla Modjadji acted on behalf of his sister's daughter, Masalanabo Modjadji, as she had not yet reached the age of maturity.[56] The fact that Mpapatla acted on behalf of Masalanabo is not surprising since he is her uncle.

Mulaudzi avers that the political organisation of the Vhavenḓa is very similar to that of adjacent communities while leaning more towards the Sotho, apparently referring to the Balobedu, rather than the VaShona.[57] However, the author of this chapter differs with Mulaudzi's assumption because the evidence from various sources cited earlier stresses the socio-historical origin of the Vhavenḓa and Balobedu to the VhaLozwi/VaRozvi/VaShona. Therefore, Balobedu's place within the commonality of their origin from the VaRozvi and VaShona *vis-à-vis* Vhavenḓa must remain an equally important aspect. The commonality between the Balobedu and Basotho/Bakone was borne out of their closer living together, especially with the southeastern Basotho, which apartheid's 'ethnic' separation policy categorised based on a created and imposed diversity, instead of a socio-historical origin and commonality. On this basis, Lestrade had provided the Department of Native Affairs with more insight into the political organisation of Vhavenḓa communities regarding their language, customs, traditions and culture (*lushaka*: 'tribe;' *mutupo*: totem; *tshiila*: taboo).[58]

Among the African people of Southern Africa, and those of the Limpopo Province in particular, political organisation is the cultural aspect on which the government revolves, and wherein the power assigns legislative, judicial and executive powers to different governing organs, above which the king/*thovhele*/*kgoshikgolo* resides.[59] As is the case with the Balobedu and Vhavenḓa, all adult males constitute an assembly of people as the ruler's advisers (Council of Elders), including members of the ruling family. In this regard, one may refer to the ruling family including the ruler's mother (*vhakoma* in Tshivenḓa, or *masetšhaba* in Khelobedu/

Sepedi), his sister or half-sister (*khadzi* in Tshivenḓa or *kgadi* in Khelobedu/Sepedi), his father's younger brother (*khotsimunene/ rangwane*) and his father's sister (*makhadzi/rakgadi*).[60] In both cases, all three personalities feature prominently as important counsellors within royal circles of the Balobedu and Vhavenḓa, especially regarding their roles in matters of succession and the business of administration, the religious life of the people and socio-political stability, wherein *makhadzi* in particular, serves as a powerful mediating force in ruling circles.[61] Equally, a ruler cannot be deposed although it is possible to disqualify a successor to the office in the event of gross misconduct. This is with the exception of the Balobedu where a female successor is a ruler.[62] Corroborating this, Mulaudzi posits that the Vhavenḓa and a few of their Northern Sotho neighbours, who logically include the Balobedu, were considered to be exceptional in that, among them the *khosi/kgoshi(ši)*, could appoint one or several of his sisters or *gota* (*mokgoma* or village head) for administrative purposes.[63] This commonality could be explained in terms of the cultural affinity that the Vhavenḓa share with the Balobedu, as well as the historical acculturation and enculturation that the Vhavenḓa share with the Bapedi. This socio-political organisation is responsible for the royal family and the commoners who exist communally in the spirit of sharing that guides African values and is in line with *vhuthu/botho* and African-ness.

### The discussion on the linguistic commonality

Languages, surnames, culture and the intangible cultural heritage of the African people of South Africa are their proud collective heritage. Having said this, earlier in the chapter, John Illife alludes to a gradual change in lifestyle from nomadic to cultivation, pastoralism and domestication, which translated to a degree of social stability. He also mentions how the interaction between the pastoralists and cultivators shaped social organisation.[64] One would expect that the social organisation resulted from social and eco-cultural interaction, which depended on the mode of linguistic communication, social proximity of the people concerned, their cultural intercourse, acculturation and enculturation; wherein there is an overlap in linguistic-cultural influences which fostered commonality. Essentially, between the north of the Limpopo and the Zambezi Valleys the dominant ancestral language was that of the cultivators, who were Bantu-speakers. They unevenly and sparsely occupied Southern Africa and South Africa in the Soutpansberg of Limpopo. Some of them spoke ancestral languages close to those of the ChiShona/ChiKalanga, of the kingdoms of Mapungubwe, Great Zimbabwe, Munhumutapa, Changamire, Rozvi and a subordinate dynasty among Vhavenḓa people, if the reference to the Soutpansberg plains is anything to go by. One senses an overemphasis on the 'ethnic,' linguistic, and cultural diversity of African people. It is also the promotion of the negation of their 'ethnic,' linguistic and cultural commonality, which is responsible for the popular, hegemonic and dominant position that there are so many African languages in South Africa. In fact, this was the most effective strategy for whites to divide Africans so as rule them. Central to this strategy was preventing them as the decisive majority of the South African population from cohering into a unified group.

Neluvhalani is of the view that the relationship between the same people is not easy to gainsay because the dynastical commonality of their languages, culture and religion, which are/ were found to be in practice long before the arrival of the Europeans, supports this fact. This assertion is in line with the opening of this chapter since it corroborates the existence of commonality among Africans, and thus dispels the wholesale European and hegemonic claim of linguistic diversity. Significantly, the essence of commonality is what characterises the communal existence of *vhuthu/botho*, which derives from the African values of tradition and customs that are interwoven in socio-historical connections, if not origin. This assertion also pours cold water on the so-called 'originality' currently found in the Eurocentric and missionary created language groups as evidenced by the coming paragraph, which has a calculated mission to control the Africans of South Africa separately on the one hand, but collectively at their whim on the other hand. In this regard, Nyameko Barney Pityana posits that Africans are by nature moral creatures and never live their lives in isolation. They are part of a community of people imbued with a character of mutual interdependence, since without norms or rules, if everybody lived as they pleased, the fabric of society would collapse.

If one were to interrogate the notion of the process of collapse, one would attest to the fact that its stage is what the missionaries were aiming at the inculcation of separatist diversity among Africans, in order to weaken them socio-politically. We hasten to say that the protagonist in the form of the colonial rule and its agents seems to have succeeded. Therefore, what the apartheid system and some bantustan leaders sought to impose, were selectively 'common' African customs and traditions that only served to subjugate and subordinate African people, making them doubt their sense of identity, self-respect and cultural systems, thereby subordinating their values, and diversifying and marginalising them in their country.

This chapter invites the reader to pay attention to the similarities in African proverbs and other figures of speech, such that there cannot be exception to the evidence of a common dynastical origin that dates from the past to the present. These experiences place the missionaries, European anthropologists, historians and ethnologists at fault for being agents of the colonial authorities because they served their whims as to the separatist, oppressive, repressive and suppressive policies. They cannot escape the blame for their complicity in the process of demeaning everything that related to the Africans of South Africa. According to Pityana, missionary education and Christian values were pervasive, and looked down on African values with the aim of rendering African people less human. It was for these reasons that Christianity declared some African socio-cultural practices pagan, considering African dress code and language uncivilised, resultantly making Africans more secretive and apologetic about their cultural practices.

Generally, Africans were compelled to adopt European names

that were described as Christian, replacing their own, regardless of the fact that in many cases there was a common name and language and a shared interpretation of the past, implying a common origin, in particular, that served as a starting point, provided one fully recognises that even these criteria need not coincide. Neluvhalani posits that for reasons that served their hegemonic Eurocentric purposes, the Europeans, and the missionaries, in particular, observed and created specific orthographies in order to distinguish in their eyes three groups of (A)baNguni-Bakone-Vhangona. Neluvhalani and Mulaudzi further argue that the distinction was apparently based on the usage of orthographies by the various European missionary societies that had intentionally changed the original spoken language into different language groups with evangelical cultural nuances to suit the objectives of diversifying and linguistic 'tribalising' of the (A)baNguni-Bakone-Vhangona.[14] The Europeans and the missionaries applied English, Swiss and German orthographies, during the corruption and reduction of African spoken languages into written form through their specific spelling patterns. To further strengthen this argument, Neluvhalani mentions P.E. Schwellnus as having shaped Tshingona into Luvenḓa/Tshivenḓa; Clement Martin Doke as reducing Nguni into Xhosa and Zulu languages; Ernest Creux as crafting Sekone into Southern Sesotho, Sepedi as Northern Sesotho and Xitsonga; while Robert Moffat as having come up with the written form of Setswana (Western Sesotho). This boils down to a process of diversification of the three groups and their sub-groups, and that European linguists had no interest in acknowledging that the Ngona-Nguni-Kone share the same origin.[15] This is evidence of the paternalistic approach to the socio-historical welfare of a people, placing them on the periphery of issues that mattered to them, by regarding them as spectators, researching about and for them instead of with them and through them. In this regard, Neluvhalani asserts that the European orthography:

> replaced place and personal names, religion and culture and so westernized them in such a way that they even looked

down upon their own... According to the Europeans, the Africans had no history until it was written on their behalf ... as if history becomes a narrative when the author has written his story, whereas it is an episode of note taking place daily with or without an influence of anyone.[16]

Neluvhalani further argues that one presents one's own history and experiences better as the first witness of such experiences and circumstances, especially if presented in the language of the affected subject. Therefore, the intention of the author of this chapter is to enable the reader to understand that language is the primary means of communication among the peoples, be it through word of mouth or by means of body language. In the cultural context, one needs to comprehend that in many cases a common language and a shared interpretation of the past implies a commonality in origin that needs to serve as a starting point.[17]

Stayt corroborates the claim that the Vhavenḓa are a composite people who have gradually welded into a compact whole such that their language is sharply associated with that of the VhaKalanga/VaKaranga/VaShona. This means that linguistically and culturally the Vhavenḓa have a place in the congeries of people between the area north of the Zambezi and somewhere beyond the south of Vhavenḓa into the Balobedu,[18] who share the same origin as alluded to earlier in the chapter. Based on oral traditions it shows that important migrations of small sibs, or sections thereof, came from the north of the Vhembe River, and the names of such sibs/small sibs overlap among the Vhavenḓa, Vhakalanga and Vhakwevho (Bakgwebo) of the Balobedu, Nḓou and Makwinḓa of Vhaḓavhatsindi group. According to Stayt and Mahosi, this confirms the evidence of cross-cultural infiltration during these important historical migrations of the people of Rozvi/Lozwi/Kalanga/Karanga origin: Vhavenḓa/Masingo/Vhasenzi/Balobedu.[19] This is further evidence of a common origin from the Changamire of Munhumutapa, who had in the past conquered and subjected the Vhavenḓa south of the Vhembe River and established a Rozi kingdom.[20] According to historical evidence, a kingdom that conquered and established themselves as lord over indigenous Vhavenḓa, the Vhangona, south of the Vhembe River is that of Ṱhohoyanḓou, the son of Vele-la-Mbeu, who is the son of Dimbanyika (Dambanyika),[21] the king of Vhasenzi, resulting in a fusion of dialects. In corroborating this assertion, Mulaudzi avers that the Vhangona were the authentic speakers of Tshivenḓa and that the Vhasenzi language was a dialect of Chishona, such that during conquest and the establishment of ruleby the Vhasenzi over the Vhangona, they also integrated their linguistic element.[22] One needs to understand this against the background of the fact that the VaRozvi and VaKalanga historically originated from Malawi, Zambia and Zimbabwe.

This makes it safe to say that people pronounce some Tshivenḓa, and by implication Tshingona as well as Khelobedu wordsthe way they do, either because of their origin or from the mixing and/or mutual influence of the indigenous languages of the Limpopo Province, with those of the Vhasenzi and Balobedu/Bapedi/Bakone, respectively.

Flowing from this, the Balobedu dialect shares some similarities with the Tshivenḓa language, which also originated from across the Vhembe River.[23] According to Mohale, we only find the most common Khelobedu wordsin the Tshivenḓa or Tshishona languages.[24]

It is of vital importance to mention these words as a way to illustrate this point. Some of the common words we find in Khelobedu and Tshivenḓa or Tshishona are "go loba" (Khelobedu) or "u luvha" (Tshivenḓa), both of which mean to pay allegiance to a particular ruler. It is important to identify the phonological commonality of the concepts as we continue with the examples. In the language of royalty, we refer to the wives of the ruler as "vatanoni" in Khelobedu, while in Tshivenḓa we call them "vhatanuni." Regardless of the orthography, it is worth noting the commonality in meaning and phonology. The words "vamakhulu" (Khelobedu) or vhomakhulu (Tshivenḓa) refer to parents of one's spouse depending on who we are addressing. In the African sense, life revolves around a people's interdependence or communalism and the principle of *vhuthu/botho*. During the ploughing or harvest season, people work in a collective as "zunde/dzunde" in Khelobedu and "dzunde" in Tshivenḓa. The use of the same word for this kind of communal life supports the commonality between the two linguistic-cultural groups, who have agnatic links with the VaRozvi. In the same vein, the discussion that precedes the immediate statement informs one of the linguistic commonality between Vhavenḓa and Balobedu. We further find evidence of a phonological relationship between Vhavenḓa and Balobedu when we refer to a girl who reaches the stage of puberty as "khomba" in Tshivenḓa, while in Khelobedu the word is "khopa." Therefore, although there is this slight difference in the orthographic phonology because of the presence of the 'mba' in Tshivenḓa, the two words nevertheless mean maiden in both Khelobedu and Tshivenḓa. The process of initiation has its own concepts as well; "vusha" in Khelobedu and "vhusha" in Tshivenḓa refer to female initiation, which further confirms the linguistic commonality that exists between the two languages. "Vuhwera" is a Khelobedu concept for a masked dancer who performs on the occasion of the return of initiates, either female or male, while in Tshivenḓa the concept "muvhira" has the same meaning as in Khelobedu.[25] Below the author of this chapter gives examples of commonality in Balobedu and Vhavenḓa names.

## What is in a name? A look at the commonality between Vhavenḓa and Balobedu names

There is a certain core of valued features such as a common names and shared language characteristics, between Vhavenḓa and Balobedu. These include a particular conception of the history of a people, and their moral attributes or institutions that link people historically.[26] The author does not wish to belabour the origin of such names, but to list the phonology of a number of Tshivenḓa names as compared to those of the Khelobedu and their commonality in meaning. In order to do this, the author presents a Khelobedu name alongside a Tshivenḓa name. In this regard,

Neluvhalani asserts that this attests to both languages giving the same name to some geographical features, flora and fauna, as evidence of their intertwined deep past as rendered by these names. He further says that this reveals, proves and supports their common dynastical origin that dates back to antiquity.[27] He refers to some of the names that exude phonological commonality and attempts to give meaning to those he knows the meaning(s) of. Here are some of the names the Neluvhalani and Mohale present in their respective sources:

Dzugudini (Khelobedu) and Dungunudzini in Tshivenda refer to a thick dark forest; vutuhazindi/vhuṭuwadzindi share a common phonology; Tswaing (Khelobedu) and Dzwaini (Tshivenda) mountains refer to the Soutpansberg, and mean mountains of salt in both languages. Mohale (Khelobedu) and Muhali (Tshivenda) are surnames in both cases, share a common phonology and mean the brave one in both languages. BuLozwi (Khelobedu) or VhuLozwi (Tshivenda) means the place of the BaLozwi. Mokone (Khelobedu/Sepedi) and Mungona (Tshivenda) mean a member of the BaLozwi cultural group, respectively. Seepe (Khelobedu/Sepedi) and Tshiembe (Tshivenda) mean an axe in both cases and may either refer to a name or surname in both cases. Maropeng (Khelobedu) and Marubini (Tshivenda) are both names and surnames in both languages, and commonly refer to a deserted settlement or homestead. Motaung/Motau (Khelobedu) and Mudau are surnames but could also mean a clan names in both languages.

Mampuru (Khelobedu/Sepedi) and Mamburu (Tshivenda) are surnames. Despite the difference of 'p' (Mampuru) and 'b' (Mamburu) there is commonality in phonology, and both refer to the VhaLemba subgroup of Vhavenda. Balobedu (Khelobedu/Sepedi) and Vhalovhedzi (Tshivenda) refer to a cultural group, although Neluvhalani claims that Balobedu is actually a Sepedi orthographic corruption of the Tshivenda original name Vhalovhedzi, through the Eurocentric linguistic-cultural impact of Sepedi.[28] Ntwampe (Khelobedu) and Nndwambi (Tshivenḓa), meaning a war/dispute/conflict that has gone badly, can appear as both a name and surname in both languages. Makgoba (Khelobedu) and Makhuvha (Tshivena)) is both a clan name and a surname. The Makgoba people attest to be relatives of the Ramabulana/Mphephu dynasty, and the Makhuvha clan who reside in Venḓa in particular.[29] Seoka (Khelobedu) and Siaga (Tshivenḓa) are surnames; note the phonological commonality. Khiedeulu (Khelobedu) and Tshiendeulu (Tshivenḓa) is a burial place/cemetery for the royal family that ordinary members of the community are generally prohibited from entering or accessing, especially because family rituals are performed as a send-off to the deceased, or during such occasions that rituals need to be performed.

Letaba (Khelobedu/Sepedi) and Ṱavha (Tshivenḓa) are the names of a river that flows between Tzaneen and Modjadjiskloof; Mogodo/Mokoto (Khelobedu) and Mugodo (Tshivenḓa) are surnames in both languages and share a phonological commonality. Mokwena (Khelobedu) and Mugwena ((Tshivenḓa) are both surnames and names and depict a phonological commonality. Khikhutini (Khelobedu) and Tshikudini ((Tshivenḓa) are place names that mean a place where people hide, especially during times of war or upheavals. A village bearing the same name exists east of the town of Ṱhohoyanḓou). Makhaphele (Khelobedu) and Khambele/Nekhambele (Tshivenḓa) can be a name, clan name or surname. Banarini (Khelobedu/Sepedi) and Vhanarini (Tshivenḓa) are clan names. Bakgwebo (Khelobedu) and Vhakwevho (Tshivḓḓa) are clan names and refer to those who taboo a wild pig, and both use it as their totem. Barwa (Khelobedu) and Vharwa (Tshivenḓa) refer to people of Khoisan origin. Khameli (Khelobedu) and Khameli are clan names and surnames in both cultural groups. Ramaru (Khelobedu) and Ramaru ((Tshivenḓa) are clan names and surnames in both languages, and usually refer to people of Balepa/Vhalemba. Muduvhadzi (Khelobedu)/ Tubatse (Sepedi) and Muduvhadzi/Ḓuvhadzi, can be names or surnames. In both Khelobedu and Tshivenḓa, Mphanama is a surname. Bakgaga (in Khelobedu) is a clan name and Makhaga is a surname in Tshivenḓa. Muthebuli (Khelobedu) and Muthevhuli (Tshivenḓa) are surnames. Muthabuli (Khelobedu) and Mutambuli (Tshivenḓa) are both surnames. Kgabo or Makgabo (Khelobedu) and Makhavhu (Tshivenḓa) are surnames.

Seko (Khelobedu) and Singo (Tshivenḓa) are surnames but may also refer to clan names. Sekone (Khelobedu) and Tshingona (Tshivenḓa) refer to a language in both cases, but also to any cultural practice. Mmakau (Khelobedu) and Magau (Tshivenḓa) are surnames and place names. Tlou (Khelobedu) and Nḓou (Tshivenḓa) are names, surnames or clan names. Batwanampa (Khelobedu) and Vhaṱwanamba are clan names. Balaodi (Khelobedu) and Vhalaudzi (Tshivenḓa) are clan names. Kgomommo (Khelobedu) and Khomummu (Tshivenḓa) are both surnames and clan names. Rapholo (Khelobedu) and Raphulu (Tshivenḓa) are surnames. Seshoka or Sešoka (Khelobedu/Sepedi) and Tshishonga (Tshivenḓa) are surnames. Sebola (Khelobedu/ Sepedi) and Tshivhula are both clan names and surnames. Machete (Khelobedu/Sepedi) and Matshete (Tshivenḓa) are both clan name and surnames. Moraba (Khelobedu/ Sepedi) and Muravha (Tshivenḓa) are surnames. Maelula (Khelobedu) and Mailula (Tshivenḓa) are both place names and surnames. Manaka (Khelobedu/Sepedi) and Managa (Tshivenḓa) are surnames. Mathuka (Khelobedu) and Maduka (Tshivenḓa) are surnames. The surname Maduka also refers to a particular clan of VhaSona/VaShona/ BaShona that we find to the north of the Vhembe River. Sebola (Khelobedu/Sepedi) and Tshivhula (Tshivenḓa) are clan names and surnames of those who are relations of the Machetes (Khelobedu/Sepedi) and Matshetes

(Tshivenḓa), the Lešibas (Khelobedu/Sepedi) and Ḽishivha (Tshivenḓa), and the Ramalebanas (Khelobedu/Sepedi) and Ramalivhanas (Tshivenḓa), who all claim socio-historical and cultural aboriginality to the kingdom of Mapungubwe. The author of this chapter wishes to make categorically clear that these are not the only names common to the Vhavenḓa and Balobedu.

### Culture and intangible cultural heritage: interrogating the culture of Vhavenḓa and Balobedu

In her thesis on the Khelobedu language, Mohale advances the definition of culture to capture its essence as a way of leading to the Khelobedu culture. She defines a people's culture as the very particular manner in which they celebrate themselves to the world and into the arena of history, "making the concept all that is and that one has, as it is more than folklore, music and dance but embraces a people's world-view."[30]

However, given some of the assertions that Andre Chris Myburgh advances above, it is prudent to wake up to the reality that human beings are bound to experience a socio-cultural interaction in many ways, such that acculturation and enculturation end up having a mutual impact on a people's culture. Barbara Oomen posits that cultures are not coherent because they "show a murky and smudged picture of blending lines and uncertain culture," which Mohale supports by asserting that Khelobedu is no exception in being contaminated by other cultures.[31] Eileen Jensen Krige corroborates the preceding authors on these assertions by arguing that being in contact with western cultures had brought with it some disturbances, which affected institutions and cultural patterns such that they cannot be compared with the major cultural evolutions not only of Balobedu, but of many other cultural groups.[32]

We choose to interrogate the assertions by Krige, Myburgh and Mohale, more so because even if socio-cultural interactions can result in mutual acculturation and enculturation, the core elements of cultures do not get lost; if anything they are "enriched in the mixture of the melting pot," as happened with the Vhavenḓa, according to Nkhumeleni Matodzi Nemakhavhani Ralushai.[33] Secondly, the mention of disturbances, murkiness, a smudged picture of blending lines, uncertain culture and disturbances echoes a negativity that implies that socio-cultural interaction is destructive, divisive and leads to diversity, instead of enriching and welding people together in commonality, as Ralushai opines. It is my informed view that the main objective of inculcating the notion of diversity of cultures was in order to entrench 'ethnic' and 'tribal' division and prejudices, and thus dilute the belief in the existence of commonality inherent within the cultures of black South Africans. As a result, although these commonalities are/were identifiable, the dent of 'ethnicity' and 'tribalism' pours(poured) cold water on such a notion, because these defeatist tendencies are the reason 'tribal' tensions occasionally appear twenty-nine years into democracy; hence the inability to realise social cohesion and nation-building. Regardless of the above assertions regarding culture, Mohale posits:

Culture refers to an interaction among people with negotiated, shared values, understanding, norms, ideals, way of life and a way of looking at the world and their place in it. It refers to the acquired life style of a group of people with patterned, repetitive ways of thinking, feelings and actions that are characteristic of members of a particular society or segment of society. It applies to a distinct group of people and involves the habits of those people, distinct from other peoples. Culture tends to bind a people together very strongly and instils certain values very effectively.[34]

Flowing from this passage, culture is a socio-interactive process that has relevance to the mind-set, feelings and the conduct of a particular people as a collective, on the one hand, as well as members of that society, on the other, and thus implicates the uniqueness of a people as compared to others without detaching a mutual influence. It is for this reason that cultural evolutionism also has a bearing on the adoption of and adaptation to new circumstances. Therefore, in this section, the discussion focuses on the common culture traits of the Vhavenḓa and Balobedu by examining their characteristics in terms of their transmission through time.[35] While the author of this chapter agrees with the cultural evolutionist theory, he argues that the basic cultural traits and characteristics of a people remain intact within the "melting pot" perspective, especially taking into account the two-tiered and circumstantial possibility of their culture dominating or adjacent cultures dominating them,[36] thereby making it an adaptive process. In view of the intent of the opening discussion on culture and earlier discussions regarding the origin of Vhavenḓa and Balobedu, this section interrogates the commonality of their cultures, especially in view of Balobedu having later predominantly settled among the Bapedi/Bakone. According to Murimbika, continuous cultural sequences offer an opportunity to derive explanatory models from descent societies, more so because there is strong archaeological evidence for cultural continuity from Mapungubwe to Mutapa (Monomotapa) in Great Zimbabwe throughout the political development into historical Venḓa.[37] The preceding statement by Murimbika, links to the above background discussion on the common origin of the Vhavenḓa and Balobedu. It is this origin of the Vhavenḓa and Balobedu that sets the tone of the interrogation of their commonality in order to defeat the notion of cultural diversity, since both are descendants of the Vhalozwi/VaRozvi/ VaKaranga/VhaKalanga/MaShona, of Malawi, Zambia and Zimbabwe.

Having the above in mind, Myburgh mentions the collective standardisation and variation, by asserting that culture "does not comprise everything man produces but only those products of his activity that have become part of his collective adaptation within the context of a people." Culture "implies norms or standards that may apply to thought, speech and other actions as well as material objects which are then standardized or stereotyped ... over a period of time."[38] One is thus inclined to postulate that any process that evolves within a people over a period of time points to dynamism that may be related to evolutionary adaptation from one generation to the next in their socio-historical-cultural, political, economic, legal, religious or ritual responsibilities.[39] All of them reveal inherent socio-historical-cultural commonality. This assertion negates the claim of cultural diversity among Africans – diversity the colonial authorities subjectively used to whitewash the commonality of African values in relation to socio-historical and cultural tenets. Their intention was to inflict a lasting effect on the essence of dignity, *botho/vhuthu*, which relate to African values, in opposition to the maxim "history has no blank pages."[40]

There is a misconstrual of the essence of socio-historical-cultural dynamism among the Africans of South Africa as lack of mutual cultural influence, as the hegemonic Eurocentric discourse would have it. Significantly, mutual cultural influence is a treasure to share among people. It involves a process of learning, acculturation and enculturation, adoption of and adaptation to the changing environment, which is the essence of human dynamism.

**The aspect of respect amongst Vhavenḓa and Balobedu**
Lesiba Teffo encompasses the assertions carried in this paragraph by positing that *botho/vhuthu*, which means humanness, implies respect for human nature as a whole, and a common spiritual ideal by which the Africans of South Africa give meaning to life; a spiritual foundation of all African societies.[41] He uses the essence of respect that both a Muvenḓa and a Molobedu woman usually extend to acknowledge seniority, respectively:

> A typical Muvenda woman would not look at her husband in the face when making an offer of any kind. She would rather crawl towards him, whilst facing downwards or sideward until she offers what is at hand. A typical Molobedu woman shows almost a similar mode of respect along these lines to every man with yet a greater degree of reverence. On meeting such a person, a Molobedu woman would stand to curtsy and greet with both her hands held together on her left whilst her face looks downward in modesty.[42]

While to the reader Teffo's words might sound patriarchal or be interpreted as gender oppression, they carry the hallmarks of customary practices that intend to show respect to senior members of a society. He mentions the common act of looking sideways and not straight in the face, as well as the act of clasping left hand, clasping left and right hands and moving them to the left by a Muvenḍa or Molobedu woman. This cultural practice of looking either downwards and sideways to the left or clasping one's hands to the left as a sign of respect to elderly people is common to both Vhavenḍa and Balobedu women. This further points to the commonality of cultural and traditional African values as well as the virtues of *botho/vhthu* that exist in the norms, rules, respect and morals that are prevalent in the African social fabric of the Vhavenḍa and Balobedu. Essentially, it is no coincidence that Teffo is knowledgeable about such an important aspect of cultural commonality, a reminder of the essentiality of African values. Teffo's example unearths the commonality in the socio-cultural behaviour embedded in the Vhavenḍa and Balobedu, which has transcended generations.

The above discussion creates and maintains an interwoven and intra-woven connection and integration of the core socio-cultural components such as the religious-cultural, socio-economic, political organisation and way of life. The intention is to serve particular purposes of national cohesion and nation building, and to define Africans,[43] Vhavenḍa and Balobedu in particular, and their African values, as the author attempts to depict. In the end, this may assist the project of socio-cultural cohesion and solidarity among the Africans of South Africa, especially if there is recognition and appreciation of the existence of socio-historical-cultural commonality between these two cultural groups, the Vhavenḍa and Balobedu. If the essence of communal life and *vhuthu/botho* among Africans is anything to go by in the Afrocentric sense, then the African values that define commonality would overshadow cultural diversity and/or exist side-by-side. This would help defeat the intention of cultural disintegration and disappearance of commonality, thereby helping to promote the merging or coalescence in accordance with the vicissitudes of Africans.[44] However, it is the informed view of the author of this chapter that the essence of commonality in the African values of *vhuthu/botho* cements the foundations of a peoples' socio-historical-cultural fabric.

## On marriage: The marriage of close relatives and the essence of *magadi* (Khelobedu) or *lumalo* (Tshivenḓa) ('bride-price')

Mohale advances that civil laws and cultural preferences have a bearing on marriage choices, and that the marriage of close relatives conforms to cultural preferences as an open secret in a number of societies, with the reports of marriage between cousins a common practice in many African societies. Mohale, a Molobedu by birth, confirms the practice of cross-cousin marriage as being a norm among the Balobedu, with matrilateral marriage being the most common.[45] Under such practices, in matrilateral marriage a brother's daughter marries a son of her paternal aunt (*rakhadi* in Khilobedu or *makhadzi* in Tshivenḓa, which means paternal aunt). The patrilateral cross-cousin marriage also occurs among the Balobedu, but not as often as it does in the previous case.[46] Such a practice is also found among the Vhavenḓa, with both patrilateral and matrilateral cross-cousin marriage, and by extension, being even more pronounced within the royal family setup. Within this conundrum would be four influential figures, the son's paternal aunt (*rakhadimakhadzi*) as the most powerful figure during marriage negotiations, although it is/was imperative that the paternal uncles should be part of the marriage delegation as well.[47] The intention of this paragraph is to capture the cultural commonality evidenced by the practice of the cross-cousin marriage, which is the norm between the Vhavenḓa and Balobedu, as more evidence of their cultural commonality.

It is important to interrogate the significance of *magadi* or *lumalo* during Vhavenḓa and Balobedu marriage negotiations and ceremonies. *Magadi* or *lumalo* are/were central to the marriage ceremony, and they were symbolised in the form of cattle, although gradually down the centuries, a *magadi* or *lumalo* equivalent of cash is used. Importantly, as Mohale avers, the use of the concept 'bride-price' creates an unpleasant perception and implication of gender relations. In addition, it appears as if this Eurocentric translation of the two concepts reduces women to the level of articles for sale, hence an infringement on women's rights.[48] The translation *magadi* or *lumalo* into, as well as the equation of the concept to, bride price shows the Eurocentric orthography, which in instances attaches status and prestige to the family into which the daughter is married.[49] Such a discourse denigrates the socio-cultural symbolism and essence of the marriage ceremony of the Vhavenḓa and Balobedu.

## Intangible cultural heritage

According to the United Nations Educational, Scientific and Cultural Organisation's (UNESCO) Convention for the Safeguarding of the Intangible Cultural Practices (ICP), intangible cultural heritage includes practices, representations, expressions, knowledge and know-how that communities recognise as part of their cultural heritage. The government should help preserve and respect this heritage through the relevant Ministry of Culture. The principal objective of UNESCO in preserving the ICP is to raise awareness of intangible cultural practices, to strengthen the recognition of their holders and practitioners and to improve the conditions for exercising, transmitting, safeguarding and disseminating such practices.[50] Intangible cultural heritage is a peoples' collective proud heritage. Therefore, it would not be prudent for anyone to gainsay the existence of commonality, which is inherent in the cultural heritage of a people, as supported by the dynastical commonality of their languages, culture and religion found to be in practice long before the arrival of Europeans.[51] As if to consolidate this argument, Edwin Hanisch postulates that frequently there is an underlying similarity between studying less tangible facets of the cultures concerned, and when the presumed differences are actually the reaction of the particular community to different circumstances and stimuli.[52] The discussion below looks at religious practices within Great Zimbabwe: the VaRozi/Vhavenḓa/Balobedu's socio-cultural-historical link.

## Religious practices

Illife asserts that Africans of Great Zimbabwe held to a belief especially strong among the patriarchal peoples of Southern Africa that access to spiritual power came only through the dead ancestors, who they approached by sacrifices of cattle.[53] Although it may be that they held this view and engaged in such spiritual and cultural practices, it is unfortunate that this author chose to diminish the importance of the 'supreme being' to Africans, apparently because this reverence may not be according to western methods. Such a Eurocentric and hegemonic interpretation of African socio-cultural issues tends to distort and hold insignificant the historical evidence from other sources about the this belief in the essence of a 'supreme being', who they referred to as Mwari/Mwali/Khuzwane/Raluvhimba.[54] The information from these sources goes a long way to show that these people believed in a 'supreme being' who they occasionally called upon for intervention, and whose intervention the ruler in the apex position mediated as a secular representative.[55] This showed that Africans of Great Zimbabwe also had their spiritual side, which was inherent in religious beliefs and practices.

In corroborating the above cited sources in response to the claim by Illife, Mohale posits that religious practices have been at the forefront of determining wholeness in many societies. Illife adds that cultural theories identify religion as one of the sources that trigger changes in many societies.[56] He further asserts that ancestral spirits form the foundation of the southern Bantu religion such that all Bantu-speaking groups have special names to refer to their ancestors (badimo in Khelobedu and vhadzimu in Tshivenḓa) whom they revere and show great respect to. In relation to this, and according to Vhavenḓa tradition, on their southward migration, Vhasenzi/Masingo kings had a magic drum known as Ngomalungundu, of Mwali/Ṅwali (or ChiShona variant of Mwari), the Great God of the Vhasenzi.[57] The drum was their magic shield, which they believed worked miracles since it had magical killing power and was not supposed to touch the ground. The drum was accompanied as well as complemented by a magical golden pipe, also given to them by Mwali(ri). Accordingly, they called the magic drum the voice of the 'Great God,' "Mambo wa Denga" (King of Heaven) or "Dzomo-la-Dzimu" (mouth of 'God'), left by the high priest. They believed that Mwali (Mwari) spoke through the drum when he was angry when people quarrelled or fought among themselves.[58] In the same instance, the Balobedu also have/had reverence for Mwari (the 'supreme being'), whom they equally regarded as the 'God' of heaven and earth, which the Vhavenḓa and VhaLozwi and Balobedu referred to by common names as above such as Raluvhimba or Khuzwane, who they believed had the effect of stabilising political power.[59] The author of this chapter believes that the evidence on the common religious practices between Vhavenḓa and Balobedu further vindicates the existence of religious-cultural commonality.

Other common religious practices between Vhavenḓa and Balobedu that Mohale has captured in her thesis are identifiable by similar pronunciation of such concepts and phrases that share similar names even if they refer to Tshivenḓa on the one side and Khilobedu on the other.

## Common language related to religious practices: Balobedu and Vhavenḓa

The religious practice of appeasing ancestors by pouring beer on a sacred place that the Balobedu or Vhavenḓa culturally regard as a shrine, during a special ceremony, is referred to as "go phasa," by the Balobedu, while the Vhavenḓa call it "u phasa;" another phonological commonality which refers to the same religious-cultural practice. The shrine, located in the courtyard of the house of the ruler or head of the family, is a place where people make ancestral offerings. However, it is worth taking into cognisance the fact that "go phasa" or "u phasa" follows the performance of the process of "u thugula" (Khilobedu) or "u tungula" (Tshivenda) that precedes the "go phasa" or "u phasa" ceremony. Such a stage in religious-cultural practice is the responsibility of the 'diviner' who uses his/her divining items/bones to perform such a ritual.[60] Another reference to the phonological commonality between the Tshivenḓa and Khilobedu languages refers to the concept "badimolalane," which means "the ancestors/gods must rest" or "let the ancestors/gods rest." The Tshivenḓa equivalence of "badimolalane" is "vhadzimulalani" or even "vhadzimukhavhalale." The reader may once again identify and/ or experience the phonological commonality in the two concepts, "badimobalale" and "vhadzimuvhalale."[61] During difficult times or periods of hardship, both the Vhavenḓa and Balobedu would call on the peaceful intervention of Mwali/Mwari/Khuzwane/ Raluvhimba. During such an appeal, Balobedu would say "wa va li mulalo shako la lala," while Vhavenḓa would exclaim "ha vha na mulalo shongo lia lala."[62] The phonological commonality in the phrases simply means that when peace descends in the land, people experience some normalcy or degree of socio-political stability. A ceremony of "malopo" (in Khilobedu) or "malombo" (in Tshivenḓa) (note again the phonological commonality of the concepts) refers to a specific dance or a ritual-performing dance-group which is usually held for a particular appeasing ceremony or during the graduation ceremony of a traditional healer.[63] During such a ceremony, a "lilopo" (singular of "malopo" in Khilobedu) or "lilombo" (singular in Tshivenḓa), who is a member of "malopo"/"malombo," performs on a "tshele" (in Khilobedu and Tshivenḓa) (again note the phonological commonality in the name of the instrument), which is a traditional tambourine. The performance on a "tshele" goes hand in hand with the beating of special drums (meropa, plural or moropa, singular in Khilobedu or miromba, plural or murumba, singular in Tshivenḓa).[64] This discussion on the concepts that relate to religious practices mainly aims at exposing some of the phonological commonalities between Tshivenḓa and Khilobedu as a way of illustrating another level of socio-cultural commonality that exists between Vhavenḓa and Balobedu.

According to Mohale, the Balobedu also perform or sing "kosha" and even perform a dance in order to show sympathy and sorrow to the queen on behalf of the people who should have been ploughing in the summer season but, due to drought, no cultivation has taken place; hence the sympathy which they direct at the queen. The corollary is that the community may still perform "kosha" during celebratory occasions.[65] In the case of the Vhavenḓa, they express such a celebratory mood of plentiful harvest or sorrowful occasion during the death of a ruler with the "tshikona" dance, which is a mass pipe performance by males, although today even females perform "tshikona." "Tshikona," which raises an occasion to a celebraton during the birth of a prince or the enthronement of a ruler.[66] Another common aspect between Vhavenḓa and Balobedu is the reverence of "vhadzimu" or "badimo." In both cases, "vhadzimu" or "badimo" refers to the ancestors, who are also the 'living-dead.' The 'living-dead' are the shade or protectors of those who are still living, for whom senior traditional leaders perform rituals, the purpose of which is to free individuals from bad luck during job-seeking occasions, for example. Accordingly, most people of the Soutpansberg (the Vhavenḓa) and the eastern region (the Balobedu) continue to respect their rulers because they see their religious positions as a guarantee for the well-being of all inhabitants.[67] It is for this reason that traditional leaders work with traditional healers to perform such rituals in order to remove bad luck, bad omens or misfortune, which they refer to as "muridi"/"moridi" in Khelobedu or "murunzi" in Tshivenḓa. The essence of such a ritual performance is to appeal for protection from the ancestors/"badimo"/"vhadzimu" who society believes offer a different kind of "muridi" or "murunzi" that instead relates to a shade of protection and good-luck.[68]

### Initiation ceremonies

Vhavenḓa and Balobedu generally called on Mwali/Mwari/Ṅwali during the season of initiation ceremonies, such that it becomes clear that the significance of the supreme being is moral, social and spiritual.[69] It is the cultural practice of 'domba' (Vhavenḓa python dance) initiation for young girls, just as it is with the Balobedu girls who partake in initiation ceremonies, that the initiates wear short wraps around their hips. Their initiation rites would involve six days of seclusion in a hut where they experience lessons in considerable hardship as future wives, where they are taught, 'molao'/'milayo' (rules).[70] Such a similarity exposes itself when one revisits the initiation rites of the 'domba,' which signals the final stage in the fertility celebrations conducted to mark the transition into adulthood.[71]

Secondly, the preceding statements show the commonality of the transition to adulthood for the Vhavenḓa and Balobedu girls. It also captures how central Mwali is in many ways in their lives. Thirdly, the fact that the training of initiates includes the experiences of the hardships of family life indicates that in both instances conditions in the initiation schools are quite vigorous. In addition, Mohale makes mention of moments during which the initiates are not allowed to mention male names, but to reveal personal secrets ("dikoma"/"dzingoma" in Tshivenḓa, or mummeries) which they do standing all night. This vigorous experience is referred to as "khilalaowemi" (Khelobedu) or "tshilalawoima" (Tshivenḓa).[72] While we make reference to these practices as further proof of the commonality found in "khilalaowemi" and/or "tshilalawoima," we end up deducing that this could serve as a discouragement for girls, especially those of the current era (the born-frees) to consider attending initiation schools. In support of this conclusion, one source reveals that the number of females who presently show interest in undergoing initiation rites has dropped exponentially.[73]

When referring to life in the Vhavenḓa socio-cultural setup, Edwin Hanisch posits that in early African society, there was traditionally no formal schooling until children reached the age of puberty when they would hold a series of initiation schools separately for boys and girls to teach them to be responsible members of the adult community.[74] This supports Mohale's assertion of the age in which young girls attend(ed) initiation schools. However, regarding male initiation, Caroline Jeannerat maintains that the male circumcision ritual was only introduced in the Soutpansberg in the 19th century when a young Makhado, son of Ramabulana and grandson of Ṱhohoyanḓou, was secretly circumcised. This corroborates the fact that the ritual was practised at a young age, as in the case of Balobedu girls and "domba,' the youth had reached adolescent stage.

It is important to note that the Vhavenḓa had copied the circumcision ritual from the Bapedi, who had already socio-culturally welded with the Balobedu through acculturation and enculturation. The essence of initiation rituals was to teach the initiates moral lessons of behaviour within society, and humility, respect and obedience to the elders, and to treat brides of fellow initiates with respect, to remain faithful and loyal subjects to the ruler, and to be good future husbands and fathers.[75] Therefore, as in the initiation of young females, the form of male circumcision is regarded as a rite of passage from adolescence to adulthood, during which the "tshikona" is performed for those who are preparing to go to Ha-Madala (to the mountain). The reference to Ha-Madala is part of the Tshivenḓa and Khelobedu culture, which exposes a commonality in a ritual that is as important to teach future husbands and wives the art of womanhood and manhood for the benefit of the broader community.[76]

## Rainmaking process

Africans commonly invoked God directly when seeking rain and they performed rituals in shrines (frequently associated with caves and water) where resident mediums and priests concerned themselves with the fertility of the region, from southern Tanzania, the Dzivaguru rain-shrine of the northern edge of Zimbabwe in Munhumutapa, to the Limpopo Province.[77] Similarly, the Queen of the Balobedu, well known down the years in history for her rainmaking powers, is celebrated/importuned during an occasion in which the community performs certain rituals, including a dance performance for rain that starts with the headman coming with his male followers to the royal kraal to dance for the Queen. During this occasion, the presence of the rain doctor is of paramount importance. He uses his divine bones to appeal to Mwali/Khuzwane to bless the community with rain, especially after a long period of drought. Females who are menstruating do not attend the ritual performance for fear of them inviting bad luck.[78]

Importantly, as they invoke the presence of Mwali/Khuzwane, they worship their ancestors, starting with the basic family unit, with the rainmaking ceremony continuing throughout the year during which they perform rituals using rain medicines. It has been explained how Mwali/Mwari/Khuzwane/Raluvhambi was the common factor between the Vhavenḓa and Balobedu, where the ruler is the mediator between the community and the 'supreme being,' whom they revere and obey at all costs in order not to incur his wrath.[79] The Vhasenzi, VaRozvi and Vashona called on Mwali/Mwari through Ngomalungundu when they appealed for rain, fertility, a good harvest, and peace and calm by performing *thevhula*.[80]

During the *thevhula* ceremony, the performers spill or pour traditional beer on the ground as thanksgiving for rainmaking, seed-blessing and a good harvest. This commonality in the practice of the ritual cements the socio-cultural essence that linked culture with religion that underpins African societies. In this instance spirits, supernatural forces, gods, cults, witchcraft, sorcery, sacrifices, rituals, taboos, veneration of ancestors, ceremonies of rites of passage such as naming ceremonies, initiation rites and customs associated with deaths and burials represent(ed) culture and religion.[81] Throughout this discussion on rainmaking, it flows that this religious practice reveals a ritualistic commonality between the Vhavenḓa and Balobedu.

## Conclusion

As part of discussion and disputing the Eurocentric claim of the existence of diversity among the Africans of South Africa in general and Vhavenḓa and Balobedu in particular, the author attempts to show that they share commonality in a number of aspects. As a starting point, the discussion illustrates how the two cultural groups shared a socio-historical origin, with the discussion showing that they share agnatic links with the VhaLozwi north of the Vhembe River. The author also identifies other issues for discussion in addition to the origin to argue for commonality and demystify as well as defeat the hegemonic approach that is used to divide Africans linguistically into different 'ethnic' or 'tribal' groups in creating homelands. The chapter also demonstrates the commonality in the political organisation between the Vhavenḍa and Balobedu, wherein *rakhadimakhadzi* occupy an important role, especially during marriage ceremonies and succession to the throne. The linguistic commonality relating to a number of concepts that the author discusses also proves that the Vhavenḍa and Balobedu have much in common regarding the words that form the core of their languages. A number of names and surnames that we attach to identification among the Vhavenḍa and Balobedu demonstrate various phonological commonalities in a number of ways to consolidate the claim that the two groups have more in common and were not as diverse as the colonial regime had wanted Africans to imbue. Culture and the intangible cultural aspect prove how cultural practices have transcended the ages and refuse to disappear to hide this commonality in order to oblige the policies of the colonial rulers. A number of issues, such as cross-marriage between cousins, that we find taking place on both side of the spectrum, continue to prove this commonality.

# Chapter Three
## The Socio-Historical Relationship between Basotho and the Nguni: Issues of Ethnicity, Languages, Surnames, Culture and Intangible Cultural Heritage

Sehlare Makgetlaneng

This chapter produces and provides understanding of the socio-historical relationship between Basotho and the Nguni as the process of their ethnic, linguistic, cultural and intangible cultural heritage commonality. Their surnames are an integral part of their commonality in this relationship. This commonality is of strategic importance to the resolution of the national question through nation building project. As a means to achieve this objective, this chapter produces and provides understanding, firstly, of the construction of ethnic, linguistic, cultural and intangible cultural diversity of Africans of South Africa in the service of a settler colonial and racist rule by apartheid's anthropologists in working closely with their German allies and colleagues. Secondly, understanding of ethnic, linguistic, cultural and intangible cultural heritage commonality of Basotho and the Nguni and the case of the Edwin Thabo Mufatsanyana, Robert Mangaliso Sobukwe, BaFokeng and the Xhosa. Thirdly, the commonality of surnames between Basotho and the Nguni. Fourthly, the understanding of the linguistic commonality between Basotho and the Nguni. Fifthly, the understanding of the commonality of surnames between Basotho and the Nguni.

## Apartheid's Anthropologists: The Construction of Ethnic, Linguistic, Cultural and Intangible Cultural Diversity of Africans

Knowledge is power when it is organised to achieve strategic and tactical objectives. The role and significance of intellectuals is of paramount importance in this task. Ideas are critical in any struggle for power and its exercise. Despite the fact that power comes out of the barrel of the gun, ideas cannot be articulated through guns. They are articulated and propagated through a shrewd and skillful use of the media and requisite manipulation of issues, processes and developments of the members of the society whose support is needed for the achievement of objectives and their sustenance. This truism was recognised in theory and practice by organic intellectuals of settler colonial and racist rule in South Africa in their collaboration with their German allies and colleagues.

Other chapters of this book deal with the socio-historical relationship among Bapedi, Batswana and Basotho, the socio-historical relationship between Bapedi and the Nguni focusing on the relationship between Bapedi and the Swazi, the socio-historical relationship among the Nguni focusing on issues of ethnicity, languages, surnames, culture and intangible cultural heritage and on the strategic importance of their ethnic, linguistic, cultural and intangible cultural heritage commonality in the service of the nation building project. They challenge and dispute the dominant, hegemonic and dominant thesis of their ethnic, linguistic, cultural and intangible cultural heritage diversity. On the Southern African regional level, Paul S. Landau maintains that popular politics of South Africa is an integral part of the Southern African regional history and the history of its people should be viewed dialectically and organically as a process which is interlinked with the history of the people of the region. His point is that, firstly, the "nationalist understanding of popular politics as the twentieth-century movement to transcend tribes and chiefs unwittingly accepts an imperialist and ultimately apartheid vision of Africans' history." Secondly, the history of South Africa "over the centuries should not be abstracted from the history of Lesotho, Botswana, even Zimbabwe (nor Swaziland and Mozambique." Thirdly, that Lesotho was "a mass political movement in the heartland of the country before it became a bordered labor reserve and "nation-state."[1] On the regional level, Thato Mabolaeng Maryanne Monyakane maintains that "the boundaries" created among the African people of South Africa into "Nguni and Sotho" and those of Southern Africa are "artificial" and should be brought to an end for them to truly "reclaim their shared heritage of culture and identity."[2] In demonstrating Pan-African linguistic and cultural unity, Siphiwe Sesanti maintains that, on the continental level, contrary to the view that Africa has many ethnic groups whose cultures and languages are not related, scientific research supports the reality that African languages are interlinked or connected, and by extension, demonstrate African cultural connectivity and unity.[3] Central to this continental, regional and national view of the African people is the issue of ethnic, linguistic and cultural commonality which has continues being fought against in the name of their ethnic, linguistic and cultural diversity or differences.

Given this provision of ethnic, linguistic, cultural and intangible cultural heritage relationship of the African people nationally, regionally and continentally, in this chapter we share with the reading audience the role played by German scholars, missionaries and colonial state officials working together with Afrikaner anthropologists in the service of a settler colonial and racist rule in South Africa. This required South African intellectuals for the resolution of the national question through the national building project to study those works that produced and disseminated knowledge and understanding inimical to the ethnic, linguistic, cultural and intangible cultural heritage commonality of the African people on the basis that theirs were ethnic, linguistic, cultural and intangible cultural diversity or differences. Ethnicity was used by the settler colonial and racist state in dividing and ruling Africans on the basis of what was regarded as their ethnic diversity, differences or separation. It was at the heart of the settler colonial and racist rule. The study of ethnic identities among Africans by volkekundiges[4] as ideological justification of the divide and rule policy continues as the practical task as Africans strive to be a chain without weak links in their efforts to successfully complete decolonisation of their country. According to Susan George, this task calls upon those who are for the equality of the material conditions and rights to:

Study the rich and the powerful, not the poor and powerless ... not nearly enough is being done on those who hold the power and pull the strings. As their tactics become more subtle and their public and their public pronouncements more guarded, the need for better spade-work becomes crucial ... Let the poor study themselves. They already know what is wrong with their lives and if you truly want to help them, then the best you can do is to give them a clearer idea of how their oppressors are working now and can be expected to work in the future.[5]

This key reason behind this call is

The fact is that there is far more systematic information available on the poor, on farmers, workers ... than on the men and women of the rich and the well-born, on those who make up the 'upper strata' - of not the 'capitalist class' - of our society. Yet now it ought to be apparent ... that we must discover as much as we can about those who occupy the upper reaches of ... society if we are to understand ... the present as history.[6]

This call is required by the fact that: "Of all classes, the wealthy are the most noticed and least studied."[7] This call is relevant in the South African case where white intellectuals of different and antagonistic political, economic and ideological positions studied Africans as if they were their main enemies. Afrikaners intellectuals studied Africans so as to understand them the key issue being to defeat and control them. This intellectual tradition in the history of South Africa has survived the end of a settler colonial and racist rule. Africans and organisations they led are studied as if they are problems to be solved and main enemies to be defeated as a means to achieve the equality of the material conditions and rights of the South African people.

The production and dissemination in Germany of racist knowledge and understanding of Africa and Africans was primarily linguistic. It linked language dialectically and organically to culture and national identity. The German missionaries played a pivotal role in this linguistic theoretical and practical task. They maintained that the best and most effective way to penetrate the minds and hearts of Africans religiously was through their native languages. It is for this reason that they learned African languages as a practical necessity to achieve their objectives. They used English as a primary language of scholarship and engagement. German missionaries working and living in African countries, linguists at the universities like those of Hamburg and Berlin and Afrikanistik scholars using languages and culture in categorising Africans for political, economic and ideological strategic purposes played a leadership role in the execution of this task. African studies in general and the study of African languages in particular was viewed as of vital importance in the advancement of the German colonial project[8] in particular and to serve the "Western cultural hegemony in enormously complex ways"[9] in general. Members of the triple alliance of missionaries, scholars and colonial officials "all wanted to use African languages to extend European power" or to serve imperialism.[10] Without African as collaborators, they should not have successfully executed their tasks and achieved their objectives. They relied on native Africans as interpreters and translators. This African agency providing organic intellectuals of colonialism and racism with the concrete understanding and knowledge of the way Africans used their customs, traditions and culture in reasserting their humanness and integrity essential for their material conditions and rights served as an integral part of intellectual native authorities in helping in imposing colonialism upon the African people.

The colonial state and its intellectuals understood that the use of customs, traditions and culture of African people was "part and parcel of the human struggle for self-preservation, self-identity, self-representation, liberation, and freedom."[11] Central to their task was to rob Africans not only of South Africa as their country and its natural wealth, their products and services, but also importantly of their history and culture interlinked with its social fabric. It is in this context that Amilcar Cabral's special focus on the importance of culture in the national liberation struggle and development, that "national liberation is necessarily an act of culture"[12] and that the national liberation movement guiding this popular re-creation of culture is "the organized political expression of the culture of the people who are undertaking the struggle"[13] can be fully understood. This "reconversion of minds – of mental sets' is "indispensable to the true integration of people into the liberation movement."[14] The need for training "people with a mentality which could transcend the context of the national liberation struggle"[15] and providing them with knowledge, skills, and experience as the collective and proud national assets through the mediation of the progressive state and governing political party in the political governance of the society and the conduct and running of its affairs is of vital importance in that their cultural, economic and social "liberation should be the work of the people themselves, who should rely primarily on their own resources to attain this goal."[16] The task of the political party as cultural re-creation and transformation is education whose aim is to new social human beings as social agents of their own transformation and development who are "fully conscious" of their "national, continental and international rights and duties."[17]

Cabral's view of the political party as a national liberation movement engaged in popular cultural re-creation and transformation is essentially not different from Antonio Gramsci's view of the political party as "the Modern Prince" whose task is to awaken and develop "a national- popular collective will"[18] by imparting the insights of its organic intellectuals to the masses of the people to "burst simultaneously into political life."[19] It "must be and cannot but be the proclaimer and organizer of an intellectual and moral reform, which also means creating the terrain for a subsequent development of the national-popular collective will towards the realization of a superior, total form of modern civilization."[20] As the modern prince of politics of the revolutionary change, the political party should act

> like one single head that thinks through a thousand brains, the cross-roads of all knowledge, of all cultures, of all specializations, precisely because it is called upon to know and to dominate the national and international reality in toto, to act upon it in order to transform it; it is force capable of lifting the masses up to the highest degree of a vanguard intellectual consciousness; a sort of collective man or homogeneous intellectual force susceptible of articulating the complex relationships: masses-party-leadership.
>
> Viewed from this perspective, the "collective intellectual" must strive to educate, to turn each follower into an intellectual. Thanks to a well-designed resocialization program, each member is prepared to assume leadership. In other words, the party must create the conditions for the political man and woman to be transformed into an expert, a specialist or, if you prefer, a cadre, a skilled person.[21]

The role of Afrikaner intellectuals in the production and provision of leaders, experts, specialists or skilled individuals was indispensable in preventing the possibility or "the potential" of Africans from materialising into independent, self-reliant, just and prosperous political, economic and ideological social formation.

The central target of their role was the nation building project of Africans on the basis of their ethnic, linguistic, cultural and intangible cultural heritage commonality enabling them to correctly handle contradictions among themselves and to serve as a chain without weak links in dealing with their allies and enemies and friends and opponents. The role of African intellectuals well-versed on the ethnic, linguistic, cultural and intangible cultural commonality of the African people and judiciously using it in the advancement of their national popular interests was indispensable in this national task. Werner Welli Max Eiselen called upon the Afrikaner intellectuals in particular and Afrikaners in general to act against the potential of Africans as inimical to the success of their project of national building and assumption and exercise of state political power as follows:

> The potential of the Bantu is largely unknown and the success of our great experiment will naturally be determined thereby. But we feel that the way of "eiesortige" (autochthonous) development is the only healthy way whereby real community growth can be promoted. [22]

Pieter Johannes Schoeman in 1941 called upon the Afrikaners to resolve the "native question" as "a bigger and steadily growing issue" they were confronting in their project:

> In this country of our love and dreams of the future, which is crisscrossed with war graves, we are confronted with a bigger and steadily growing question mark which is a sombre black silhouette on the horizon of our future. [23]

Central to the project of the Afrikaner minority was to end their subordinate status through the politicisation and mobilisation of their ethnic power. They assumed and exercised state political power by being victorious in the 1948 elections. They confronted the challenge poised to their project by the African majority by defeating them through their divide and rule policies. They executed these interlinked tasks by answering the strategic question as to who were their allies and enemies, friends and opponents in their national project. They used their role within public institutions and organisations, their leadership of public and private organisations, their knowledge, skills, experience and determination as the collective and proud Afrikaner assets to assume and exercise state political power so as to restructure South Africa for their interests.

These Afrikaner intellectuals were Afrikaner anthropologists who played a key role in constructing ethnic, linguistic, cultural and intangible cultural diversity or differences of Africans. This task served the forces of settler colonialism and racism in their socio-political, cultural and economic governance and control of Africans. Nicolaas Jacobus van Warmelo and Eiselen were some of these Afrikaner intellectuals Robert Gordon refers to as "apartheid's anthropologists."[24] They had a crucial and tangible impact on the settler colonial state's policy "out of all proportion to their numbers" and "completely overshadowed" their English-speaking white anthropologist counterparts in having "impact on South African "race theory."[25] They called their discipline, ethnology or anthropological style or tradition, volkekundige as they practiced it in the country. Theirs was not only anthropological theory. It was also practical. It was anthropological praxis they controlled in the service of the colonial control, domination and exploitation of the African people. It is in this context that volkekundige as an ideological justification of the settler colonial and racist divide and rule policy for the control, domination and exploitation of the African people in the name that their ethnic self-determination and the free, independent exercise of their sovereignty and domestic and foreign policies in the so-called bantustans or homelands as their countries were advanced can best and concretely be understood.[26] This was opposition to the right to their national self-determination and the free, independent exercise of their sovereignty and domestic and foreign policies in their country.

Apartheid's anthropologists rendered invaluable service to the colonial state through its Department of Native Affairs in dealing with the national question or the native question in managing common affairs of political and economic rulers. The creation of diverse or different African ethnic groups was of strategic importance for excluding Africans politically and territorially in the name that they had the right to the separate national self-determination and the free independent exercise of sovereignty and domestic and foreign policies sovereignty for their separate development of the national ethnic, linguistic and cultural identity.

Germany, through Carl Friedrich Michael Meinhof, well-known German Africanist linguist and ethnologist and head of the Faculty of Bantu and Pacific Languages at the University of Hamburg, rendered invaluable service to the colonial state in dealing with the native question. He served as a professor of African languages at the Colonial Institute, the forerunner of the University of Hamburg. The chairperson of the Seminar for Colonial Languages, the first chair for African Studies at the University of Hamburg, a member of the National Socialist German Workers Party, the Nazi Party, in 1933, he was one of the signatories of the commitment of the professors at German universities and colleagues to Adolph Hitler and the Nazi state. He had decisive and intangible impact on a group of young Afrikaners who left for the University of Hamburg in Germany in the 1920s for their doctoral studies in ethnology and linguistics. Among them were Van Warmelo and Eiselen, a son of a German missionary, who came to play a key role in African affairs within the state as intellectuals and senior officials. They studied under him. He also supervised them in their doctoral studies. They were followed, among others, by Johannes Anthonie Engelbrecht, Bernardus Izak Christiaan van Edeen and Dirk Ziervogel in the 1930s.

According to Ernest Fred Dube, as young intellectuals they were sent to "study Nazi ideology and organizational tactics." Hendrik Frensch Verwoerd, Ebenezer Donges and Eiselen were some of them. Upon completion of their studies and return to South Africa, they fashioned "apartheid and developed structures that paralleled the Nazi SS and Brown Shirts in the form of the Ossewabrandwag and the Grey Shirts."[27]

Grey Shirts or Gryshempte in Afrikaans was a common name given to the South African Gentile National Socialist Movement, a South African Nazi movement that existed during the 1930s and 1940s. Its members were also members of the National Party. Afrikaner nationalist movements that admired German Nazism such as Grey Shirts and Ossewabrandwag were popular among Afrikaners before the Second World War. John Balthazar Vorster and other members of the Ossewabrandwag opposed South Africa's participation in the Second World War and carried out sabotage actions against the administration of Jan Christian Smuts. His administration acted severely against the Ossewabrandwag movement and put its leaders including Vorster in prison throughout the Second World War.

The Department of Native Affairs played a leadership role in the formulation and implementation of the policy of separate development and its consequence principle that Africans were not South African nationals but nations of so-called bantustans or homelands regarded by the National Party as their countries and nations. It operated on the basis of their constructed ethnic, linguistic, cultural and intangible cultural heritage diversity or differences. It relied on the Ethnological Section under the leadership of van Warmelo who played a leadership role from 1930 to 1969[28] as Chief State Ethnologist. The perspectives of African informants and researchers profoundly shaped the writings of van Warmelo as Chief State Ethnologist.[29] Some of them were teachers and reverends. He collected manuscripts on the customs, traditions, culture and intangible cultural heritage of Bapedi, Batswana, Basotho, Shangaan-Tsonga, Swati, Venda, Xhosa and Zulu written by Africans.[30] He has been honoured for the role he played in studying and conducting research on the ethnicity, languages, surnames, culture and intangible cultural heritage of Africans as transformed by their internal migration within South Africa in the service of a settler colonial and racist rule.[31] He has published works including dictionaries on these issues, processes and developments individually as their sole-author and together with African experts. He also collected extensive information on them working with African informants and researchers for the settler colonial state through its Department of Native Affairs.

Van Warmelo was proficient in several African languages of Southern Africa,[32] and Eiselen, anthropologist and linguist fluent in a number of African languages, an ally and associate of Verwoerd, an intellectual architect of "apartheid" and of Bantu Education who served as the Secretary for Native Affairs and the Minister of Native Affairs. Eiselen's academic knowledge and writings served the state in its theory and practice in preserving "Bantu institutions" and using language in promoting "ethnic culture."[33] They were central aspects of the political project of the state in studying and understanding ethnicity, languages, culture and intangible cultural heritage of the African people the key issue being to control them.

Van Warmelo were mentored by Meinhof who worked closely with him as Chief State Ethnologist. He collaborated with him in translating his book, *Grundriss einer Lautlehre der Bantusprachen* into English as *Introduction to the Phonology of the Bantu Languages.* Providing description of six African languages, its English translated version importantly served British and Afrikaner colonial forces in their programme of action against Africans of South Africa.

Van Warmelo's works most of them written by Africans as informants and researchers in their African languages on ethnicity, language, cultural and intangible cultural heritage issues, processes and developments of Africans served political purposes of the settler colonial state in its control of Africans. They included in particular or specifically detailed information about their history, traditions, laws, warfare, religion and way of life. Sara Pugach maintains that the purpose of the classification of African languages and "tribes" was "very political."[34] In the case of van Warmelo, "fixing 'tribal' ethnicity provided order to what, for whites, may have appeared a jumbled mass of peoples whose relationships to one another were not immediately discernible." His works were of vital importance in that they were collected, written and published during the time when "detribalisation and urbanisation" among Africans were of "increasing concern to white South Africans." His "ethnic construction" provided a policy direction for resolving these "perceived crises."[35]

Meinhof's impact on van Warmelo's is helpful in fully understanding "the role of German philology and anthropology in shaping South African anthropology in general and Afrikaner volkekunde in particular."[36] The role played by racism and racist ideology in South Africa is reflected in the literature on the history of volkekunde, Afrikaner nationalist ethnological tradition that played a key role in legitimising a settler colonial and racist rule. Its roots are German movement led by Meinhof in his racist theories of African linguistics. Van Warmelo's book, *A Preliminary Survey of the Bantu Tribes of South Africa,* served as the blueprint for the social engineering of ethnic identities explained in Meinhof's book, *Foundations of Bantu Phonetics.* His South African disciples included van Warmelo's predecessor as State Ethnologist Gerard Paul Lestrade, the linguist Clement Martyn Doke,[37] Johannes Anthonie Engelbrecht, van Eeden and Eiselen.[38] Engelbrecht, van Eeden and Eiselen were students of Meinhof at the University of Hamburg.

Van Warmelo's second source of inspiration in his work upon whom he relied extensively was Hermanus Cornelius Martinus Fourie's doctoral thesis in divinity completed at the University of Utrecht in The Netherlands. Fourie called for the establishment of an ethnological bureau to serve the state in acquiring knowledge of Africans and in using it as power to control them. In his words:

> The failure to solve the native question in South Africa is largely due to the ethnological ignorance of the authorities … it is necessary that the government of South Africa should as quickly as it is possible establish an ethnological bureau and a chair in Bantu languages.[39]

This was the ideological front of the struggle with ethnology regarded by Fourie as "a political and religious necessity" used to rule Africans. He maintained that the "knowledge of the Bantu" was of vital importance in that it "will lead to expert rule: and for the Bantu – a knowledge of the Evangelism of Jesus Christ."[40]

Meinhof's passing away was regarded as a great loss by those who studied under him. Upon hearing that their intellectual mentor passed away, his former students, van Eeden, the Reverend Walter Bourquin, a Baptist Minister who studied African languages and worked on them, and Eiselen praised him in their obituary in June 1946. Gerard Paul Lestrade wrote that

> in his work as a teacher and guide of others interested in African languages and allied subjects, he gathered round him, both in his own school in Hamburg, and in places geographically far removed from that Mecca of the African linguist, an ever-growing band of pupils and collaborators, whom he inspired, stimulated, and in every way aided in the quest for knowledge of the African and his tongues.[41]

He also wrote that "South Africa, fortunately for itself, is able to count among its linguists several of Meinhof's former pupils and collaborators" and that he conducted a "special studies of goodly number and range of individual Bantu languages (among which, in the South African area, Northern Sotho, Venda, Xhosa and Zulu" which are of "practical necessity in colonial administration."[42] Doke and Lestrade thanked Meinhof, firstly, for his study of Sotho and Nguni languages. Secondly, for "a realization of the value of African-language study" or its "practical angle part it can and must play in the government and administration of Africa." Thirdly, for his insistence "with apt proof" of "the theoretical significance of language-study for allied disciples such as anthropology" and its "practical necessity in colonial administration."[43]

Writing that with his "robust stature" cutting "an impressive figure," Eiselen maintained that Meinhof "is no more, but his name and his work shall live on, also here in South Africa."[44] Meinhof had a profound "lasting influence on South African intellectual and political life"[45] of the settler colonial and racist rule and its continued consequences. The point is that unlike his later disciplines, Eiselen came to "operate from within the very heart of the apartheid government, crucially assisting in framing the ideology and practice of racially differential governance during the 1940s and 1950s." He played a key role in

> one of a fundamental separation of the European race from the Bantu race: an ideology of difference bred on a Berlin mission station in a former Boer republic and given a "scientific" framework in Meinhof's home, office and seminar room at Hamburg University between 1921 and 1924 – with lasting consequences for the political history of South Africa.[46]

Eiselen, the well-known intellectual product of Meinhof, highly appreciated and treasured racist impact of Meinhof on himself and his racist position on Africans in 1923 as follows:

> The sexual drive is particularly strong [in the African] and therefore the marriage between an African and a white woman is always unhappy ... "The animal in him will awaken [if we do not lay a new, Christian, foundation threaten our [white South African] society," that the "black peril of the German Empire is also our peril; the African stands low spiritually; it is our duty towards our fellow whites to lift him [the African] up and to bring about a cultural movement of which our children will reap benefit."[47]

This was basically a call for the Immorality Act which was passed by the parliament in 1927 for the socio-political and ideological regulation of the relationship between South Africans on the racial lines. The legislation was primarily socio-political and ideological in that without it, should it have been difficult if not impossible to justify the settler colonial and racist rule in the name of separate development of racial groups.

With political decolonisation gaining momentum and South Africa being forced out of the Commonwealth of Nations, and Africa as an increasing battleground of what was referred to as the

Cold War, Verwoerd called for survival of white South Africans as a whole not only Afrikaners. He now called for "the necessity for preservation of European civilization, specifically associated with race" and urging "white unity, regardless of differences in history and culture."[48] It is interesting to note that he continued being against African unity, "regardless of differences in history and culture" of Africans specifically as members of one race. He increasingly viewed South Africa as a staunch formation against communism and a strategic geopolitical "lynchpin of white civilization" in Africa and internationally.[49]

Children and grandchildren of Eiselen and other apartheid anthropologists still "reap benefit" of the socio-cultural, political, economic and ideological movement brought into existence and well-entrenched by their grandfathers. The reason behind this socio-historical reality is the fact that misfortunes of capitalism and racism faced by Africans and benefits of capitalism and racism enjoyed by whites since their inception in South Africa survived the end of the settler colonial and racist rule in 1994.

### Ethnicity, Language, Surnames, Culture and Intangible Cultural Heritage Commonality of Basotho and the Nguni: The Case of Edwin Thabo Mofutsanyana, Robert Mangaliso Sobukwe, Bafokeng/Bakwena and the Xhosa

Some scholars maintain the position that there was a time when Africans were not divided into ethnic and linguistic groups and that ethnicity did not exist. Patrick Harris, one of these scholars, maintains that "many of the ethnic divisions that are today a concrete reality did not exist, even in a conceptual form, before the end of the nineteenth century"[50] and that "Many of the linguistic givens and truths believed by the Swiss missionaries to be scientifically incontrovertible were, in fact social constructs whose roots may be traced to nineteenth European codes of thought."[51]

One of the key characteristic features of the socio-historical relationship between Basotho and the Nguni in terms of ethnicity, languages, surnames, culture and intangible cultural heritage is that while some Basotho split from the Nguni, other Basotho were integrated into the process of the building the Nguni group. Central to this relationship was their migration from one place to another place until they settled either for a long time or permanently. This movement transformed their ethnicity, languages, surnames, culture and intangible cultural heritage as they settled among the people into which they were integrated. They acquired the ethnicity, languages, surnames, culture and intangible cultural heritage of their fellow Africans who welcomed them within themselves.

Peter Becker maintains that some Basotho people split from the Nguni people while others were integrated into the process of building the Nguni group and that King Moshoeshoe welcomed the refugees escaping the consequences of the Difagane into the Basotho nation.[52] He maintains that the Basotho nation was born at Thaba Bosiu, Moshoeshoe's stronghold where he protected the refugees and others by providing them with food, shelter and other forms of life-support needs, a precipitous, flat-topped hill which he transformed into an impregnable fortress. The victims of suffering from the settler colonial onslaughts knocked at his doors at Thaba Bosiu for food, shelter and other forms of life-support needs in increasing numbers. Moshoeshoe and his advisors, personally and collectively addressed by their plight, welcomed them into this stronghold. There are different and antagonistic views and interpretations of what is the socio-historical development referred to as Difagane or the Mfecane. It is referred to as Difagane in Sotho and the Mfecane in Nguni. We agree with Julian Cobbing that, as used by "white historians" supportive of a settler colonial rule, it is "essentially a concept that evolved or developed for mainly propaganda purpose" to "account for and legitimise the South African homelands"[53] policy of dividing Africans so as to conquer and rule them. Central to it is to justify "the unequal land distribution between blacks and whites in today's South Africa" in the name that it originated from "an orgy of African self-destruction in the 1820s and 1830s which depopulated the Orange Free State, the Transvaal and Natal just in time for the occupation."[54]

One of the consequences of this migration is that some Africans who are referred to or are regarded as Basotho and the Nguni were originally not Basotho and the Nguni. Edwin Thabo Mofutsanyana is one of these Africans. He was referred to as Mosotho. His surname is originally the Nguni surname, Mfuzunyane. One of its popular and well-known bearer is Edwin Thabo Mofutsanyana, a leader of the African National Congress and the South African Communist Party and its General Secretary during the time it was called the Communist Party of South Africa before it was banned. He was born in 1899 in Qwa Qwa in the Free State Province. His was related to King Moshoeshoe, the founder of the Basotho kingdom, through his mother, Linkhapa. She was a daughter of Molapo, a son of Moshoeshoe. His father was a descendant of the Nhlapo or AmaNhlapo, a member of the Zulu clan originally from the Mashishini area near Pietermaritzburg in KwaZulu-Natal Province. Members of the Nhlapo clan were forced to leave after their tensions with Matiwane, a tradional leader of AmaNgwane during the intensified conflicts of the 1820s throughout the area. A branch of the Nhlapo clan under the leadership of Mfuzunyane settled among the Basotho in Qwa Qwa, formerly Witzieshoek. Upon their integration into Basotho, their surname, Mfuzunyane was transformed by Sesotho into Mofutsanyana.[55] Their ethnicity was transformed from that of the Zulu, an integral part of the Nguni group, into that of the Basotho, an integral part of the Sotho group. Govan Mbeki's admiration of Mofutsanyana as a political leader led him to give his middle name to his son, Thabo Mbeki, the former deputy president and president of South Africa and the ANC.

This development relating to the socio-historical relationship between Basotho and the Nguni in terms of their ethnicity, languages, surnames, culture and intangible cultural heritage applies also to Robert Mangaliso Sobukwe, a son of a Sotho father and a Xhosa mother. His grandfather was from Lesotho.[56] He is referred to as Xhosa. In his response to this position, Sobukwe maintained that:

I call my clan 'Baboons' because that is the totem of my clan. There are thus crocodiles, baboons, monkeys, lions, etc. You'll, therefore, realise that those who claim to know me do not in fact know me because if I am not mistaken, I have been described as a Xhosa. I am not, as you can see.[57]

Sobukwe, who according to Nyameko Barney Pityana, "spoke several languages," was "a linguist, comfortable in many South African languages," who besides "his mother tongue isiXhosa, was proficient in English and Afrikaans. In Kimberely, in the Methodist Church and at funerals, he often acted as an interpreter,"[58] was a representative of "multi-ethnic" African identities"[59] against ethnic, linguistic, cultural and intangible cultural heritage diversity thesis in the service of the settler colonial and racist rule and its present consequences. He is one of a popular and well-known Pan-Africanist and the first and founding president of the Pan-African Congress. The surname Sobukwe is originally the Sotho surname Rabogoe.[60] The locals in Queenstown in the Eastern Cape where Sobukwe's grandfather migrated to mispronounced Rabogoe as Sobukwe. Their mispronunciation of Sesotho surname Rabogoe transformed it into Xhosa surname Sobukwe. The combination of migration and the Xhosa as the Nguni language transformed Sesotho surname into the Xhosa surname.

Migration served as a key socio-historical process in the formation and transformation of ethnic, linguistic, cultural and intangible cultural heritage identities in Southern Africa. It served in the formation and transformation also of names and surnames of people.

Bafokeng acquired their name from a period of living in a region or place with a lot of dew (phoka). They call themselves "Ba-Phokeng" (people who live in a place of dew). Ba-Phokeng over time evolved into Bafokeng. They still use a term "phoka) when they call each other. Bafokeng venerate the rabbit (mmutla). Those who come from Phokeng near Tlhabane (Rustenburg) venerate crocodile (koena/kwena). At one point, all Bafokeng venerated crocodile. Bafokeng are descendants of Bakwena who currently speak Setswana as their mother tongue. Citing a "well-known Bafokeng tradition" according to which the name of the people is derived from the time when they "reached their present location," Bernard Mbenga and Andrew Manson regard Bafokeng as "People of the Dew." Their reason is that Bafokeng encountered thick dew (phoka) covering the valleys in the morning.[61] This is a socio-cultural tradition and practice among the African people.

There is a difference among scholars on the origin within South Africa of Bakwena whose surname is Mokuena or Mokoena. While some maintain that they originated in the KwaZulu-Natal Province, some maintain that their origin is the North-West Province.

James Walton maintains that Bafokeng split into two sections in the Magaliesberg area in the North West Province. The other section was subdivided into a number of clans which migrated southwards across the Vaal River. They are the first Tswana to cross the Vaal River.[62] Bafokeng are an integral part of Basotho. Basotho whose surname is Mofokeng are part of Basotho. Bafokeng became Bafokeng-baMmutle. They named themselves after their traditional leader Mmutle.

The Bafokeng intermingled and intermarried with the San people near the hill Ntoanatsatsi or Ntsuanatsatsi between the Free State towns of Frankfort and Vrede where they settled.[63] A son of their traditional leader married a daughter of a San traditional leader. While this marriage was not disapproved, some members of the Bafokeng community and Bakoena who also settled in the area refused to be led by a son of a San woman when his father passed away.

It was forbidden for some Basotho to marry San daughters. It was for this reason why so some Sothos objected to being led by a son of a San. As the consequence of this disagreement, Bafokeng clan split. The main section under the leader of mixed Bafokeng-San blood migrated until they reached the Transkei in the Eastern Cape Province. Upon introducing themselves among the Xhosa, they were asked as to who they were. They answered: "Re baMmutle" (we are ba ga Mmutle) or the Bafokeng of the hare. Their totem was mmutla or the hare The Xhosa mispronounced ba ga Mmutle as Mvundla. Mmutle is a Sotho word for hare. Bafokeng adopted the kwena (crocodile) as their totem to mmutla (hare). The language and culture of the Bafokeng, an integral part of the Sotho group, were transformed through migration into that of the Xhosa, an integral part of the Nguni group. Ba Mmutle were transformed in the Eastern Cape into the Amavundle or Ama-Vundle clan.[64]

Manti Teboho Pitso conducted fieldwork research in which he interviewed scholars, experts and community members on the socio-historical background of Basotho in QwaQwa and social context of QwaQwa for his Master of Philosophy thesis in Indigenous Studies. South Sotho individuals of Southern Africa he interviewed provided him with the socio-historical background why they settled in QwaQwa.

Manti in his study produced and provided evidence that Bakoena or Bakwena are originally the Zulus from the KwaZulu-Natal Province. They were members of the Ngwenya clan. Some members of the Ngwenya clan are still in KwaZulu-Natal with Ngwenya as their surname. They left the KwaZulu-Natal as a result of Difaqane or Mfeqane. Upon arrival at Ntsoanatsatsi or Ntsuanatsatsi, they settled on top of the mountain for them to be able to see their enemies approaching so as to protect themselves from their attacks. They became Bakwena. They were attacked at Ntsoanatsatsi. As a result of these attacks, some left for various places. There are those who left for Bopedi for safety and security. According to Mokoena, some members of the Ngwenya clan left KwaZulu-Natal for Bopedi in the Limpopo Province.[65] Sepedi transformed their Zulu surname, Ngwenya, into Sepedi surname, Mokwena.

The case of Mofutsanyana, Sobukwe and the key characteristic features of the relationship between Basotho and the Nguni in terms of ethnicity, languages, surnames, culture and intangible cultural heritage support the position articulated by Harris that "many of the ethnic divisions that are today a concrete reality did not exist, even in a conceptual form, before the end of the nineteenth century"[66] and that "Many of the linguistic givens and truths believed by the Swiss missionaries to be scientifically incontrovertible were, in fact social constructs whose roots may be traced to nineteenth European codes of thought."[67]

## The Linguistic Commonality between Basotho and the Nguni

There is commonality between Sesotho and Ndebele languages. Ndebele is used in this chapter for the Nguni language-cluster. They belong to Sotho and Nguni language-clusters. Sotho language-cluster consists of Sesotho or Southern Sotho, Sepedi or Northen Sotho and Setswana or Western Sotho. Nguni language-cluster consists of Ndebele, Shangaan-Tsonga, Swati, Xhosa, Venda and Zulu. Elsabe Taljard and Sonja E. Bosch maintain that Sesotho and Ndebele "languages are basically agglutinating in nature since prefixes and suffixes are used extensively in formation."[68] They correctly maintain that Sesotho and Ndebele languages "belong to a large grouping of languages, i.e., the Sotho and Nguni language groups respectively. Languages belonging to the same language group are closely related and to a large extent mutually intelligible."[69] They have mutual impact. They have not developed in isolation from each other. Central to these features characterising them is the issue of their commonality. In addition to these features is the issue of interaction between Basotho and the Ndebele people. According to Richard Nordquist, interaction between speakers of languages as the process is "the social and linguistic phenomenon by which speakers of different languages (or different dialect of the same language) interact with one another, leading to a transfer of linguistic features."[70]

Nicholas Jacobus Van Warmelo, appointed Chief State Ethnologist in the Department of Native Affairs on 7 April 1930 until his retirement in 1969, maintained that Sotho-speaking South Africans can read and understand what is written in Ndebele as spoken in Limpopo and Mpumalanga provinces. According to him, the point, among others, is that Sotho has impact on the Ndebele language and that Ndebele words are pronounced in Zulu.[71] To the extent that the majority of the Ndebele people particularly of Limpopo and Mpumalanga understand and speak Sepedi and that Sepedi is common with Sesotho and Setswana which are members of Sotho language-cluster, they are Sotho-speaking people.

Richard Bailey makes serious efforts in producing and providing evidence of linguistic communality of Africans of South Africa and in demonstrating commonality of Sotho and Nguni words and common origins of Sotho and Nguni languages.[72] Not understanding this socio-historical development of common origins of Sotho and Nguni languages and their commonality which survived their separation from each other, some scholars view their relationship in terms of assimilation or integration. Vernon George John Sheddick, one of these scholars maintain that "certain grammatical features of Nguni, as well as vocabulary and idioms, have been assimilated into Southern Sotho."[73]

The following table provides the commonality of Sesotho and Zulu words. This is conclusive, irrefutable evidence of linguistic commonality between Sotho and the Nguni as represented by Basotho and the Zulu.

**Commonality of Sesotho and Zulu words**

| Sesotho word | Zulu word | English word |
|---|---|---|
| mosadi | umfazi | woman |
| basadi | abafazi | women |
| haholo | kakhulu | a lot |
| hosasa | kusasa | tomorrow |
| hosing | ekuseni | in the morning |
| hantle | kahle | well |
| phetolla | phendula | translate, change |
| ho hlompha | kuhlonipa | to respect |
| kgosi | inkosi | traditional leader |
| maswi | amazi | milk |
| meetse | mazi | water |

**The Commonality of Surnames between Basotho and the Nguni**

Basotho and the Nguni share surnames such as Mokoena, Mokuena or Ngwenya (crocodile). The surname Mthimkhulu, Moremoholo, "mthi" or "more" or "tree" and "mkhulu" or "moholo" "great" or great tree, is shared by Basotho and the Nguni. Shabangu, the Nguni surname, was transformed into Chabanku (a person who is afraid of sheep) as Basotho surname. Xaba was transformed into Seteka. This socio-historical reality is conclusive and irrefutable evidence of the ethnic and linguistic commonality of Basotho and the Nguni. It is evidence also of the commonality of their surnames.

## Conclusion and Recommendations

This chapter produced and provided understanding of the socio-historical relationship between Basotho and the Nguni as the process of their ethnic, linguistic, cultural and intangible cultural heritage commonality and their surnames as an integral part of this commonality in their relationship. This commonality is of strategic importance to the resolution of the national question through nation building project.

Apartheid's anthropologists played a key, leadership role in establishing nationalist identity for Afrikaners and in crafting a policy of dividing Africans in order to rule them on the basis of ethnic, linguistic, cultural and intangible cultural diversity. This was for the purpose of preparing a ground for the assumption and exercise of state political power. Calling for the imposition of political power and authority over Africans and upon the state to mobilise and deploy resources in defence of the national status quo, they called upon the state to deal with challenges posed by Africans as the decisive majority of the national population. Their key role in the state's socio-political engineering was characterised by the structural need of preventing Africans from constituting the socio-political and cultural forces against the realisation of their political project and of responding to the demands of the African people for the political change in an African country. They worked closely with their allies of Germany in transforming Africans to view themselves primarily in terms of ethnic, linguistic, cultural, intangible cultural heritage and other affiliations such as clans and regions. Central to this task was to ensure that these affiliations blunt edges of the struggle against settler colonial and racist domination, oppression and exploitation as the immediate or natural arenas of political, economic and ideological tensions. Understood in this context, separate development or apartheid was a broader ideological attempt to rationalise the operations of domination, oppression and exploitation through ethnic, linguistic, cultural and intangible cultural heritage policies and mechanisms of divide and rule. This serves as a call for the abandonment of the thesis of ethnic, linguistic, cultural and intangible cultural heritage diversity of the African people and its replacement with the thesis of their ethnic, linguistic, cultural and intangible cultural heritage commonality.

# Chapter Four
## The Socio-Historical Relationship between Bapedi and the Nguni: The Case of Bapedi and Swazis: Issues of Ethnicity, Languages, Surnames, Culture and Intangible Cultural Heritage

*Molapo Rachidi*

## Introduction

This chapter is concerned with socio-historical relationship between Bapedi and Swazi focusing on ethnicity, languages, surnames, culture and intangible cultural heritage. Their ethnicity, languages, surnames, culture and intangible cultural heritage as historically impacted upon by their migrations are central to the discussion. In other words, a historical perspective will be provided to give a better understanding of the socio-historical relationship as members of the South African society.

Precolonial Africa had social and political institutions that are important in shaping some of the ethnic, linguistic, cultural and intangible cultural heritage identities that are critical to the focus of this chapter. Therefore, a historical lens is critical and of vital importance and relevant in looking at the issues that are important for contemporary relationship between Bapedi and the Nguni particularly relationship between Bapedi and Swazis, ethnic member of the Nguni group.

Few scholars have looked at the aspect of Bapedi-Swazi relationship with a different focus. Reflecting on 19th century Transvaal history, the relationship of this two groups was hostile It was impacted upon by quest for regional dominance in the midst of a situation of flux with Boer, British and other South African interests.

## Historiography

Historiography refers to some scholars whose work has a direct relationship with the subject matter of the chapter.

The work of Peter Magubane, *"The Vanishing Cultures of South Africa,"* shows how communities have come under serious cultural pressures.[1] These vanishing cultures show that societies are not static and how they have adapted to the changing situations facing them. In the process of change, some aspects are lost while others are modified or acquired in different versions.

A common thread in Magubane's book is that ethnic groups of South Africa have been exposed to the same internal and external factors. It is for this socio-historical reason that their changes are common. His book is important as far as it tackles cultural and intangible cultural heritage changes over time. However, its shortcomings relate to language and internal migration as applied in this chapter. External dynamics alone are not enough to explain why some people left their original places for other places where they settled permanently.

Thabani Thwala's work focuses on how the ruling Dlamini dynasty in Eswatini, formerly Swaziland, used its daughters as a form of control of other traditional leaders through their marriages to them. Through this practice, the heirs in some of the chiefdoms that emerged would have Dlamini blood.[2] In these areas which did not have Dlamini dominance, such as the Magagula, a Sotho community, a shift took place in terms of this impact and placing of some or certain places under their sphere of influence. This tactical means is a common practice as found in other communities.[3] Peter Delius states that:

> The paramount also delegated and designated rank and legitimacy through dispensing wives and daughters to subordinate chiefs. These were mainly the sisters and daughters of the paramount and became the principal wives of the chiefs to whom they were married and thus potentially mothers to the successors to the chieftainship.[4]

According to this practice, the king's daughters would be given out to junior traditional leaders wherein their heirs would maintain relationship with the particular kings and therefore be favoured by kings or senior traditional leaders.

Philip Bonner's book has direct relations with some key aspects of this study.[5] An aspect that links with this study is about Swazi dispossession and labour migration into the Transvaal. White settler penetration into Eswatini had devastating impact on its future. The ruling Dhlamini dynasty welcomed whites into their land and gave them huge chunks of land through concessionary companies.[6] It was during the reign of Mbandzeni that this major land alienation of the Swazi people took place.

Added to this socio-historical development, was the fact that at the end of the 1899-1902 Anglo-Boer War or the South African War, many Swazis enlisted as mine and farm workers in South Africa. Eswatini's independent status changed drastically as it had to export many of its able-bodied men and women to the South African labour market as migrants.

Another work that has relevance to this study is that of Joseph Mandla Maseko. It deals with the history of the members of the Maseko clan, Swazi people, and their struggles for power.[7] Maseko's scholarship is interested in documenting the history of the Ncamanes Masekos (Swazis) who had lost the kingship position to the Dhlaminis and, as a result, are scattered in Southern Africa. Despite the fact that reasons for their being throughout the region are varied over time, they are all linked to their history as Amacamanes. They are also found in Limpopo, Gauteng and other provinces of South Africa. This documentation of their history is very useful especially when dealing with their names and surnames. Its major shortcoming is being one-sided focusing on the Amacamanes and losing the changes that were affecting the Swazis as a whole when they migrated to other places and what had become of them in other regions when adapting to changes overtime. It is of vital importance to see the changes as dynamic and not the creation of stereotypes about Swazi identities so as to have a concrete understanding of their history. The other aspect of the book is in tracing some of the Amacamanes from Eswatini, Lesotho, Zimbabwe, Malawi and Mozambique. This migration can be likened to the Mfecane era which had scattered scores of Africans to various parts of Southern Africa. This may be true of internal conflicts for power within Eswatini itself and coupled with the Mfecane in terms of the impact of the migration. The Free State and Lesotho have created refuge for the Masekos in their places. The book also deals with some aspects of intangible cultural heritage such as spirituality of the ndau people or what in South Africa would be called Batau (Pedi), vhadau(Venda), and ndau(Shona). An interesting issue about them is that they have a common totem. This is despite the fact that they are nationals of various countries of Southern Africa.

Leroy Vail has also provided an interesting scholarship in one of the issues, processes and developments related to the subject matter of the study.[8] According to him, tribalism is seen from two angles. These angles are that of the coloniser and the colonised in its creation.

The Transvaal was populated by various ethnic groups with socio-historical relevance to the study. One of these groups was the Koni group which was located between Ohrigstad and Carolina in Mpumalanga. The study that investigated this area, was concerned with history and the material culture of the people who lived in it.[9] Combining archaeology and history, it gives an interesting approach to Bokoni.[10] Bokoni as applied in this study implies more a geographic formation than people who lived in it.

There is a tau group which traces its origin to Eswatini. Through the process of migration, it ends up in terms of settlement in Badfontein which falls within the boundary of Bokoni. Bokoni the place, as a geographically big formation, may have included multiple ethnic, linguistic, cultural and intangible cultural heritage groups that did not share the same origin.

African migrations of the late 19th century have impact on the African people internally and externally. The penetration of European settlers through expansion as a form of migration into Southern Africa negatively affected Eswatini and its people. The arrival of white settlers on Swazi shores, led to the political governing Dhlamini aristocracy ruling the country entering into deals with the white settlers. Land was the major transaction medium between these two actors. By the early 1900, Swazi people were enlisting their services as farm workers, while others had taken contracts as migrant labourers on South African mines. Their service to South African mines and farms owned by whites had far-reaching consequences as the majority of Swazi citizens had lost land and transformed into workers.

Some nationals of Eswatini were dispatched by the king to guard its northern and western borders against Bapedi, members of the Sotho group, and the Zulus, members of the Nguni group, from any invasion. In the process, some wives of the king joined their fellow Swazi males to establish Swazi outposts in places such as Badplaas. This group of people were able to spread in Mpumalanga, the former Eastern Transvaal, places such as Barberton, Badplaas, Carolina, Machadadorp, Badfontein, Belfast and others.

Nineteenth century Transvaal politics were such that there was a quest for dominance of the region since the discovery of diamonds and gold. The relationship of the four groups were hostile. Some forms of alliances were established in the process.

The Transvaal under the political leadership of the Boers in the nineteenth century was strategically located in the interior. It had access to the eastern coast. However, what made the Transvaal more strategic or central in South Africa was the discovery of huge deposits of gold in the Witwatersrand. This socio-historical development attracted scores of people far from South Africa to its shores. On the one hand, this was one factor that led to the contestation for power between the Boers and Britain. In a fluid situation, the Boers entered into some alliances with indigenous traditional leaders with the hope of pushing their adversaries away and defeating them. The Swazi, who were in constant threat of attacks from Bapedi and the Zulu, saw an alliance with the Boers as a tactical means to balance regional forces in their favour.

As the mining industry progressed, there was a huge demand for cheap labour. Africans of Southern Africa were targeted as the solution to this labour demand. Harsh taxes were imposed on African communities. This was not enough as many of these communities had access to land, livestock, and other resources which made it possible for them to survive as money economy had not become a dominant factor in their lives.

### Language dynamics of Bokoni

From the study conducted at Bokoni, the dominant language spoken within it was Sepedi. From evidence of people who lived in it, there was an articulated combination of Sepedi, Swati and Pai under the dominance of Sepedi. The issue of the language spoken by the majority and the minority in Bokoni was the consequence of the demography of the area.

### Names and Surnames

The people who were residents of the area also reflected the demographic of the settlement. There were names and surnames such as Lingwati, Letswele, Mhlanga, Ngomana, Mkhabela, Hlatswayo, Ngwenya, Manzini, Mdluli, Mgiba, Ngele, Mnisi and others. These names and surnames were Swazi in origin. They found themselves in a dominant language in the area. This language is Sepedi. This process affected the type of Sepedi spoken in the area.

Other surnames that appear to be that of Bapedi have origins in Eswatini. The tau (lion) people of Mokwena, Selwane, Masemola,

Mogashwa, Phaahla, Marishane, Moima, Nkwana, Bapela and others are found in some parts of the Limpopo Province. They share the same totem of a lion (tau).

There are acceptable names while others may offend people. This forms part of labels by outsiders of particular people. The Swazi are derogatorily called or referred to as lepono in singular or mapono in plural. Bapedi and Vhenda use these names because of their dress code. They appear "naked" bhunyu in Tshivenda and ponoka in Pedi. Bapedi refer to the Swazi as mapono because at one time they served as allies of the Boers in the war against Bapedi.

Swazis are also known to have been "used" by Boers to raid a number of chiefdoms in the Transvaal, such as the Bapedi, Makgoba, Moholoholo, Venda and others. It should be noted that this socio-historical development was not a one-sided affair. It was a situation of conflict whereby material interests were paramount. The struggle for regional power dominance was impacted upon by a number of factors. While the Boers feared British domination of the Transvaal, the Swazi feared Bapedi and the Zulu. Therefore, the issue of entering into alliances was a necessary way of preventing the enemy from being dominant and challenging enemy dominance as a collective.

## African migrations and their consequences

As people moved out of Eswatini looking for greener pastures on the mining and agricultural sectors particularly on the farms and in the mines and other sectors of the South African economy. Some never returned back to their country. This process of migration and the consequence process of urbanisation had deep social consequences as people moved to the small towns such as Nhlazadze, Machadadorp, Belfast, Lydenburg or Mashishing, Carolina, Barberton, and Dullstroom.

Some Swazis settled at Badfontein near the Crocodile River and worked on the neighbouring farms. Ruins and graves were left in the area during the process of their migrations. Apart from these material cultures, there were fields for ploughing and livestock breeding. This was during the time when the African economy depended heavily on pastoralism. Other Swazis moved to farms around Lydenburg or Mashishing and surroundings. The material culture found in the area is linked to their movement.[11]

A word needs to be said about Mokwena, Selwane, Masemola, Mogashwa, Phaahla, Marishane, and Moima. They trace their origin to Eswatini. They then settled at Badfontein and then some parts of the Limpopo Province. In the Steelpoort valley and Eastern Leolu mountains there are a number of Swazi communities. Their movement has to do with the balance of forces that took place in the Transvaal at the turn of the century. The creation of trust lands later the so-called homelands or bantustans whose existence was facilitated through the Bantu Authorities Act, the Group Areas Act and other legislations had an impact on the creation of Bapedi ethnicity. As a result of these migrations, a generational gap developed in terms of language and culture. For example, the people I spoke to during the fieldwork research, acknowledge their Swazi origins. They also acknowledge that in terms of language and cultural practices, they have been integrated into Bapedi social systems.

Another group with Swazi origins found itself living on the farm Boomplaas in Mashishing or Lydenburg. The roots of this settlement are linked to Bapedi converts who left Sekhukhuneland for Botšhabelo or Middleburg in Mpumalanga because of cultural conflict.[12] However, their stay in Botšhabelo was short-lived as a result of class and race relations. It is for these reasons that they moved to Lydenburg or Mashishing where they sought to establish their independence. By the time of the 1899-1992 South African War, conflict in the area had polarised consequences. Due to the conflict, there were Swazis who found refuge among Bapedi and Bapedi who found refuge among the Swazis. In other words, human security and survival tactical means were more important than ethnic divisions or ethnic affiliations.

The emergence of the apartheid system with the passing of the Group Areas Act, in which Boomplaas was declared a "black spot" and by 1956, the settlement was moved further North in the Ohrigstad valley to Sterkspruit (Phiring). A number of families bear Swazi surnames such as Hlatswayo, Ngele, Manzini, Ngwenya, Mlangeni, Mnisi, Nkosi, Mhlanga, Maphanga, Mgiba and others. With the dominance of Bapedi institutions such as schools and churches, the development of the Swazi language was hampered. The elderly generations are the ones still able to understand and communicate in Swati. Over time, Sepedi would become a lingua franca in the village. This is a generational gap that emerges on the cultural front.

A small village as Sterkspruit with this language composition or dynamics means that Swati as an official language recognised in the national constitution can be spoken informally. The fact remains it will not develop in its own right with Sepedi dominance which obtains institutional support while others do not get this support.

One of my informants in the study, Mr Vusi Lingwati, whose family was based in Nhlazadze saw his family been torn apart by forced removals. They then moved to Badfontein and the family split into five groups. While some members of the family went to Barberton, others went to Bushbuckridge, Phiring, Kgautswane (Rietfontein) and Monsterlus.

Mr Lingwati stated that, "Rena language ye re e shomishago ke Sepedi because seSwati sa rena ga se pure. Ke gore re dula le Bapedi. Sa rena ke sa Sekhukhune ga nnyane. So, language ya rena ya Seswati e ya moyafala. Ge ba ka fihla ra bonana ra bolodishana re ka kwishishana ka siZwati."[13] What he means is that the language they are using is Sepedi because their Swati is not pure. Sepedi they speak is a bit of that spoken in Sekhukhune as their language has been lost in the process. However, if we meet the Swazi and we speak we will be able to understand each other.[14] He stated that:

the language breakdown started around 1966/68 when relatives were evicted from the farms. Others went back to Nelspruit, side of Barberton, relatives who speak Swati, others went to Bushbuckridge, tone changed to Pulana, others in Phiring where you (researcher) have relatives and Marulaneng, Jane Furse.[15]

The group that went to Barberton still speaks pure Swati. This is because of its close proximity to the majority who speak Swati. The groups that moved to Phiring, Monsterlus and Bushbuckridge have a diluted Swazi because they have moved away from the majority of the Swazis who speak Swati or from Swati as the core mother tongue dominance.

The Bushbuckridge group speaks Sepedi that is impacted upon by Sepulana, a dialect of Sepedi language spoken in the area. The Monsterlus group speaks both Sepedi and Ndebele. The Kgautswane (Rietfontein) group speaks Sepedi as the area is dominated by Pai group which forms part of the Eastern Sotho. In other words, their Sepedi developed over time.

The movements of the Swati people imposed some linguistic constraints on the development of the language. Many of the people had to send their children to Bapedi schools or churches which in turn affected the development of their language which had become a hybrid of the original version of the language.

Another important dimension to this variable is intermarriages among the groups. People marry across ethnic lines. This led and continues leading to integration and acceptance of members of the other ethnic groups. Multilingualism becomes important medium for communication in such environments.

Multilingualism as an important feature in a democratic settings means that, learning multiple languages is helpful in communication and cultural development. This aspect can be said to be a contributory factor to social development. A society such as South Africa with various languages and cultural groups means that some forms of new identities are needed or encouraged to develop.

## Culture and Intangible Cultural Heritage
Culture is a dynamic process. It is not static. People have various cultural identities in the form of language, dress codes, belief systems, history and others. The "invented traditions," according to Eric Hobsbawm and Terence Ranger, give the impression that this "culture" is "natural."[16] The reality is that it evolved over time.[17]

With the movements of people, the culture kept on changing and reshaped by the people in various situations. Therefore, the "invented traditions" address complex dynamics of "past and present." At times, the culture in its "original" form is lost or given a different flavour. As Lingwati states, "Aowa Prof, I think re adoptile culture ya Bapedi le ge go na le negotiation lobola, bontši o no bona ba dira Sepedi ga ba sa dira sizwati, sometimes siZwati o bona ge ba apara dituku tša sizwati gore ke mohlobo mang wa batho. Almost 99% ke Sepedi."[18] (No Prof, we have adopted Sepedi culture in that during times of lobola, you see people following Pedi practice. Often you see women dawning Swazi attire to show what type of people they are but the practice is 99% Pedi.)

Culture as a socio-historical process is affected by a number of various factors. One of these factors is, firstly, the integration of people by the dominant groups into themselves. Secondly, institutions and processes such as schools, churches, koma and others contribute to the development of culture and demise of some cultural practices. This means that with various generations, culture develops and is integrated into the dominant culture. The process of integration discussed in this study is "mild" not the same as the "institutionalised assimilation" or "colonial assimilation"[19] as applied in countries such as Angola and Mozambique. In other words, integration took place but not as practised and enforced by colonial and racist governments through their policy principles. Colonial and racist governments applied policy principles of indirect rule such as British or assimilation by French and Portuguese governments.

## Ethnic affiliations

African nationalists shun ethnicity as a colonial construct. This accordingly was used by colonisers to divide and rule oppressed communities. Therefore, the promotion of "nationalist consciousness" is better than "ethnicity" as it divides than "unites" people. Some scholars have viewed ethnicity as "false consciousness" and " backwardness" in a contemporary society.

However, it is important to look at how ethnicity was constructed and applied over the years by the same African nationalists. To say a person is Mopedi, Swazi, Zulu, Ndebele, Coloured and others is to give a particular label, which may be accepted or rejected. Some people prefer to call themselves Africans rather than externally imposed labellings, affiliations of the "tribe," "ethnic group," the "bantu" and others. These labels were problematic especially during the apartheid era as they were seen as reinforcing the ideology of the National Party of "separate development." The creation of "homelands" was seen as re-enforcing those ethnic divisions to serve political interests of the ruling white social forces. Settler colonialism was also seen as deriving interests when the colonised, exploited and oppressed people were divided and deliberately made ignorant of the political situation affecting them. Political formations were created or formed along the lines of these labels and in turn created confusions among the people. The emphasis by national liberation movements was for people to overcome ethnic divisions and move towards embracing nationalist consciousness which pushed them to accept their thinking albeit their different ideological orientations. In other words, "nation" building was seen as the major target or objective to be achieved in the fight against the oppressors. According to Leroy Vail, most African states are driven by "ethnic particularism commonly known as "tribalism." In other words, the "tribe" and "ethnic affiliation" are contributory factors to the problems of "nation" building.

In 1911 two years before the formation of the South African National Native Congress, Pixley ka Isaka Seme one of the leading intellectuals, lawyers and nationalist politicians called for unity among the oppressed people of South Africa. He had made profound impact in his thinking as a student at the Columbia University in New York City when he took part in student debates when he presented his paper on the "regeneration of Africa" which was the foundation or basis of the earlier black intellectual thought in South Africa diaspora and on the African continent. During the era of segregation in South Africa, the situation was very harsh for both the African middle class and the masses of the people as a result of a settler colonial and racist rule. Seme was disturbed by the ethnic and tribal divisions that were plaguing the African people in the country. He stated the following:

> The demon of racialism, the aberrations of the Xosa-Fingo feud, the animosity that exists between the Zulus and the Tongaas, between the Basutos and every other native must be buried and forgotten; it has shed among us sufficient blood! We are one people. These divisions, these jealousies, are the cause of all our woes and from all our backwardness and ignorance today.[20]

According to Seme, these divisions arose out of the settler communities and some of the oppressed people had embraced them. It appears that these divisions were real especially with people who were well educated and saw their fellow Africans of South Africa who were not well educated as the "other." The "jealousies, ignorance and hatred" were personalised and not seem as products coming for the oppressors with their system. Some of the African leaders of the time expected the British qualified franchise at the Cape to be extended to the Africans in the other provinces. This was not to be as structural racism and class exploitation were the foundations of the society and to get rid of such a system was very difficult. As seen from the first twenty years into democracy, the popular support for the liberation movements was great especially during the first ten years but since then, the support has declined significantly.

The challenges of building a nation were encountered in other African countries as demonstrated in Mozambique, South Africa's neighbour. In their efforts to build Mozambican nation, Samora Machel as the president of the Front for the Liberation of Mozambique (FRELIMO) pointed out that:

> FRELIMO, in its twenty years of existence and in this path of struggle, turned us progressively into Mozambicans, no longer Makonde and Shangane, Nyanja and Ronga,

Nyungwe and Bitonga, Chuabo and Ndau, Macua and Xitsua .... Ours is not a society in which races and colours, tribes and regions coexist and live harmoniously side by side. We went beyond these ideas during a struggle in which we sometimes had to force people's consciousness in order to free themselves from complexes and prejudices so as to become simply, we repeat, simply people.[21]

In Africa where there are "tribes" or "ethnic" groups with historic cleavages sometimes conflicts emerge along ethnic or racial and class lines. The nationalist consciousness was to transform these divisions into nationalist world views which saw their problems as the exploitative racialist systems which contributed towards these conflicts. The situation of Mozambique may reflect the total colonial situation in which the oppressor was stripped off his humanity with the direct policy of assimilation. The challenge as applicable here is that of Pan-Africanism in which it was not a problem in a particular country but the universal human conditions Africans faced in different parts of the world. Their conditions were almost similar where they found themselves.

There is caution that needs to be taken note of. Although nationalist leaders condemn ethnicity, they often use it when it suits them especially when their political fortunes are under threat. As a solution to their political problem, they use ethnicity against their opponents for their survival.

It can also be said that challenging oppression by African varied over the years. There was the moderate era of petitions to the open conflict of mass demonstrations and armed confrontations. Therefore, building the nation was long and protracted struggle.

### Conclusion and Recommendations

This chapter explored issues of ethnicity, languages, surnames, culture and intangible cultural heritage through a historical lens. The study used the socio-historical relationship between Bapedi and the Swazi within the context of the socio-historical context of the socio-historical relations between Bapedi and the Nguni to explore issues of ethnicity, languages, surnames, culture and intangible cultural heritage. Periodisation of the study was the late nineteenth century leading to the contemporary period.

Findings of the study are that there are identities that evolved overtime which when seen from the current perspective can be confusing. A number of families who are found in the Limpopo and Mpumalanga provinces originated as Swazis. The process of their migration has since transformed this socio-historical reality. This kind of transformation or change is that there is nothing "swazi" in their everyday life or ethnic and linguistic affiliations and cultural and intangible cultural heritage activities as well as in their surnames. The process of migration has transformed their ethnicity, language, surnames, culture and intangible cultural heritage. It can be said that they have totally integrated into Bapedi with being Bapedi in terms of ethnicity, language, surnames, culture and intangible cultural heritage.

Internal migration has taken different dimensions. Internal migration of African people within South Africa has transformed their ethnicity, languages, surnames, culture and intangible cultural heritage as their left their original places for other places where they permanently settled among their fellow Africans whose ethnicity, languages, surnames, culture and intangible cultural heritage are different from theirs. They acquired ethnicity, languages, surnames, culture and integrable cultural heritage of Africans their permanently settled among them as their own.

Capitalism on the one hand has drawn men and women into its folds irrespective of their ethnicity, languages, surnames, culture and intangible cultural heritage affiliations, making them a new working class in a modern capitalist society. Ethnic cleavages of the past are no longer relevant as people seek to express their identities in a changed environment. These identities are mobile or dynamic, ever changing with time.

The new identity that is dominant is a nationalist one that exists within a class society that is littered with cleavages of unemployment, poverty and inequality. The old identities coexist on the margins of the nationalist or a working class consciousness.

The tribal barbarians of yesteryear have been replaced by a hybrid of African who advocates heritage gatherings once a year. Therefore, people can embrace multiple identities. These multiple identities are critical in an environment that has been transformed by many factors such as the state, capital and politics. Identity formations have evolved overtime and keep on changing.

Lastly, it appears backward to propagate ethnic or tribal identities when democracy has received acceptance by African political and economic leaders who were marginalised by the former settler colonial and racist oppressors. In other words, African political and economic leaders have become hybrids which is living in two worlds.

Decoloniality embraces the formation of the new "nation" that has emerged from the colonial setting. Part of the old has not been completely erased in the "new" with serious structural consequences of the economy being in white hands, unemployment, poverty and inequality being so rife. The scores of the people who are poor and who do not have the skills for a competitive capitalist society survive on a welfare system of grants. Their sustainable security and well-being call for a capable state which is developmental in form and content as well in operation which through government theoretically and practically regards as its first function the socio-economic and financial protection of citizens.

Languages and cultures have evolved over the years. Some of the people who have embraced multilingualism are in a position to survive better than those who opted not to learn other languages but depend on one. Bapedi and the Swazis may have originated from the same or common backgrounds but many found themselves living in the same space and therefore the "other" no longer features much as they are in a position to speak common language and Sepedi and Swati have not developed in isolation from each other and as such Bapedi and Swazis communicate among themselves as speakers of these two languages. The consequences are that there is a considerable number of Bapedi who are Swati speakers and a considerable number of Swazis who are Sepedi speakers.

# Chapter Five
## The Socio-Historical Relationship between Batswana and the Nguni: Issues of Ethnicity, Languages, Surnames, Culture and Intangible Cultural Heritage

Sehlare Makgetlaneng

This chapter produces and provides understanding of the socio-historical relationship between Batswana and the Nguni by focusing on issues of ethnicity, languages, surnames, culture and intangible heritage. Their surnames are an integral part of their commonality in this relationship. This commonality is of strategic importance to the resolution of the national question through nation building project.

### The Case of Ba ga Seleka as the articulated combination of Zulu, Northern Ndebele and Batswana and their relationship with Bapedi

Ba ga Seleka are the articulated combination of the Nguni as represented by the Zulu and the Northern Ndebele socio-historically in terms of ethnicity and Tswana linguistically and culturally. They have a close socio-historical relationship with another member of the Sotho group, Bapedi particularly through

Tompi Zacharia Seleka. They are a classical representation of the socio-historical relationship between Batswana and the Nguni in the areas of ethnicity, languages, surnames, culture and intangible cultural heritage. Ba ga Seleka are historically Zulu people. They are descendants of Mazwe. Mazwe was a traditional leader of Northern Nguni group of the Zulu people who later become ba ga Seleka. They left the KwaZulu-Natal Province in the seventeenth century for Lesotho. They settled on the banks of the Phuthihatsana River on the border of Lesotho. They adopted customs, language and other factors of their Sotho neighbours which come to characterise them. While in Lesotho they adopted phuthi (duiker) from Baphuthing as their totem. Phuthi is venerated generally by Bapedi and Basotho who are members of the Sotho group. There are people who maintain that tlou (elephant) is their totem. Tlou is venerated also by some Northern Ndebele groups. Briefly, their intangible cultural heritage is duiker and elephant. They are also totems of Sothos and the Nguni.

Their history is characterised by migration from one place to another place since Mazwe passed away. They moved from Bophuthaditjhaba, formerly Witsieshoek, in the Free State Province on the banks of the Wilge River until they permanently settled at Lephalale in the Limpopo Province. Mazwe's successors who include Motlhabya, Tselapedi 1, Maila, Mfatla, Nawa or Naoa, Bogosi 1, Mmelana, Bogosi 11, Seleka 1, Radipabe, Madidimala, Seleka 11, Mananya and Seleka 111 have Setswana, Sepedi and Sesotho names. Some of these names are also surnames such as Tselapedi, Maila, and Nawa. This is supportive of the fact that ba ga Seleka adopted customs, language and other factors of their Sotho neighbours which come to characterise them. It is also supportive of the position that Mazwe's successors were given Sotho names.

Ba ga Seleka are regarded as part of the original Northern Ndebele people before they were subdivided into ba ga Mokopane, ba ga Laka, the Mauwana, ba ga Letwaba and boo Seleka. Ba ga Kekana, ba ga Langa and ba ga Letwaba as the major divisions constitute the Northern Ndebele people.[1]

Ba ga Seleka admit their Northen Ndebele ethnic identity and also as descendants of Mazwe. Despite the fact that they are regarded as Batswana because of the language and culture, they are still conscious of their original identity as more Northern Ndebele than a Tswana way of life characterised, among others, by language and culture. They maintain that it is through their socio-historical contact and intermarriage with Batswana, especially Bakwena, that they have "virtually become Tswana in language and culture."[2] They once left for Botswana where they settled among the Bakwena. They returned to South Africa where they permanently settled as South Africans.

Their socio-historical relationship with other Northern Ndebele groups, Batswana and Bapedi is characterised by the fact that for many years they

> relied on assistance and asked for support from other Northern Ndebele groups far to the south while Tswana and Northern Sotho neighbours were at hand.[3]

Ba ga Seleka's socio-historical relationship with Bapedi is characterised, among others, by the fact that Tompi Zacharia Seleka as a regent served, firstly, as Minister of Agriculture and, secondly, as Minister of Justice in the Lebowa bantustan or homeland government. Thirdly, the Lebowa government honoured him by renaming Arabie College of Agriculture in Marble Hall, next to what used to be Boaparankwe College for sons of traditional leaders and councillors of Bapedi, Venda, Shangaan-Tsonga, Ndebele of Mpumalanga Province, Ndebele of the North West Province and others, as Tompi Seleka College of Agriculture. There has never been a reported opposition to these forms of honour to Seleka and appreciation of his capability and experience to serve in these capacities from Bapedi. Like the Ndebele of the Limpopo Province, ba ga Seleka are fully regarded as an integral part of Limpopo.

Ba ga Seleka live in a geographical area mainly between Africans whose mother tongues are Sepedi and Northern Ndebele on the one hand and the Tswana-speaking people where South Africa shares a border with Botswana on the other hand.[4]

The major source of this information on ba ga Seleka is from a journal article by Michael de Jongh and Frik C. de Beer of Department of Anthropology and Indigenous Law at the University of South Africa. They interviewed Tompi Zacharia Seleka, ba ga Seleka councillors, elders and those knowledgeable about their "tribal history and traditions."[5] They had extensive discussions with them.[6] They spell their place as Lephalala. It being called Lephalala is more appropriate to the fact that it means to flow. Despite this being its meaning and the fact that it is how it is spelt in some literature, it is officially spelt as and known as Lephalale.

### Culture and intangible cultural heritage of Batswana and the Nguni

This chapter uses the role and significance of matriarchy in the culture of Batswana and the Nguni and the right of African women to marry in explaining culture and intangible cultural heritage of Batswana and the Nguni.

### The Role and Significance of Matriarchy in the Culture of Batswana and the Nguni

This section of the chapter deals with the role and significance of matriarchy in the cultural well-being and intangible cultural heritage not only of Batswana and the Nguni of South Africa but also of other African people of the country and the African continent. They are of vital importance in the preservation of the senior traditional leadership as intangible cultural heritage among not only within Batswana and within the Nguni but also within Africans nationally, regionally and continentally. They are characterised by the centrality of women in their cultural well-being and intangible cultural heritage such as the institution of traditional leadership which has been preserved in time and space. Matriarchy is viewed in this chapter as a social system and practice in the communities in which women exercise power and authority in the leadership of the allocation of resources, including preservation of the society. Its practice by African communities through various forms has ensured its preservation in time and space. African women as persons who preserve the institution of traditional leadership by giving birth to those who succeed their predecessors as traditional leaders is one of the key roles they play in their centrality in their cultural well-being. Women exercise their right to marry not only men, but also females among African communities in South Africa. It is through this right to marry they exercise that they play a central role in preserving African families in South Africa. The role and significance of matriarchy in the socio-cultural well-being among the African people of South Africa is an issue marginalised and neglected by those who spent time, energy and resources over-emphasising the role of patriarchy in their socio-cultural life.

## The centrality of women in an African cultural and intangible cultural heritage setting

This chapter provides analysis of the role and significance of matriarchy in the cultural well-being and intangible cultural heritage not only of Batswana and Nguni of South Africa but also of other African people of the country and the African continent as a means to contribute towards a concrete understanding of the centrality of women in an African cultural and intangible cultural heritage setting. It takes issues with the cultural practice of placing male human beings at the centre of one's view of the society and its culture and history. The androcentric view of the world and its societies, a product of the Western socio-cultural civilisation, has helped and continues helping to distort the role and significance of matriarchy in the cultural and intangible cultural heritage well-being among the African people. It uses maleness as a basis of defining and explaining the world and its societies. It is Eurocentric. Eurocentric is affirmed mostly linguistically in the sense that androcentric is inherent in European languages. While African languages like Setswana and Nguni languages are gender-free, European languages are not. They are not like European languages which are gender-centric perpetuating the definition and explanation of the world and members of its societies on the basis of maleness.

Setswana and Nguni languages and other African languages accept "the fact that humanity consists in equal parts of men and women and that the experiences, thoughts, and insights" of both males and females "must be represented in every generalisation that is made about human beings."[7] The acceptance of this socio-historical reality points to the centrality of women in the creation and reproduction of the society. It is against androcentrism. In her criticism of the androcentric view of the world, Gerda Lerner maintains that:

> By making the term "man" subsume "woman" and arrogate to itself the representation of all of humanity, men have built a conceptual error of vast proportion into all of their thought. By taking the half for the whole, they have not only missed the essence of whatever they are describing, but they have distorted it in such a fashion that they cannot see it correctly. As long as men believe the earth is flat, they could not understand its reality, its function, and its actual relationship to other bodies in the universe. As long as men believe their experiences, their viewpoint, and their ideas represent all of human experience and all of human thought, they are not only unable to define correctly in the abstract, but they are unable to describe reality accurately.
>
> The androcentric fallacy, which is built into all the mental contracts of western civilization, cannot be rectified simply by "adding women." What is demanded for rectification is a radical restructuring of thought and analysis which once and for all accepts the fact that humanity consists in equal parts of men and women and that the experiences, thoughts, and insights of both sexes must be represented in every generalisation that is made about human beings.[8]

Contrary to Lerner, the androcentric approach is not the

monopoly of men. There are women whose discourse on issues, processes and developments of their societies is male-centred. The successful struggle against androcentric approach lies not in attributing it to males, but in ensuring that it should not be used by both men and women in their view of their societies and their issues, processes and developments. To attribute androcentric approach to males and to argue as if it is their monopoly is to do injustice to the struggle against it by those who are opposed to it irrespective of their gender. There is structural and fundamental need, politically, economically and ideologically to view the struggle against this approach not in terms of gender. Directly related to our position is the fact that it is of vital importance in the struggle against this approach not to perpetuate the thesis of sisterhood - the thesis that females or women are together in the cause against social injustice on the basis of their gender. One being either for or against social justice is the process because of one's political, economic and ideological position. It is not because of one's gender that one is for or against social justice and gender equality.

It is of vital importance in the struggle against the androcentric approach and in the cause for gender equality not to view gender as if it is a social class in which it is implied that women are waging a war against men. This struggle calls for a truly progressive perspective. Mamphela Ramphele explains the "major flaws" in some variants of feminist thinking that, firstly, conceals rather than illuminate the analysis of women's issues, processes and developments. According to her, these "major flaws" include, secondly, the tendency on the part of some feminists to see "sisterhood" in Africa and globally as the solution or "the answer" to all socio-political and economic problems faced by women in their societies. In this view, social relationship is reducible to the domination of men over women. Thirdly, there is the tendency towards arguments according women "moral superiority" over men. This implied that women would necessarily or ipso facto be caring, progressive leaders and members of institutions, including government. Being women is viewed as automatically trusted with power progressively advancing popular interests of members of their societies. She maintains that the risk of "sexism in reverse" exists in this view as its holders "fail" to distinguish between "male power structures" and "men."[9]

Ramphele maintains that "men do not hold the monopoly over the potential to dominate," especially in the context in which members of the society are ranked according to race, class, age and geography or location. Failure to take into account her position and to act accordingly leads to "fragmented and unsatisfactory" approaches that do not correctly address socio-political and economic problems faced by members of the society and how best and most judiciously to solve them. Her position is of vital political, economic and ideological importance. It calls for the structural need for a coherent and appropriate approach relevant to the solution to the problems confronted by members of the society irrespective of their gender. It is helpful to the formulation, adoption and implementation of policies and tactical means to solve problems faced by male and female members of the society. Women, like men, are not homogeneous. Their different and antagonistic positions, experiences, material conditions and rights they use means to defend and change should be recognised in theory and practice. There is no alternative to have a coherent and appropriate approach informed by these experiences and conditions shaping and shaped by gender in the formulation, adoption and implementation of measures in solving problems faced by male and female members of the society.

A coherent and appropriate approach which is not "fragmented and unsatisfactory" is needed in providing a critical analysis of power relations. According to Ramphele, this approach calls upon feminists to be "just as fervent in their opposition to racism, economic deprivation and exploitation, hierarchical and undemocratic practices, as they are in relation to sexism."[10] Feminists and their movement need this approach as it strengthen them in supporting "those sectors of society who have to grapple with the impact of these other power differentials in their lives."[11]

Implementation of policy measures within the framework

of this approach have risks. They demand that we take risks, make courageous acts and live a principled life as scholars and activists. It calls upon scholars to criticise in public their fellow scholars, among others, for their "fragmented and unsatisfactory approaches" and positions which do not serve the struggle for social justice of men and women. They demand that we mobilise action for the realisation of the qualitative improvement and progressive change in the material conditions and rights of men and women. In Ramphele's words, these risks include "having the courage to face up to the contradictions within ourselves, first and foremost - our own vested interests as individuals, as well as our fears and hopes."[12] There is also the risk that powerful men and women are likely to be against "analysts who pose a threat to fundamental power relations."[13] The qualitative leap forward for African women "lies in taking risks to address unequal power relations at all levels."[14] To do justice to this cause, they must avoid the tendency to see as a zero-sum game that is either with men or women and not as shared by men and women.[15]

A coherent and appropriate approach which is not "fragmented and unsatisfactory" is needed in providing a critical analysis of power relations is of critical importance given the fact that:

> much contemporary analysis of gender discourse is celebratory in tone, and consequently largely uncritical where the broader issue of non-gender politics is concerned. Within such framework, gender-specific discourse depicts women not just as empowered but – more importantly politically – as self-empowered: that is to say, women are represented as having become emancipated as a result of their own grassroots agency. One outcome of this celebratory approach is that any and every form of gender-specific activity or mobilization is regarded as empowering and thus desirable, regardless of its politics, political direction or political effect.[16]

Gender is used in this chapter as the state of being a female or a male, especially with reference to socio-cultural differences rather than biological dissimilarities. By definition, gender is the meaning given to femaleness or maleness. Being a female or a male varies from one socio-cultural context to another in a particular society or within it among given communities. Elizabeth Spelman supports this reality in the case of women and females when she maintains that:

> Women are what females of the human species become, or are supposed to become, through learning how to think, act, or live in certain ways. What females in one society learn how to think, act and live can differ enormously from what females in another society learn; in fact, ... there can be very significant differences within a given society.[17]

Gender is viewed differently in particular societies. Culture and its preservation and inheritance dynamics can be fully understood in a particular social-cultural setting. This view of gender is of crucial importance in understanding the role and significance of matriarchy in the cultural well-being among the people of a specific society or within it among particular community and its members. It is in this context that the role and significance of matriarchy in the cultural well-being among the African people of South Africa can be fully understood as a particular socio-historical development in a specific society. Africans of South Africa are characterised by cultural commonality whose aspects of cultural differences are products of their migration since they went into different parts of South Africa were they permanently settled. The concrete understanding of this process of migration in time and space characterised by push and pull factors requires a requisite attention of the history of the African people.

African women derive their socio-cultural power and authority from the role they play in raising and keeping families. This provides them with a direct authority and a vital role in the society in fostering, developing and maintaining cultural values at a critical and the most vulnerable stage in the life of human beings. This is the stage of childhood. The centrality of women in the preservation of cultural and intangible cultural heritage of the African people can clearly be understood, highly appreciated and treasured if we consider the indispensable role they play in the preservation of the institution of traditional leadership. They give birth to children who upon being male and female adults serve as traditional leaders. In some African communities in South Africa if a family does not have a male child, a problem emerges which should be solved. A solution to this problem, firstly, is that a male child is married for him to preserve the family in question. The second cultural option the family has is to marry a female for her to bear children. The last-born male child born out of this marriage is the one who does not leave the family house. His task is to preserve the family in question. If a woman who is married has children, her last-born male child is the one who does not leave the house of the family. His task is to preserve it. At issue is the indispensable role women play in the preserving key factors characterising socio-cultural well-being and intangible cultural heritage of Africans. Briefly, motherhood is a dominant aspect of their centrality. When Africans find children in the house, they ask them a question where is your mother, not where is your father. They ask them a question where is your father provided they know their father. Motherhood is the role of cultural significance among Africans. Africans of South Africa attach primary importance of women being mothers over being wives. Women are regarded in their role as mothers rather than as wives. They are greeted as mothers not as women. African mothers are known more as protectors of their children than supporting their husbands and marriage as the institution per se[18] cannot seriously be said to be submissive and passive in their role as wives. Albertina Sisulu articulated the role and significance of motherhood in the cultural well-being among Africans of South Africa in her approach to white South African mothers as follows:

> My approach to my white sisters is: "Our children are dying in the townships, killed by your children. You are mothers.

Why do you allow your children to go to train for the army? There is no country that has declared war on South Africa. Do you want your children to come and kill our children?" Because that is what is happening. We want to know from our white sisters why there is not a word from them about this. Our children are being killed mercilessly, but what do they say? How can they, as mothers, tolerate this? Why don't they support us?[19]

Central to Sisulu's approach to white South African mothers is a recognition of the difference in the role and significance of matriarchy in the cultural well-being between Africans and whites of South Africa. This is the demonstration of the fact that the value attached to the role and significance not only of matriarchy, but also of motherhood is not the same and similar or common within societies, especially those which are racially diverse such as South Africa. Being mothers does not have the same meaning among people who are different racially and culturally.

Motherhood is central to and respected in African societies. It is not unilaterally linked to wifehood as it is the case in Western societies. A mother is a central person in African societies. According to Oyeronke Oyewumu:

In all African family arrangements, the most important ties within the family flow from the mother, whatever the norms of marriage and residence. These ties link the mother to the child and connect the children to the same mother in bonds that are conceived as natural and unbreakable. ... The idea that mothers are powerful is very much a defining characteristic of the institution and its place in society.[20]

Ifi Amadiume agrees with Oyewumi. Defending this position with formulations like "the logic of motherhood" and "the motherhood paradigm," she maintains: "The mother is the pivot around which familial relationships are delineated and organised."[21] She argues: "The recognition of the motherhood paradigm means that we do not take patriarchy as given, or as paradigm."[22] Her emphasis of "the motherhood paradigm" is not only to raise awareness of the fact that patriarchy is not a paradigm, but also to register her opposition to the acceptance of patriarchy as a paradigm. According to Oyewumi, the problem with the Western view of "woman" is that it regards patriarchy as given and as a paradigm. Her point is that the "woman" in the Western theoretical view, including the Western feminist theoretical view is basically a wife.[23] It is for this reason that she maintains that the Western view of woman is overloaded with implications and associations which are irrelevant within the African socio-historical context. It is here that "the motherhood paradigm" is of vital importance. Its focus is not on woman, but also on the mother-child relationship as central in a social relationship. This means that basically the central issue is not femaleness, but a social relationship.

Motherhood is central in the resolution of the disputes over traditional leadership. If two males are fighting over traditional leadership, the first question asked is who are their mothers. The second question is what is the purpose their mothers were married for. The issue is that the community under the leadership of a traditional leader marries a woman, especially a daughter of a traditional leader for her to bear a first-born male child to be a traditional leader when he becomes of age. The biological father of the children is not the main issue. The main issue is that the male adult who gave her a child should be a member of the royal house or of royal blood. This is one of the significant aspects of the centrality of women in an African cultural setting.

### The Right of African Women to Marry

One of the significant aspects of matriarchy in the cultural well-being of Batswana and the Nguni in particular and Africans in general is that African women have the right to marry. They are not only married, they also marry. They have been exercising their right to marry since many years back. They marry both males and females. This cultural practice renders the notion of the same sex marriage anomaly in an African cultural setting. The notion of the same sex marriage is a contradiction in itself. It is a combination of issues which are different. They are a sexual act as an action and the marriage as an institution. The combination between a sexual act as an action and the marriage as an institution does injustice to the marriage as an institution. It is appropriate to refer to the marriage between individuals of the same gender as same gender marriage not same sex marriage. Gender is not sex. It is interesting that South Africa as a country in which Africans are the decisive majority of its population, as a social formation in which issues of Africanity, African Renaissance and decoloniality are extensively raised and discussed and books, journal articles and occasional papers, monographs continued being published on them, a formation which was regarded as an integral part of the West does not seriously in practice do justice to its African cultural identity. Culturally and sociologically, Africans of South Africa are minority demanding other South Africans to affirm them. There is a structural and fundamental need for Africans of South Africa to substantiate in practice the cultural identity of South Africa as an African country in which Africans are the decisive majority of its population. South Africa is an African country not simply because it is in Africa. The brutal cultural reality of South Africa is that its African population, especially members of the executive, legislative and judicial branches of government have been compromising when it comes to key issues, processes and developments. The consequence is that issues such as botho or ubuntu, linguistic, ethnic and cultural diversity and nonracialism have been pursued at the expense of its African population. Demands raised by African university students in the country relating to African national issues, processes and developments are demands that this injustice be brought to an end for Africans to walk tall culturally in their country.

We have pointed out that African women in South Africa have the right to marry. There are some specific cases in which women marry. Firstly, when there is no male child in the family. A widow can marry the female to serve as her daughter-in-law to bear children for the family. The purpose of this process is for the family to have a male child in order to preserve it. Secondly, a daughter whose parents have no male child can marry a woman with children for her male child to preserve the family of her parents. It does not matter whether her parents are still living or have already passed away.

Some individuals who do not understand this practice accuse Africans of preferring male children over female children. Far from being a preference of male children over female children by Africans, the issue is that female children, upon being married, leave the family. In most cases they acquire surnames of their husbands. By not leaving the house of his parents, the male child preserves it by having children. One of these children being a male in turn preserves the house of his parents by not leaving it. He is referred to in Sotho as moshalalapeng or the one who remains with the house of his parents. This is how the family among Africans of South Africa is preserved from generation to generation through a male child.

The centrality of African women in the cultural and intangible cultural heritage well-being of the African people can best be understood if we come to grips with the critical importance of the care economy in the form of domestic work broadly. The broad view of domestic work is the service African women render not only to their families, but also to their communities, societies and economy. Centring on the pivotal role in the household and domestic labour, they perform two key functions for capital. Firstly, by bearing and rearing children, they produce new workers for capital. Secondly, by feeding and clothing children until they are able to feed and clothe themselves, they reproduce working class for capital on a daily basis.[24] Through their reproduction of labour power, African women render the service in the accumulation capital process.[25]

Despite challenges faced by African women, Fatima Sadiqi maintains that they are not "inert and powerless."[26] According to her:

> They transmit the culture as well as the domestic functions which give them power inside the household. Further, they

manage the domestic economy (annual renewal of food) and
have a role in family planning and the everyday running of
the household. In addition, in traditional settings, co-wives
often support each other when confronting the husband's
authority. Finally, the mother has real and symbolic power
over their children and husband. Although this type of
power is not publicly recognised at the community level,
it is nevertheless real. These types of power are diffuse and
latent, as they are neither expressed openly nor claimed.
Women's public appearance and utterance 'sexualizes'
the public domain where 'serious' non-sexual matters are
discussed.[27]

In order judiciously to do justice to the role and significance of
matriarchy in the social-cultural and intangible cultural heritage
well-being among Batswana and the Nguni in particular and
Africans in general in the context of the centrality of women
in their culture and intangible cultural heritage well-being, we
should take into account the strategic importance of creation
and sustenance of resources giving and sustaining life and "how,"
firstly, "they are embedded in wide sets of ideas and social and
political relations concerning gender."[28] Secondly, we should
deal with "resource access and control" in a way which "both
necessities and orientates the detailed understanding of women's
and men's interactions with specific environments, and their
own perspectives on these interactions."[29] Despite considerable
changes in their material conditions and rights, they still operate
within the framework of their cultural well-being they have
sustained over time.

The view of matriarchy and patriarchy by the Western scholars
has negatively affected the view of Africans culturally. This has been
sustained by the racist position that Africans have no movement
of their own and that they are extensions of other people and that
their continent is a field of action acted upon by external actors
and powers for their own interests. This position means that
Africans have no socio-cultural and historical movement of their

own. This is basically Eurocentric view of the world that Africa and Africans should be understood within the socio-cultural and historical framework of other people particularly of the West.

This cultural and intangible cultural view of the decisive minority of the world subjecting the cultural well-being and intangible cultural heritage of the decisive majority of the world does not acknowledge that culture occupies a pivotal space in the social well-being of people of any particular society. As the theoretical and practical achievements of the society, it consists of products produced and preserved by its members, the way it organises and uses knowledge and understanding, ideas, organises and uses beliefs and accepts patterns of behaviour and practices. Understood in this context:

> Culture structures all of our lives, whoever and whenever we may be. Our culture channels how we think, how we act, how we relate to other people, how we work and relax. At the same time, we as human beings create and control the culture of our communities, either unconsciously by repeating and passing on patterns of behaviour that we have been taught, or consciously, as cultural workers who change and develop the culture around us.[30]

This cultural view recognising the particularity of the cultural well-being of the people of a specific society within the universality of the people of the world is of vital importance in understanding the role and significance of matriarchy in any particular society. This view is of vital importance in understanding of the African societies which are gender egalitarian social formations. Gender egalitarian formations are societies in which members of the society irrespective of their gender have their own sphere of power and authority in terms of division of labour in the society. Women play a critical role in the socio-cultural well-being in these societies by binding them together by being keepers of families, workers of the land and distributors of food. These are societies whose social cultural rules are based on the thesis of Mother

Nature, conceptualised in mythologies, proverbs, idioms, songs and sayings. Setswana proverb, mmangwana o tswara thipa ka bohaleng or Sepedi proverb, mmago ngwana o swara thipa ka bogaleng (the mother of the child holds knife on its edge) is one of the proverbs supporting the centrality of women in the cultural well-being and intangible cultural heritage of Batswana and the Nguni. The saying that women carry mountains on their backs is also supportive of their central role in the well-being of the African people. A mother will go out of her way, even taking risks at times, for the safety and welfare of her children. A mother is a mother of the nation not only of children.

## Conclusion and Recommendations

This chapter has produced and provided understanding of the socio-historical relationship between Batswana and the Nguni by focusing on issues of ethnicity, languages, surnames, culture and intangible heritage.

It viewed Ba ga Seleka as the articulated combination of the Nguni as represented by the Zulu and the Northern Ndebele socio-historically in terms of ethnicity and Tswana linguistically and culturally. It helped in understanding their close socio-historical relationship with Bapedi particularly through Seleka who served for a long time as its regent. They are a classical representative of the socio-historical relationship between Batswana and the Nguni in the areas of ethnicity, languages, surnames, culture and intangible cultural heritage. They are also related to Bapedi in terms of geographical residential proximity which has helped to forge and sustain their relationship with Bapedi in time and space.

It made serious attempts in contributing towards understanding of the role and significance of matriarchy in the cultural well-being and intangible cultural heritage not only of Batswana and the Nguni of South Africa but also other African people of the country and the African continent. As a means to achieve this objective, it discussed, firstly, the centrality of women in an African cultural and intangible cultural heritage setting and, secondly, the right of

African women to marry. This right is a socio-historical process in the sense that it is an integral part of the history of African people.

The role and significance of matriarchy in the cultural well-being and intangible cultural heritage of African people should be viewed as a process in its own merits. It should not be subordinated to patriarchy. Its subordination to patriarchy reduces its role and significance. This is broadly within the context of view of Africans. They should not be viewed within the context of other people. To view them within the context of other people is the same view of Africans as an extension of other people as if they have no movement of their own. The fact that Africans are different from other people, among others, in terms, of ethnicity, languages, surnames, cultural and intangible cultural heritage is the objective socio-historical reality. This is characterised by the fact that the role and significance of African women in the cultural well-being and intangible cultural heritage of Africans are different from the case of other people.

# Chapter Six
## The Socio-Historical Relationship among Ndebele, Swazi, Tsonga-Shangaan, Xhosa and Zulu: Issues of Ethnicity, Languages, Surnames, Culture and Intangible Cultural Heritage

*Busile Cynthia Ndhlovu and Monicca Thulisile Bhuda*

**Introduction**

The Nguni/Abangoni people, who originated in the Great Lakes region of Africa and moved south between 900 and 1290, were divided into smaller groups, each with its own cultural characteristics and dialects.[1] According to Erna Oliver and William Hosking Oliver, the majority of people once lived in a vast formation that spanned from Eswatini in the south to KwaZulu-Natal and the Fish River.[2] Within this wide formation, the Mtamvuma River has historically divided the Cape, or Southern Nguni (e.g., Xhosa and Mpondo), from KwaZulu-Natal, or Northern Nguni (e.g., Zulu and Swati). While other groups can be found in Malawi, Mozambique, Zambia, and Zimbabwe, smaller groups can still be found on the interior plateaus of the provinces of Limpopo and Mpumalanga.

Although the anthropology, history, and material culture of many Nguni people have been extensively studied,[3] their archaeology and ancient history are still less understood. Alfred Thomas Bryant, one of the scholars who have written about Nguni culture, maintains that the Nguni people were divided into multiple groupings, each of which underwent linguistic change as a result of encounters with other linguistic groups as they travelled down various routes to the south.[4]

South Africa's Nguni group consists of the Zulus, Ndebele, Swati, and Xhosa. It is only recently that the Tsonga people, based on evidence of history, have become to be regarded as part of the Nguni group. The historical Nguni kingdoms of the Ndebele, Swazi, Xhosa, Tsonga, and Zulus in modern-day South Africa are found in the provinces of Gauteng, KwaZulu Natal, Limpopo, and Mpumalanga.[5]

Sibusiso Ngubane argues that due to migration driven by wars, some Nguni groups have blended and accepted other people as their own.[6] Migration changed ethnicity, languages, surnames, culture and intangible cultural heritage of African who left their original place for other places where they permanently settled among their fellow Africans who did not share their ethnicity, languages, surnames, culture and intangible cultural heritage.[7] The aim of the study is to investigate socio-historical relationships among Ndebele, Swati, Tsonga, Xhosa, and Zulu.

## Definition of Socio-history

In this study, socio-history is defined as history that emphasises social structures and the interaction of various groups in society rather than affairs of state. According to Charles Tilly, the word social history can apply to both a branch of the historical sciences and a broad method of studying history that emphasises society.[8] Social history saw a triumphal development from the 1950s to the 1980s in both expressions after emerging from marginal and nascent beginnings at the end of the nineteenth and the beginning of the twentieth century. Throughout, social history can best be described in terms of what it strives to avoid or in opposition to what it offers a substitute for.

Eric Allina-Pisano argued that in social history, the structures of societies and social change, social movements, groups and classes, working and living conditions, families, homes, local communities, urbanisation, mobility, ethnic groupings, etc. were all taken into consideration.[9] Social change is emphasised as a central dimension around which historical synthesis and diagnosis of the contemporary world should be organised, challenging dominant historical narratives that were constructed around the history of politics and the state or around the history of ideas.[10]

## Methodology

The study uses secondary data sources from scholarly articles, books, and documents on the history of the Nguni people in particular and the African people of Southern Africa in general. It further looks at literature that focuses on the Nguni languages and their similarities, the history of surnames, and the consequences of migration. The study thereafter focuses on recently published articles on the culture of the Nguni people.

## The migration history of the Nguni people

The Nguni people left Central Africa and moved south along the eastern coast of Southern Africa. While some groups dispersed and settled along the road, others continued in their journey to other places. As a result, the Swazi settled in the north, the Zulu in the east and the Xhosa in the south. They have a common ancestor. It is for this reason that their languages and cultures are common. The history of the Nguni people's migration has been preserved through oral tradition. Patricia Jolly stated that they were a group of people who migrated from Egypt to the sub-equatorial Great Lakes region. They then made their way south, tracing the eastern coastline of Southern Africa. They landed in what is now South Africa some 2,000 years ago. In 1400 AD, there was a second, larger wave of migration.[11] This evacuation occurred roughly 100 years before Europeans rounded the Cape of Good Hope.

The Nguni people share common surnames, clan names, cultural practices, and dialects. Monica Wilson maintains that the

Nguni people are said to have arrived in South Africa around 2,000 years ago and that around 1400 AD, a second, more significant wave of migration started.[12] About 100 years before Europeans crossed the Cape of Good Hope, this exodus took place. The Nguni people are recognised today for their love of vivid colours and for their use of beads, animal skins, and other materials for body ornamentation.[13]

### The history of Zulu migration

James Gump and Mathieu Deflem maintain that Zulu kaMalandela formed the Zulu in 1574 as a small clan in what is now Northern KwaZulu-Natal.[14] As part of the African migrations, Nguni communities have moved down Africa's east coast over the centuries. Shaka's rule brought the clans together to forge a single Zulu identity and consequently Zulu ethnic group started to take shape.[15]

### The history of Swazi migration

Percy Alfred William Cook stated that the Nguni-speaking clans that moved from north-east Africa and eventually settled in south-east Africa in the fifteenth century are the ancestors of the Swazi people.[16] They first travelled to southern Mozambique before arriving in the then-San-populated area of modern-day Eswatini. They are still referred to as bakaNgwane ("Ngwane's people") instead of Swazis.

Eswatini was home to Sotho and the Nguni groups in the 19th century. After 1820, Rita Astuti and David Price Williams maintained that the Ngwane group flourished under the leadership of King Sobhuza.[17] He was replaced by Mswazi, who either expelled the Sotho groups from the country or integrated them into his group. He ruled from 1840 until 1875. The Swazi nation began to take shape as a result of these changes. It was given Mswazi's name. Swazis crossed the border into the Transvaal in small numbers. These individuals made up groups like the Nkosi, Shongwe, and Khumalo who now reside in the Barberton and Mbombela (formerly Nelspruit) areas in Mpumalanga.

## The history of Ndebele migration

Philemon Buti Skhosana maintains that any of the many African peoples who largely inhabit the South African regions of Limpopo and Mpumalanga are known as Ndebele. They are also known as Transvaal Ndebele. The primary Nguni people's ancient offspring, the Ndebele, started migrating to the Transvaal in the 17th century. In the course of the 17th century, some Nguni communities moved from KwaZulu-Natal to Transvaal.[18] The Northern Ndebele group made their home in the vicinity of Mokopane (formerly Potgietersrus) and Polokwane (formerly Pietersburg). They intermarried with Bapedi or the Northern Sotho. This process led to linguistic alterations.[19]

Thomas Neil Huffman maintains that the majority of the Transvaal Ndebele trace their genealogy to Musi, or Msi, who, together with a small group of Nguni migrants, split off and finally settled in the Transvaal at the location of present-day Pretoria.[20] In the 18th and 19th centuries, Nguni people who had fled the wars of Dingiswayo and Shaka in KwaZulu-Natal joined the descendants of Musi's people. By hiding in the bushes, the Transvaal Ndebele avoided the Zulu raids. But as a result, they were geographically separated into various groupings. After Msi's passing away, his two sons, Manala and Ndzundza, established two groups and divided the Ndebele people in the south. Bronkhorstspruit, Bethal, Belfast, Middelburg and other nearby towns served as their new homes in Mpumalanga or the former Eastern Transvaal.[21] As a tribute to their forefathers, these groups adopted names of Manala and Ndzundza as their identities.[22]

## The history of Xhosa migration

According to historical records, the Xhosa people have lived in the Eastern Cape region either since at least 1593 or earlier.[23] The Transkei region saw the arrival of the first Xhosa groups in the fourteenth century. Over time they travelled south until they eventually met the white settlers at the Fish River in 1788. The Xhosa had been residing in the vicinity of the Fish River for more than a century at this point. Conflicts with the Khoikhoi or the San people happened frequently during their journey to the Fish River. They were ultimately victorious over the San people. Various Xhosa groups decided to establish themselves along Africa's southeast coast.[24]

### The history of Tsonga migration

The Tsonga people came into South Africa and left it for more than thousand years.[25] They are thought to have come from Central and East Africa somewhere between AD 200 and 500. Alan Smith maintains that they first resided on the northern Mozambican coastal plains. They eventually moved to the Limpopo and areas near St. Lucia Bay in KwaZulu-Natal starting in the 1300s.[26]

Fumiko Ohinata highlighted that the Tsonga people are made up of numerous clans that are present in Mozambique, Zimbabwe, and South Africa.[27] They are made up of the three sub-groups. They are Shangaan, Thonga, and Tonga. The dialect they all speak and their shared history as canal traders bind them together.[28]

### The Commonality of Nguni people's languages

Julius Sikelela Zwangendaba Matsebula, David King Mlotshwa, Josephine Mafimi Mlotshwa and Nkomeni Douglas Ntiwane maintain that the Nguni group consisted, among others, of the Besutfu Nguni, emaNtungwa Nguni, and emaTekela Nguni.[29] The maNtungwa Nguni were those who are today known as emaZulu and emaXhosa. They maintain that the two groups of the Nguni resided in KwaZulu-Natal and in Mthatha in the Eastern Cape while others went to other parts of Eastern Cape.[30] Those who resided in KwaZulu-Natal speak the Zulu language and the ones in Mthatha and other parts of Eastern Cape speak isiXhosa.[31] They also maintain that the emaTekela Nguni were led by King Dlamini. They are the ones who speak Siswati as their mother tongue. There is a linguistic commonality among members of the Nguni group. They also maintain that this linguistic commonality among the Nguni is supported by the fact that their languages are interrelated and have the same root. The case of the word *ubuntu* in their languages: in Siswati *ubuntu*, isiZulu *ubuntu*, isiXhosa *umntu* and

IsiNdebele *ubuntu*[32] support this reality. The root nt/ *ntf* for all the Nguni languages is evidence that they are common. Due to the fact that the Nguni people were affected by linguistic changes, each of the group experienced variations in their languages.[33]

## The Nguni People and their languages

The Nguni languages may be better understood as a dialect continuum rather than a collection of distinct languages because they are closely related and common. Proposals to establish a single Nguni language have been made several times.[34] The linguistic classification, "Nguni" is typically thought to include the subgroups "Zunda Nguni" and "Tekela Nguni" in academic writings on the Southern African languages. This division is primarily based on the salient phonological difference between the corresponding coronal consonants Zunda (/z/) and Tekela (/t/), which gives rise to the native name Swati and the more well-known Zulu form Swazi.

According to the socio-historical background, migration of the African people was the main cause of multilingualism. Mandla Nkosinathi Ngcobo confirms that developments such as colonialism, and border propinquity relocation had impact upon the development of multilingualism.[35] The relocation of people led to variations in their common languages.[36] The Nguni people in particular and the African people of South Africa in general were related as a family that shares common languages and culture. Hence, Paul Maylam refers to the Nguni people as a group with a broad linguistic similarity.[37] He maintains that, although there are dialects within the Nguni group, these dialects are closely related or bear a resemblance to each other. This reality is supported by Ngcobo when he states that "there are numerous linguistic similarities among all these languages."[38] The table below provides evidence of the linguistic commonality among the Nguni people. He provides explanation of this linguistic commonality in the table on the following page.

| English | Siswati | Zulu | Xhosa |
|---------|---------|------|-------|
| arm | -khono | -galo | -galo |
| ash | -lotsa | -lotha | -thuthu |
| bark | -gcolo | -gxolo | -gxolo |
| big | -khulu | -khulu | khulu |
| bird | -nyoni | -nyoni | -ntaka |

The dialects stated in the above table were informed by the identification of some clicks that were adopted from the San tradition. In Ngcobo's words:

> The Khoisan people were considered as the first people to occupy the Southern District of, and they moved to Cape Town. Africa their language was the Khoisan language, and their language was characterized by clicks, hence it is known as the click language. They were known as the Khoi-Khoi or San people and were passionate about hunting.[39]

The clicks that are noted in the above table are "c" and "x." The fact that they were adopted from the San people proves that the San's language was the first language that laid a foundation for the Nguni language family. The table also indicates the commonality or relatedness of the Nguni languages. While in the word bark, Siswati uses the click "c," Zulu and Xhosa use the click "x." Despite this process of migration, isiZulu, isiNdebele, isiXhosa, and Siswati have retained their commonality in time and space. They still retain it. This reality is supported by the vocabulary they share.[40]

Matsebula, Mlotshwa, Mlotshwa and Ntiwane maintain that the Nguni people in particular and African people in general originated from the Niger Delta Basin in West Africa. They confirmed that communication with each other was easy without any barriers. They have one central belief that life and moral values are centered on an individual. African people were governed by the principle of "ubuntu "that binds them and keeps them together as Africans, hence their term of reference is maintained by the word "ntu."[41]

Peters Joyce supports this reality by referring to the Bantu people as the Ntu-speaking people.[42]

Thandeka Primrose Sabela and Busile Cynthia Ndlovu support this reality by maintaining that *ubuntu* helps to create consciousness about what is tolerable and intolerable within the community.[43] In addition, they emphasise that ubuntu reinforces a sense of respect among human beings. In other words, the principle of ubuntu binds the African people together. Sabela and Ndhlovu explored that the Nguni group moved to the East its interest being in crop farming and stock farming. As population gradually grew and increased pressure in sharing the small available land, the importance of a search for fertile land for grazing and farming increasing became a major issue among the Nguni group.[44] Migration was the consequence of this socio-historical development. The Nguni group comprises Besutfu Nguni, Ntungwa Nguni, and Tekela Nguni.[45] In addition, the Nguni group known as Mantungwa Nguni became part of those who speak Zulu and Xhosa who migrated towards South Africa.[46] Their linguistic commonality has helped to preserve other aspects of their relationship. The linguistic commonality of the Nguni people is evidence of their originality. Central to them is a high level of mutual intelligibility.

Scholars like Carl Meinhof and Wilhem Guthrie confirm that Bantu languages where the Nguni languages belong, were spoken by people of the same ethnic group.[47] However, due to migration, the united groups were separated into various sections that exposed them to new environments that resulted in linguistic variations.[48] The African people migrated from one place to another, from one country to another country and from one province to another province within one country because of factors such as border proximity, politics, and colonialism. Other factors which contributed toward the migration of the African people include insufficient food production and their search for fertile land for grazing and farming.[49]

The process of migration resulted in the variations in their languages. Variations in their languages and the constructed ethnic groups enabled the creation of ethnic and national identities among the Nguni in particular and Africans in general. This in turn enabled the National Party in their establishment of the so-called homelands for the African people.

### The Ndebele language

The Ndebele language is a linguistic formation with different clicks. Cornelis Johannes Coetzee supports the position that the people under the leadership of Mzilikazi acquired the Ndebele name from the Sotho group.[50] He maintains that the Sotho people refer to Ndebele as Matabele as follows:

> Die naam ko nook va die Suid-Sothowerkwoord - go tebela, wat beteken om te verdryf, afgelei gewees het. Die Ngunistamme, waarmee die Sotho in aanraking gekom het, sou dus 'die verdrywers' bekendgestaan het.[51]

The name Ndebele came from the interaction between the Ndebele and the Sotho group. The name came from their practice of using large war buffers during their battles. The Transvaal Ndebele has close affinities with the Xhosa than with other Nguni groups. This is supported by the Ndebele enthusiasm in their traditional attire which looks like the Xhosa attire. The Ndebele people are divided into two sections. There the Northern Ndebele and the Southern Ndebele. There is a popular position that the Northern Ndebele were absorbed by the Sotho, while the Southern Ndebele preserved its identity into two sections. They are the Manala and the Ndzundza. They have linguistic commonality.

Katjie Sponono Mahlangu presents the linguistic commonality among the two Ndebele groups[52] as follows:

| English | Manala | Ndzundza |
|---|---|---|
| destroy | -sinya | -ona |
| borrow/ loan | -glima | -boleka |
| hole | -umlidi | -umgodi |
| grandmother | -umgeguli | ugogo |

## The commonality of surnames of the Nguni people

The Nguni people have common surnames. The surname Radebe is shared by Zulus, Xhosas, Swazis and the Hlubi people or Amahlubi. The name of the clan is the name of the first person that gave birth to the clan. We may call the person where the entire clan originated from as the ancestor or *gogomkhulu* in Swati. His name became a surname of the clan. In the context of the surname Zikalala, the clan surname indicates that the ancestor of the Zikalala family originated from the Zulu clan. The clan surname for Zikalala is found among the Swazis and the Zulus.

The Nguni people have almost similar surnames. Most of the surnames are indicators of the people's places of origin. Surnames such as Dlamini Ndlovu, Ngwenya, Nkosi, are common across the Nguni group. Clan surnames were determined by traditional leaders in Eswatini and South Africa. The people who belong to a particular clan come from the same ancestor. Nkosi and Dlamini are regarded as one surname by the Swazis. Sometimes Dlamini is written as Dhlamini from the Swazi version.

Richards Patrick maintains among the Swazis, the most common surname is the Dlamini which constitutes at least 20% of the Swazi population, followed by the Simelane with not more than 3%.[53] The Nxumalo is the next popular surname. Ndwandwe and Mkhatjwa are followed by Shongwe and Khumalo. Patrick further explores the rest of the top ten surnames in descending order. They are Zwane, Kunene, Mabuza, Magagula, and Nkambule. The Zulu version of Nkambule is Khambule. The last list of known surnames is Vilakati, Mamba, Hlophe, Mavuso, and Fakudze. The Zulu version of Fakuzde is Fakude. It is followed by Nsibande, Dvuba or Dube for the Zulus, Matsebula or Mathebula for the Zulus, Shabangu and Thwala for Swazis and Zulus. Thwala is a surname used by Swazis and Zulus.

## Some Nguni surnames of Tsonga Origins

Nguni surnames are related irrespective of the type of clan they belong to. There is a socio-historical relationship between the origin of Nguni surnames and the Tsongas. This is supported by the fact that there are surnames that originated from the Tsongas that are linked to the members of other Nguni groups. The only difference is the linguistic elements. The Tsonga groups within the Nguni were affected by voluntary or forced integration into other Nguni group due to migrations.[54] In some cases, some of their surnames were adjusted to match those of Nguni in several aspects.

Batsonga (Vatsonga) people incorporate Vandzawu. This Nguni group is today found in Southern Mozambique, Limpopo province, and West of the Kruger National Park.[55] There are Batsonga people also in some areas of the Mpumalanga province, namely, Komatipoort, and Nkomazi areas that are closer to South Africa's border with Mozambique through Maputo. The Siswati language used in these areas is dominated by Xitsonga. Their surnames were not possible to be transformed into any of the surnames of other Nguni groups. They were transformed to sound more like those of other members of the Nguni group such as Zulus and Swazis. A mistranslation and misspelling were some of these reasons. The following are examples of how a mistranslation and misspelling of the Tsonga surnames occurred:

Xirindza instead of Silinda or Silindani and Silindza
Nyarhi instead of Nyathi and Nyatsi.[56]

The first surname is for Xitsonga, the second is for Zulu and the last is for Swazi.

There are instances where Tsonga surnames were given Nguni spellings. However, in their new Nguni spellings, the words end up without a Nguni meaning. The meaning has nothing to do with the Nguni languages, such as the surnames below:

from Mavunda to Mabunda
from Makhuvele to Makhubela
from Ndhove to Ndobe.[57]

The fact of the matter is that what makes a surname to be Nguni is not the similarity with a Nguni word or a Nguni-sounding surname. What is important is that a surname should be originally of the Nguni heritage. It is for this reason that, according to the Viv Lifestyle Magazine of 2 May 2017, the Nguni surnames of Tsonga origin are the following:

- *Mabona* originates from Khosa and the Tsonga group which is also Mavona-Khoseni.
- *Mthombeni* originates from Mbita-nkulu and comes from the Nhlave Tsonga group.
- *Manyisa* originates from Tembe which is the category of the Rhonga Tsonga group.
- *Masiya* also originates from the Khosa, Khoseni Tsonga group.
- *Masinga* originates from Hlungwani in the Hlengwe Tsonga group.
- *Mazibuko* originates from the Zivuko in the Nhlave Tsonga group.
- *Mkhathini* originates from the Khosa in the Khoseni Tsonga group.
- *Mbiza* originates from the Cawuke in the Hlengwe Tsonga group.
- *Mpofu* originates from Valoyi in the Lozwi Tsonga group.
- *Bvuma* originates from the Mavundza in the Nhlave Tsonga group.
- *Myiyo* and *Mlilo* originate from the Mavasa in the Hlengwe Tsonga group.
- Sono originates from Hlungwani in the Hlengwe Tsonga group.
- *Hlenga* and *Hlengwa* originate from Cawuke in the Hlengwe Tsonga group.
- *Thwala* and *Twala* originate from the Makamu in the Nhlave Tsonga group and
- *Zitha* originates from the Nkwinika in the Nhlave Tsonga group.[58]

Noel Casper Makhuba helps in explaining the socio-historical relationship between Tsonga surnames and Nguni surnames. This confirms that, for instance, Khoza is a Nguni version of Khosa which is used by communities in KwaZulu-Natal and Mpumalanga, Eswatini as well as among the Tsonga people. According to the Viv Lifestyle Magazine, Mabaso surname is used by the emaNtungwa.[59] It declares that Mabuza originates from Mavhuza in the Hlanganu Tsonga group, which is then used by the Nguni dialects by translating the V of Xitsonga into B. Hence it proposes that Mavhuza be changed to Mabuza.

According to Makhuba, in the Tsonga surnames, the word *kuthebula* means to bewitch. It means *kuloya* in Nguni. Therefore, *Matsewula is a Siswati version of Mathebula. The source relationship* and origins of Tsonga surnames and the *Nguni* surnames are revealed in many surnames, and some were affected by forced inclusion, such as the Mthembu and Themba that originate from the Tembe in the Rhonga Tsonga grouping. The Tembe people in northern KwaZulu-Natal had to use Mthembu and Themba as their Nguni surnames due to the British forced inclusion of the Tembe into the Zulu group. Makhuba maintains that the Shabalala surname originates from Chavalala in the Vaxingwidzi Tsonga group, and the Nguni version of the surname is Shabalala. In addition, the Ubisi surname originates from Rivisi in the Khoseni Tsonga group. The Nguni-translated version of Rivisi is Ubisi. Its Siswati version is Lubisi. This is supported by the fact that Lubisi surname is found in the Mpumalanga province in the Nkomazi municipality of the east of Mpumalanga. The Nkomazi is close to the border with Mozambique, where Xitsonga is spoken. Ndzimandze surname originates from Ndhimandhe in the Nkomati Tsonga group. It belongs to the Southern Sambo group that was absorbed by the Swazi group.

Viv Lifestyle Magazine of 2 May 2017 calls upon us to note that there are Ndzawu surnames that cut across various Nguni ethnic groups. These are surnames such as Ndlovu, Simango, Msimango, Sithole, Mhlanga, and Moyo.[60]

**The commonality of the cultural practices of the Nguni people**
Matsebula, Mlotshwa, Mlotshwa and Ntiwane maintain that Nguni's cultural practices and beliefs are common. They also maintain that the Nguni people easily communicate with each other.[61] This is due to the relatedness of their languages as explained.

Joyce perceives that the belief system of the Swazis is underpinned by animism, the endowment of natural structures and objects such as rock creations, trees, and streams with spiritual personalities.[62] According to him, what is called the other world is characterised by spirits of various types, some generous while others are wicked. On these practices, he maintains that the Swazis are like the other Nguni group members, such as the Zulu and the Xhosa.[63] Just like the Xhosas and Zulus, the background of the Swazis, includes the consultation with the sangoma who can be either a male or female. He further states that the selection of the sangoma is done through a spiritualist of which the choice is suggested by abnormal behaviour.

The Xhosas use *impundulu* flipping of their wings for rainmaking. The Dlamini clan has a special rain-making custodian. Matsebula, Mlotshwa, Mlotshwa and Ntiwane confirm this when they state that:

> Unfortunately, *Silo Zikodze* did not live long enough to be installed to eMaswati royal ceremony, nor dance his first *Incwala* ritual. He was struck by lightning, something considered very grave indeed as they were known as the custodians of rain and lightning. Dlamini who, through *umtfunti.* Swazis. The Dlamini clan has a special rain-making custodian.[64]

Although the Swazis also worshiped ancestral spirits, they know that there is a supernatural who is above everything.[65] Most of the Nguni people have a tendency to adhere to spiritual acts in their cultural practices in the form of sangoma or other traditional healers. The Nguni people have a custodian of doing something, like rain making as already pointed out.

Joyce maintains that God is known as the Supreme Being or *UMkhuluncadii*.[66] Just like the Swazis, the Zulu people claim that God is uNkulunkulu who is the Supreme being. While the Xhosa refer to God as a Supreme Being and call Him uMdali, uThixo, or uQamata, the Tsonga people believe that everything was created by the supreme being called *Tilo*.[67] Makhuba maintains that the Tsonga people worship *Tilo* through their ancestors. The Ndebele refer to God as Zimu. This proves that the Nguni people were acknowledging the Supreme God right before the missionaries. Mahlangu confirms that the Nguni people refer to God as Zimu as follows:

AmaNdebele a thi inkosi e phezulu ngu Zimu. Bathi: U munye. Aba M bonga nab a se bu nzimeni, na b'ehlelwe n'ugula. Bat hi: Zimu si lekelele. Ukuthi abantu ama Ndebele bay a M azi uZimu ukuthi: U khona.[68]

[The Ndebele-speaking people say the king up there is God. They say he is One. They do not worship him; they only worship him when they are in danger when they are sick, they say: God help us, whether the Ndebele people know that God is there (or not)].[69]

From the above, it is clear that the Nguni people acknowledge God as the only one with supreme powers. However, the Ndebele people are the only Nguni group who claim not to worship God in normal circumstances. They only consider God when they are faced with challenges such as sickness. The above paragraphs prove that the African people were aware of the Almighty God, and they were worshiping Him even before the arrival of the missionaries.

**Nguni Marriage and Lobola: The Case of the Swazi group**
Lobola is the basic principle to be considered before marriage among the Nguni. While the Swazi society is patriarchal in nature, women play a pivotal role within the social structure. Siswati marriage is still being guided by traditional practices.

In the past arranged marriages were the custom followed by most of the Swati people. Old and young people are nowadays free to decide on a partner of their choice. Lobola is a prerequisite for the Swati in their marriage. Lobola is a term that refers to the practice of giving cattle to the bride's father or family by the groom's family.[70] According to the Swati tradition, this is considered a sign or token of appreciation offered to the groom's family.

## Ndebele Traditional Beliefs

The Ndebele people believe in God called Zimu, the creator of nature, lightning, and rain as well as the whole universe. They believe that Zimu has little to do with them directly and no rituals or sacrifices that are connected to Him. The spirit of ancestors is considered in great esteem by the traditional Ndebele people. To them, keeping the ancestors happy is important so that they are always kept happy in order for them not to face disasters and other problems such as illnesses. The common offerings they make to their ancestors include beer, sacrifices of cattle and goats and fowls. It is the responsibility of the husband to perform such rituals on behalf of the family. They also believe in traditional healers who communicate by throwing bones. This kind of belief is practised by all the Nguni groups.

## Language and Culture of the Xhosa People

The Xhosa people use clicks like the San and the Khoikhoi people. They inherited the clicks from their closest contacts with the Khoisan. Siphokazi Angelinah Dazela explores the Xhosa pronunciation. The letter $x$ is pronounced by placing the tongue against the teeth on the side of your mouth. The letter $q$ is pronounced by clicking your tongue at the back of your mouth. The $c$ is pronounced by putting your tongue behind your front teeth. The Xhosa group just like the Zulus uses clicks. Some of these clicks such as q and x are not used by the Swazi group.[71]

A large percentage of the Xhosas are Christians. They believe in their supreme being known as uMdali, uThixo, or uQamata.

They believe in their ancestors. They call them iziNyanya. They trust their ancestors. They approach God through them. In addition, diviners are people like traditional healers known as *iGqirha*. The latter are qualified before practicing their calling. These traditional healers take care of the community and help in chasing off evil spirits. This practice applies to the other Nguni groups. Hlubi traditional healers wear distinctive white dresses. They carry spears which was shown to them by their ancestors in the form of a dream. In addition, if they are not holding spears, they believe that they will fall ill. The perception behind this is that they trust the powers or spirits of their ancestors for protection. The ancestors are believed to have supernatural powers.

The Xhosa people are part of the Thembu clan considered as the oldest of the Nguni clans.[72] Alfred Thomas Bryant maintains that a small percentage of this group joined the Ntungwa clan into the Zululand, while leaving others.[73] He further argues that the Khoisan language has a tangible impact on the Xhosa language. Hence the fact that Xhosa language has many clicks that make the language unique and different from other Nguni languages. It is closer to Zulu language than to other Nguni languages.

## Conclusion and Recommendations

Using secondary data, the study has focused on socio-historical relationships among the Nguni. It looked at issues of ethnicity, languages, surnames, culture and intangible cultural heritage. The study made the case that there are commonalities in these identities among members of the Nguni group because of migration within South Africa. Internal migration was driven by various issues, processes and developments. The study looked at the migration history of the Nguni group. Moreover, the study looked at the detailed cultural and intangible cultural heritage practices and beliefs of the Nguni people in South Africa with the aim of identifying their similarities and differences.

It also made the case that there is the battle for tribalisation among the Nguni in the name of ethnic, linguistic and cultural diversity or differences that has created a solid foundation for retaining ethnic view of the Nguni people in particular and African people in general and that some ethnic groups and their cultures are more dominant and resistive than others. Our recommendations are that this battle and its characteristic features should be fought against for it is the same policy of dividing Africans so as to rule them economically and financially.

# Chapter Seven

## The Strategic Importance of the Ethnic, Linguistic, Cultural and Intangible Cultural Heritage Commonality of the African People of South Africa in the Service of the Nation Building Project

Sehlare Makgetlaneng

Migration remains a key socio-historical process in the formation of ethnic, linguistic, cultural and intangible cultural heritage identities in Southern Africa. Over the centuries, people from others parts of Africa and the world beyond the continent migrated into what is today South Africa as their country. It is for this reason that South Africa is a number one racial, ethnic, linguistic, cultural and intangible cultural heritage microcosm of Southern Africa. The popular, hegemonic and dominant view of Africans of South Africa in terms of ethnicity, language, culture and intangible cultural heritage constitutes a challenge of how they should forge and sustain their unity. It was put in place and refined by the forces of settler colonialism in their service of their rule and interests and those of members of their race for strategic and tactical reasons. As those who became South African nationals on the basis of external expansion of mercantilist imperialism and as South Africa was thrust into rivalries of imperialist powers it and other parts of the region, the continent and the world as a theatre, this history of migration shaped the content and operations of those the country became their national homeland. As the country become increasingly of global, continental and regional strategic importance, prosperous with lush farmland and the mining of diamonds and gold and strategic location, some South Africans in alliance with external actors and powers sought to keep its natural resources and wealth for themselves and exclude other South Africans. This struggle for control of the country and its resources shaped the content and operations of their interaction. Africans as the decisive majority of the population and as the labour backbone of the operations of the economy and its mining, agricultural and manufacturing sectors became the primary targets to be defeated in this struggle. Strategies and tactics were crafted and implemented to ensure their defeat and its sustenance. Divide and conquer policy became central in the utilisation of the combination of soft power and hard power for this strategic purpose. The thesis of ethnic, linguistic, cultural and intangible cultural heritage diversity is a sophisticated ideological means to divide Africans and rule them for them to remain being economically and financially dominated in their country.

## Introduction: The Relevance and Service of the Chapter to South African Nation Building Project

The main target of this chapter is the popular, hegemonic and dominant view of ethnic, linguistic and cultural diversity of Africans of South Africa. Interrogating this view, it maintains that they share a common history of ethnicity, languages, surnames, culture and intangible cultural heritage that disputes this view of their ethnic, linguistic and cultural diversity. Central to this view is that they are ethnically, linguistically and culturally diverse or different. Rather than recognising the fact that they have continued living together in social relations of common history of ethnicity, languages and culture, this view has been successful in forging and sustaining the narrative of ethnic, linguistic and cultural differences which is popularly, hegemonically and dominantly guarded, managed and celebrated in the name of ethnic, linguistic and cultural diversity. Central to this success has been the promotion of the proliferation of guardians, managers and celebrants of their ethnic, linguistic and cultural diversity. The consequence has remained being the task of a popular, hegemonic and dominant view of Africans on the basis of ethnicity, language and culture in a country in which they are the decisive majority of its population. This is the sophisticated version of dividing them so as to continue ruling them ideologically, economically and financially in an African country in which they are the decisive majority of its population.

The relevance and service of this chapter to South Africa in its nation building project is to serve it in its efforts to achieve its national integration objectives by highlighting the strategic importance of ethnic, linguistic, cultural and intangible cultural heritage commonality of its African people as opposed to their diversity.

The history of African people is a cause for a better life and sustainable development of present and future generations. In this cause, they enjoy opportunities and face challenges. Opportunities they enjoy in their cause for a better life and sustainable development of present and future generations are directly interlinked with their being the decisive majority of the national population at the centre of the struggle for the resolution of the national question through nation building. This factor makes them indispensable to the successful nation building project and the resolution of the national question. For them to be a truly social agents for the resolution of the national question through nation building, their being quantitative majority should be transformed into a qualitative majority. This transformation requires that they are viewed as the people who have or share a common history of ethnicity, languages, surnames, culture and intangible cultural heritage. This is in the best interest of a successful cause for a better life and sustainable development of present and future generations for their socio-economic, financial and ideological status in the society to reflect their being decisive majority of its population.

Ethnic and linguistic tensions are structurally against social solidarity and unity. Social solidarity and unity are the prerequisite means of confronting social and material constrains in enhancing the advancement of material conditions and rights of the African people and their fellow South Africans. The advancement of collective material conditions and rights of South Africans is best and most effectively served if the theoretical means are not based on their view in terms of their ethnic and linguistic affiliations. The qualitative movement towards the society's sustainable development and security should be at the centre of the struggle against viewing its people primarily in terms of their ethnicity and languages. The point is that in the advancement of its sustainable development and security, its people should be viewed as individuals who are its nationals not as individuals who belong to the particular ethnic and linguistic groups. The fact that South Africans should be viewed and treated as citizens not as members of particular ethnic and linguistic groups is of vital political, economic and ideological importance in the advancement of social change and transformation of their society and its institutions and economy. The success of its social change and transformation is the process judiciously served not by ethnic and linguistic-centric view and treatment of its members.

## Ethnic, Linguistic, Cultural and Intangible Cultural Heritage Commonality of the African people as Service to the Resolution of the National Question

The ethnic, linguistic, cultural and intangible cultural heritage commonality of African people is of strategic importance for the resolution of the national question through the nation building project. The resolution of its national question through the nation building project is judiciously served through the emphasis of what its African people share in common not their diversity. This can in turn be served best and most effectively if we take into account the consequences of their internal migration within their country and its consequences as far as their ethnicity, languages, surnames, culture and intangible cultural heritage are concerned.

Internal migration of the African people affected their ethnicity, languages, surnames, culture and intangible cultural heritage as members of their particular ethnic and linguistic groups left some parts of their country for its other parts in other provinces where they settled permanently. This socio-historical development is of vital importance in the creative theoretical use of their ethnicity, languages, surnames, culture and intangible cultural heritage particularly as they confront their challenges relating to it as people who are popularly viewed as of different or diverse ethnic, linguistic and cultural groups. Not only ethnicity and culture of Africans who left their original locations for other locations in other provinces where they settled permanently were transformed. Their languages, surnames and intangible cultural heritage were also transformed.

Depending on their length, their surnames were either fundamentally or slightly transformed. While those which are long such as Mkhatshwa were fundamentally transformed, those which are brief such as Gola were slightly changed by languages of ethnic groups in which they settled permanently. There are surnames such as Swana which were not transformed even slightly. Gola or Kola and Swana are some of the surnames which are brief. While as used by Xhosa people it is spelt Gola, it is spelt Kola as used by Bapedi people. As originally a surname only for the Xhosa people, it was slightly changed upon some of them leaving their original place and arriving in a place or places in Limpopo Province among Bapedi people where they settled permanently. Swana has remained intact. Swazi surnames such as Mabuza, Mkhatshwa and Nkambule were fundamentally transformed by Sepedi into Maphutha, Mogashwa and Kgaphola upon their bearers arriving in Limpopo where they settled permanently. The Swazi surname such as Masimula was transformed into Masemola by Sepedi upon their bearers arriving in Limpopo where they settled permanently. Those who left for KwaZulu-Natal Province their surname remained intact as Masimula. The reason for this development is because Swazi and Zulu languages are more common.

Moswathupa, the surname of Bapedi in Limpopo, is originally a Ndebele surname, Masombuka, of Mpumalanga. Masombuka was fundamentally transformed by Sepedi into Moswathupa upon its bearers arriving among Bapedi where they settled permanently. The name "sombuka" means to begin. The word thupa basically means begin in the sense that moswathupa means it is the beginning of the thupa which burns.

Upon arrival among Bapedi where they settled permanently, Ndebele, Swati and Xhosa people, became Bapedi in terms of ethnicity, surnames, culture and intangible cultural heritage. They acquired Sepedi surnames and Bapedi ethnicity. In the case of those who became Bapedi ba ga Masemola, their leaders became Bapedi.[1] Those who did not become traditional leaders became members of Bapedi sub-groups under the leadership of traditional leaders. Traditional leaders whose surnames are, among others, Kgaphola, Mogashwa, Mokwena, Marishane, Nchabeleng, Phaahla, and Phaahlamohlaka are originally from ba ga Masemola. Some of them are descendants of Kgoshi Matlebjane 11. Kgoshi Matlebjane's six sons were Mokwena, Selwane, Mogashwa, Masemola, Phaahla and Photo. The fact that he was killed by his teenage son, Photo, because of the plan by his five senior sons which was concealed from him led to two idioms. They are Matlebjane o bolailwe ke tswala and ka hlagolela leokana la re go gola la ntlhaba.[2]

### The Linguistic Commonality of the African People

The over-emphasise of ethnic, linguistic and cultural diversity of Africans and its use in promoting the negation of their ethnic, linguistic and cultural commonality is responsible for the popular, hegemonic and dominant position that there are so many African languages spoken in South Africa. This is contrary to the reality that languages of the Sotho group consisting of Bapedi or Northern Sothos, Batswana or Western Sothos and Basotho or Southern Sothos are common not diverse. The same applies to the case of the Nguni group consisting of Ndebele, Shangaan-Tsonga, Venda, Swazi, Xhosa and Zulu people. Shangaan-Shangaan people, as linguistically related to Swazi and Zulu, are a members of Nguni language-cluster. They are related to Nguni group also in terms of surnames. Venda people, as linguistically related to the Nguni group, are a member of Nguni language-cluster. They are also linguistically related to the Sotho group, especially Bapedi. They are related to Sotho and the Nguni groups also in terms of surnames. This reality is supported by P. Eric Louw when he maintains that:

> The Afrikaner nationalism built on and systematized the colonial British divide-and-rule policy. Since whites constitute a minority of South Africa's population, the most effective way to rule was to prevent the 75% black-African population from cohering into a unified group. A key means of achieving this was an active state-sponsored encouragement of African tribalism in South Africa. The central feature of apartheid was the creation of tribal political 'homelands' (originally called 'Bantustans'), each tied to a separate black 'nation' with its their own language. The 'nations' and 'national languages' engineered into existence in this way were: Transkei and Ciskei ('the national language' of both of these was Xhosa); Kwa-Zulu ('national language' Zulu); Bophuthatswana (Tswana); Lebowa (North Sotho); Qwa Qwa (South Sotho); Venda (Venda); Gazankulu (Tsonga); KaNgwane (Swazi); and KwaNdebele (Ndebele).
>
> These national languages and the homelands have more to do with the geo-political divide-and-rule needs of apartheid than with linguistic criteria.[3]

It is correct to refer to Setswana as Western Sotho as an integral part of Sotho language-cluster in the same way other two members of Sotho language-cluster are referred to and Batswana as Western Sothos as Bapedi and Basotho are referred to. South Africa has two main African language-clusters. By maintaining that they are not Sothos, a considerable number of Batswana have excluded and continue excluding themselves from the Sotho group of which they are an integral member. As the result of this socio-historical development, words shared by Sotho language-cluster are incorrectly regarded as only Tswana words.

The Afrikaner intellectuals successfully used the language question in forging and sustaining their nationalism and paving a way for the assumption and exercise of the state political power by the Afrikaners for their interests. They also successfully divided African people on the basis of ethnicity and language in order to rule them. Out of the ethnic and linguistic commonality among Africans, they exaggerated minor ethnic and linguistic diversity factors to create what they regarded as Black nations.[4] This is contrary to the reality that African languages are more common making communication among Africans easier. The fact that Sotho language-cluster is essentially common and that Nguni language-cluster is also common is such that members of these two language-clusters easily communicate among themselves. African speakers of African languages are more trilingual in that they understand and speak more than three African languages. Others understand and speak more than four languages. This is the case particularly in the case of the Sotho group. Despite their limited formal education, a considerable number of Africans understand and speak Afrikaans and English. African speakers of African languages spoken in South Africa communicate freely among themselves in these languages. The point is that there are basically two main African linguistic groups or language-clusters. Their classification are Nguni (Ndebele, Shangaan-Tsonga, Swazi, Xhosa, Venda and Zulu) and Sotho (Bapedi, Basotho and Batswana).[5] This reality renders Neville Alexander's position that "Nguni (Zulu, Xhosa, Swati, Ndebele and Sotho (Southern Sotho, Northern Sotho, Tswana) can and should be standardised or unified in writing and in all formal settings (school, church, law-courts, etc.)."[6] The commonality within the Nguni language-cluster and within the Sotho language-cluster, the commonality between these language-clusters and closer interaction among Africans which has resulted into them understanding and speaking other African languages of South Africa have rendered Alexander's position null and void. His position is based on his misunderstanding of the proposal of Jacob Mfaniselwa Nhlapo, a member of the African National Congress (ANC), in his work published in 1944, *"Bantu Babel: Will the Bantu Languages Live?"*[7] who, according to him, essentially

> proposed that the spoken varieties of Nguni and Sotho respectively be standardised in a written form as the first step to a possible standardised indigenous African language, in order to help to overcome tribal and ethnic divisions.[8]

Ethnic divisions are not in themselves the problem. They cannot be solved because they are not the problem. They should be handled correctly through the judicious management of relations of members of ethnic heterogenous social formations. South Africa's division into ethnic groups is not a problem. It is its division into social classes which is the problem of different and antagonistic interests which should be solved.

Nhlapo's proposal was the task to forge African political unity through harmonising writing systems of Sotho-Nguni languages. It was a political project, not a linguistic project, centred on the strategic importance of the political economy of language in the national liberation struggle. He was calling for the rejection of division or fragmentation of Africans and the thesis of linguistic diversity.

It is for this reason that Louw is also correct: "So naturalised have the languages developed by apartheid's separate nationalism become, that many now believe that South Africa has nine reified and 'given' black languages."[9] From this, he concludes by maintaining that:

> This reified view of language is closely tied to the notion of culture as an historically given and inherited phenomenon. This view denies process and change in the formation of culture and language. Given the history of Afrikaans itself

(as the result of a process of integration between Dutch, French, German, English and the indigenous Khoi), it is ironic that Afrikaner nationalism became so wedded to the static view of language and culture.[10]

The consequence of the "apartheid state" spending "a great deal of effort and money in dividing South Africans from one another" and that a "key means of doing this has been to 'engineer' separate languages"[11] is that:

> The Nguni-cluster was split into four languages/nations. The Sotho-cluster has been split into three languages/ nations. These seven languages have been codified; taught at schools; used by the Radio Bantu channels and later by TV2 and TV3 channels. Schools have especially played a key role in teaching people to believe that they are Zulus or Xhosas or Tswanas, rather than South Africans (or for that matter Ngunis or Sothos). Through education the differences have been emphasized and made to seem 'natural.'[12]

This socio-historical development has continued in South Africa since 1994 with some Africans being in charge with the political governance of the country. What the successive colonial administrations including that of the National Party have done is continued being done through the South African Broadcasting Corporation television stations and radio stations broadcasting in African languages. It is being done, among others, at schools and universities. Some Africans in intensifying this programme of action demand that African languages be used as medium of instructions at high schools and universities. According to Louw, the solution to this problem created by the successive colonial administrations and defended by African political governors of South Africa is that "it means confronting separate apartheid languages that have taken on a degree of real material existence in the form of codifications and educative and media infrastructures (with all the vested interests which that implies)."[13]

The fact that Sotho language-cluster is common and that Nguni language-cluster is also common is such that members of these two language-clusters easily communicate among themselves. The consequence of this commonality is such these languages are unified and that there is no need for them to be amalgamated and standardised. This linguistic commonality is buttressed by the fact that the majority of Shangaan-Tsonga and Venda people even in the rural parts of South Africa understand and speak Sotho. African speakers of African languages are more trilingual in that they understand and speak more than three African languages. Others understand and speak more than four African languages. This is the case mostly or tangibly in the case of the Sotho group. Despite their limited formal education, a considerable number of Africans understand and speak Afrikaans and English. African speakers of African languages spoken in South Africa communicate freely in these languages. The point is that there are basically two main African linguistic groups or language-clusters in South Africa. There are some authors who do not understand and speak African languages who maintain the incorrect position that there are four African linguistic groups or language-clusters. This position confuses the issue of ethnicity with the issue of languages in the case of Shangaan-Tsonga and Venda people and Shangaan-Tsonga and Venda languages. It is based on the misunderstanding of the fact that Shangaan-Tsonga and Venda are an integral part of the Nguni group in the same way that Bapedi are an integral part of the Sotho group. This incorrect position is maintained, among others, by Alexander Johnston who argues that Tsonga and Venda are "minority African languages."[14] This is not the case with white South Africans and Afrikaans and English. They are people of two different languages which are not common.

Given this reality, at the centre of the task of developing the language policy in South Africa should be the focus on other South Africans particularly whites and Afrikaans and English. The point is that, firstly, the majority of them do not understand and speak a single African language spoken in South Africa. Secondly, they do not make any serious efforts to understand and speak African languages. Thirdly, the consequences is that, firstly, a considerable number of them are not able to pronounce African first names and surnames. Secondly, they are linguistically and culturally isolated from the decisive majority of the national population. These problems are maintained by the fact that the decisive majority of the national population are linguistically and culturally subordinated to the decisive minority of the population in an African country which is of global, continental and regional importance. This is an integral part of the national question which should be resolved through the nation building project by embarking upon a programme, among others, of linguistic integration.

## The Commonality of Surnames among Africans

Members of the Nguni group share surnames such as Dube, Mnisi, Tshabalala. The surname, Tshabalala is spelt differently as Chabalala and Shabalala among them. They are related to them also in terms of surnames. Venda people are linguistically related to the Nguni group and the Sotho group, especially Bapedi. Their surnames are similar to or common with those of the Sotho group. Surnames such as Khosa or Khoza is shared by Shangaan-Tsonga and Zulus, Khumalo by Swazis and Zulus, Ndlovu, Ndou, or Tlou, meaning elephant, by Zulus, Venda and Bapedi, Madlala or Matlala by Zulus and Bapedi. Some Africans have transformed their surname, Ndlovu, Ndou or Tlou, into Olifant. The surname Mokoena, Mokwena or Ngwenya meaning crocodile is shared by Bapedi, Basotho and the Nguni particularly Zulus. The surname Mthimkhulu, Moremogolo or Moremoholo, "mthi" or "more" or "tree" and "mkhulu" or "mogolo" or "moholo" "great" or great tree, is shared by Ngunis and Sothos. This socio-historical reality is conclusive and irrefutable evidence of the ethnic and linguistic commonality of the African people. It is evidence also of the sameness and commonality of their surnames.

## The Commonality of Ethnicity among Africans

Migration of the African people within South Africa and its transformation of their ethnicity, languages, surnames, culture and intangible cultural heritage applies to the social relationship within and among members of the Sotho group and the Nguni group. A considerable number of individual Africans are articulated combination of African ethnic groups. Their ethnicity, languages, surnames, culture and intangible cultural heritage are their collective proud shared national common heritage. Various forms of integration have taken place among African people across ethnic and linguistic lines. They continue taking place across ethnic and linguistic lines in their journey towards the resolution of the national question through nation building project. This is an integral part of their struggle to complete decolonisation of their country.

Ethnic, linguistic, cultural and intangible cultural heritage commonality characteristic factors including that of surnames of the African people are the consequences of migration within and at the frontiers of South Africa involving their movement. The promotion of social solidarity through social mobilisation and action, not the over-emphasise of ethnic, linguistic and cultural and intangible cultural heritage diversity of African people is the creation of conditions for the success of the resolution of the national question. Social solidarity is the process without which Africans and their fellow South Africans can successfully ensure that their linguistic, social, cultural, human and natural resources are used in putting their country and themselves first in terms of their material conditions, rights and development.

Ethnic, linguistic, and cultural diversity should be interrogated as a means to create and sustain environment of dialogue, debate and policy conducive for the resolution of the national question through nation building project. This is a means to set the stage for dialogue, debate and policy seeking a theoretical and practical basis for a concerted action by South Africans in their struggle to resolve the national question. This task should place African people at the centre of debate, advocacy and policy in the struggle for the resolution of the national question. The resolution of the national question through nation building is the process dependent upon programmes of action embarked upon by Africans and their fellow South Africans. A failure to solve the national question in the country is also the process dependent upon their programmes of action embarked upon by Africans to end the root causes of the socio-economic problems they face in their struggle to complete decolonisation of their country and its institutions and economy.

The process of social mobilisation and action in the form of dialogue, debates, policy and implementation is of vital importance in forging social solidarity to resolve the nation question through nation building. The process of social solidarity and unity in action is the process without which South African social agents of structural transformation can defeat their internal and external enemies. For them to be successful in confronting their problems for their resolution, it is of vital importance to emphasis what is common among them not what are their diversity. This is the case particularly of African people upon which the resolution of the national question through national building depends for its success.

Social mobilisation for unity in action in resolving the national question will judiciously be served by emphasing the fact that Africans share a common history of ethnicity, languages, surnames, culture and intangible cultural heritage. This task is of strategic importance in that it structurally disputes the popular, hegemonic and dominant thesis of their ethnic, linguistic and cultural diversity. Ensuring that they recognise that they continue living together in social relations of common history of ethnicity, languages, surnames, culture and intangible cultural heritage helps to shift their attention from the popular, hegemonic and dominant narrative or thesis of their ethnic, linguistic, cultural and intangible cultural heritage diversity. This serves their mobilisation into admitting that they share more in common in addition to their race. This is the service to the emancipatory political project for national structural social change. The successful movement of theory and analysis to practice through mobilisation of the South Africans as social agents of transformation and development and concrete action to achieve a new South Africa based on the equality of material conditions and rights is impossible without defeat of this popular, hegemonic and dominant narrative or thesis.

**The Zion Christian Church as an Intangible Cultural Heritage**
The Zion Christian Church (ZCC) as an organisation founded for a religious, educational, professional or social purpose rendering a public religious service is an intangible cultural heritage.[15] Its membership consists of all African ethnic groups of South Africa. It is open to members of African ethnic groups of Southern Africa and Africa as well as any African who is not a national of African continental country. It is a national representative of common intangible cultural heritage of Africans.

ZCC is located at Zion Moria City, 40 kilometres from Polokwane. Founded by Engenas Barbanas Lekganyane, it is the largest church in Southern Africa. Established by an African religious leader, it is the most expanding church in the world and one of Africa's churches with the most intangible cultural heritage impact. Hundreds of thousands of African people from across South Africa and Southern Africa, visit Moria for spiritual healing and prayer every month. The annual Easter pilgrimage to Moria is the biggest event on the church's calendar. It attracts millions of people from across South Africa and Southern Africa. Zion Moria City is a pilgrimage site of vital religious, social, cultural, educational significance as well as health and general well-being. Social practices such as dances and songs are performed and sung as folklore, customs, traditions, knowledge, and expressions of the members of the church.

The ZCC renders services such as spiritual healing from physical sickness and other social, cultural and health problems. These services and facilities are rare as they are not expensive for the majority of Africans. The ZCC's spiritual healing approaches and methods such as the laying-on-hands, the use of holy water, and drinking of blessed tea and coffee, are used by Africans as the alternative provider of health and general well-being.

The deep spirituality of these practices enjoins its members to abstain from alcohol, smoking, and violence. Directly related to this social practice is the ZCC ethos of preaching the message of peace. Central to this message is its call for reconciliation between and among parties where there are conflicts. Before one is admitted into the ZCC as a member, one is called upon to confess his or her wrongdoings, repent and ask for forgiveness. This is what Ernest Wamba-dia-Wamba, a distinguished Democratic Republic of the Congo scholar with a high academic, scholarly and multidisciplinary reputation and standing in Africa and internationally refers to as the people's conception of reconciliation:

> the necessity of a genuine national reconciliation informed by a critical rereading of the country's history exposing individual and collective responsibilities, discussed through a deballage (public self-critical palaver) forcing the accused to admit their wrong-doing, amend themselves, seeking for and obtaining pardon after having accepted to repair the damages, etc.[16]

This is reconciliation through honestly, sincerity, objectivity, truthfulness, credibility, fairness, "transparency, accountability- from below-, eradication of 'negative values' (anti-valuers) – public political hygiene" which is required for "true national self-determination."[17] It is "a prefiguration of the new society in which rules are rooted in political truth of people's sovereignty and equality."[18]

Those who are already members of the ZCC pray together with those who are being admitted. It is through confession, repentance and prayer that one obtains redemption. Moreover, the ZCC plays an important role in the education of Africans by promoting its importance among young Africans. It does so by encouraging them to go to school and providing them with bursaries to further their studies.

The church is successful in forging unity and solidarity among its members of various ethnic groups. This is one of its great achievements in an environment where ethnicity is often associated with conflicts and tensions among Africans nationally, regionally and continentally. The church can best and most effectively theoretically and practically be used in South Africa in forging unity and solidarity among Africans of various ethnic, linguistic and cultural groups. It should be used to serve as a national asset in the contribution towards the achievement of social solidarity in an environment where ethnicity is often associated with conflicts and tensions among Africans of different ethnic, linguistic and cultural groups. The achievement of this social solidarity will be a substantial and welcome addition to South Africa's policy efforts to achieve national integration through nation building and in its contribution towards Southern African regional integration and African continental integration. The leaders of the church should ensure that it earn for itself the status of a critical organisational actor in contributing towards South African national integration and Southern African regional integration and African continental integration. The church is threatening to be a Southern African regional organisation. It has branches throughout the region.

The ZCC gave birth to the International Pentecostal Holiness Church. Frederick Samuel Modise founded it in 1962 in Meadowlands, Soweto upon leaving the ZCC as its member. He built the church and began its process of praying for the sick. Like the ZCC, its membership is open to members of African ethnic groups of South Africa, Southern Africa and Africa as well as any African who is not a national of African continental country. The formation of the African independent churches was an integral part of the right of the African people to their national self-determination and the free, independent exercise of their sovereignty and domestic and foreign policies.

## The settler colonial state on a South African nation and the national question

The forces of settler colonialism and racism used the thesis of ethnic, linguistic, cultural and intangible cultural heritage diversity for their own strategic and tactical interests. The Native Affairs Act (Act No. 23 of 1920) was used to create the basis for the so-called self-determination of African people on the basis of what they regarded as their ethnic, linguistic and cultural diversity or differences. The Bantu Authorities Act, 1951 (Act No. 68 of 1951) was used to divide them by giving authority to their traditional leaders within what were regarded as their homelands. It was enacted to provide for the establishment of the so-called "Bantu authorities" and to define their functions, to abolish the Natives Representative Council, to amend the Native Affairs Act, 1920 and the Representation of Natives Act, 1936. The consequence was the Bantu Homelands Citizenship Act of 1970. It declared that Africans are citizens and nationals not of South Africa but of "homelands" regarded as their countries. It was used by the settler colonial and racist state to grant what it refers to as independence to any "homeland" as it determined.

The settler colonial and racist state used ethnic, linguistic, cultural and intangible cultural diversity in dividing African people for its purpose of denying their being South Africans and sustaining settler colonial and racist rule. This can be understood if we come to grips with the reality that it maintained, firstly, that the "population of the Republic of South Africa is heterogeneous and multinational" which "may be compared to Western Europe and West Africa" in "its diversity of cultures. Each group has its own distinctive social system, culture" and "language, hence its own distinctive political and educational aspirations."[19] Secondly, that African ethnic groups are "Black nations" with their own "Black states."[20] Thirdly, that "the Blacks in the Republic of South Africa consist of several distinct nations, each" with "its own customs and traditions. They speak nine different languages."[21] Fourthly, that "the Republic of South Africa is not inhabited by a homogeneous society with a common group loyalty, language ... or culture."[22] Fifthly, that Africans "do not form a single nation but are composed of separate ethnic groups, forming different nations, with different languages and cultures."[23]

The state continued justifying its position by maintaining, firstly, that after "the Union of South Africa was established in" May "1910, the traditional territories of the Black peoples were retained" and "were subsequently enlarged by land purchases in terms" of "the Black Land Act (1913) and the Development Trust and Land Act (1936)."[24] Secondly, that these "Acts reserved a total" of "almost 15,4-million ha for exclusive Black occupation. Consolidation is still proceeding and will probably exceed the provisions of the 1936 legislation." Thirdly, that the "British conquest of Southern Africa led" to "the inclusion of entirely different nations" in "the Union of South Africa, such as the Xhosa, Zulu, North Sotho and Venda, as well as parts of the Tswana, Swazi, Sotho and Tsonga/Shangaan peoples."[25] Fourthly, that "government policy is" to "restore to these nations the independence they enjoyed before British colonial conquest, and their territories are being consolidated" and "developed to reach this goal. Once independent, they will be free to decide whether they want to unite with other states."[26] Fifthly, that there "is no cultural uniformity in South Africa because of the vastly different cultural backgrounds of its peoples"[27] or that there is "no 'typical' South African culture, no single way of life."[28] The state emphasised its position that "the Republic of South Africa is not inhabited by a homogeneous society with a common group loyalty, language, history or culture."[29]

The state maintained, firstly, that in "the light of the country's multinational and historical realities, the conviction has grown that relations between the White, Indian" and "Coloured peoples, and the various Black peoples within the borders of the Republic of South Africa, cannot" be "satisfactorily regulated in a single integrated superstate."[30] Secondly, it can be "satisfactorily regulated" on "the historically tried basis of separate nation states, i.e., a system" of "political independence coupled with economic interdependence."[31] Thirdly, that this "policy evolved from a philosophy forged" and "determined by the realities of more than three centuries - has in both official and common parlance become known as multinational development."[32] Fourthly, that this policy "envisages the peaceful coexistence of the peoples of South Africa, modelled" on "the modern pattern of independent national communities."[33] Fifthly, that a "multinational system of this nature" is founded on "the basis of separate national states" which "are economically interdependent."[34] Sixthly, that it "will also safeguard the identity" of "each group, including that of minorities."[35] Seventhly, that when "the Union of

South Africa came into being in 1910 the territories of nine Black peoples fell within" the "geographical confines of the Union."[36] These "territories - as" they "are today known - were Bophuthatswana, Ciskei, Gazankulu, KwaZulu, Lebowa, Qwaqwa, KwaNdebele, KaNgwane, Transkei and Venda. Three - Transkei, Bophuthatswana and Venda - have already attained independence."[37] It further maintained that the "remaining seven have reached the stage where" they "are semi-autonomous with their own legislatures."[38] While "Transkei, the first Black national state to receive independence, became a republic" in "October, 1976," Bophuthatswana "followed suit in December, 1977 and Venda in September, 1979."[39] It concluded that:

> When the process of political emancipation of the national states is completed, the map of South Africa will look vastly different. Instead of one South Africa established as a result of British colonial expansion in the sub-continent at the turn of the previous century, there will be the Republic of South Africa and several independent national states completing the process of creating separate nation-states for Southern Africa's Black peoples which Britain began by granting independence to the Swazi, Botswana and Lesotho nations in the 1960s. It is envisaged that these states will be economically interdependent, perhaps linked in a common market. Through the formula of political interdependence and regional co-operation in matters of common interest, e.g., the generation of power, water supplies, soil conservation, etc., it is hoped to avoid the clash of Black and White nationalism.
>
> As South Africa's pattern of multinationalism takes shape, it is natural and necessary that there should be consultation between the component peoples. One achievement above all others may be ascribed to the policy of multinational development: it has led to the emergence of authentic representatives of the Black nations and has provided them with a platform. In recent times there have been progressively

more extensive discussions between the Government of the RSA and governments of the Black states. The Government has made it clear that future developments will be worked out in consultation with the leaders at the head of those institutions presently constituting the political nuclei of the evolving Black nations.[40]

It is, thus, clear that the incorrect and ahistorical position maintained and defended by the settler colonial racist state on a nation is also maintained and defended by Joseph Stalin. His position is that a "nation is historically evolved, stable community of people, formed on the basis of a common language, territory, economic life and psychological make-up manifested in a common culture."[41]

Central to his position on a nation is that a nation or "a national community is inconceivable without a common language"[42] and that there "is no nation which at one and the same time speaks several languages."[43] This position is based on one of key, central features of his definition of a nation that "a common language" is the characteristic feature of each and every nation.[44] This position means incorrectly that bilingual and multilingual social formations are not nations.

Lionel Forman, a member of the South African Communist Party,[45] basing his position on a nation and the national question in South Africa on Stalin's position on a nation and the national question, pointed out that:

A nation is a stable community of people who have lived together in the same territory from generation to generation, speak the same language, have an internal economic bond welding the community into a whole, and a common "psychology" manifesting itself in the common culture.

The nation is not based on race. Every nation existing is composed of a mixture of races. Nor is it tribal. Most - maybe all - nations resulted from the coming together of different tribes into one nation. On the other hand, there is no reason why a community of people, tribal in origin, could not become a nation.

What can be seen from the definition? This: that South Africa is not a nation. It is a multi-national state consisting of a number of nationalities.[46]

He continued that:

a national group (nationality) is a stable community which has existed for a long time, speaks the same language, has a common psychology manifesting itself in a common culture, and which, lacking its own territory and economic cohesion, aspires towards them.

The two characteristics of nationhood which a community may lack and still be a national group are territory and economic cohesion. But every national group aspires to acquire these.[47]

Forman continued that "We know what a nation is. It is a stable community who have lived together for a long time in the same territory, speak the same language, have an internal economic bond and a common psychology and culture."[8]

Pointing out that "socialists define a "nation" in clear terms" and that their position and/or their definition of a nation is that if "a community does not share a common language, territory, economy and culture, it is not a nation,"[49] Forman concluded that "A glance at the definition is sufficient to show that there is no South African nation. The South African people have a variety of languages and cultures. For the same reason the Africans are not a nation."[50]

He defended Stalin's position that "it is only when all these characteristics," namely, "a common language, territory, economic life" and "a common culture," are "present that we have a nation" and that "it is sufficient for a single one of these characteristics to be absent and the nation ceases to be a nation."[51] Pointing out that by "a common economy" is meant "a single national market,"[52] he concluded that in the case of "the Zulus":

> There is no doubt that they have a common territory in Natal, in a substantial portion of which they are an overwhelming majority of the population. Similarly, they have a common language and culture. In one respect only have they not yet attained nationhood, and that is with regard to the development of a single Zulu market. The government has strangled Zulu economic development because it is in the interests of the ruling class that the Zulus be kept at the level of unskilled labourers. There is no doubt, however, that this stifling of the Zulu nation will no endure, and that the Zulus are on the threshold of true nationhood.
>
> ... Other "pre-nations" in a position similar to the Zulus are the Basotho, the Xhosas, the Swazis, the Tswana, etc.[53]

He incorrectly maintained that, given the "absence of a demand for self-determination" which is "a reflection" of the fact that "there are still no nations in South Africa,"[54] Africans have no "demand for self-determination."[55] Since the inception of the national liberation struggle, Africans have been striving to end the settler colonial and racist state so as enjoy their national self-determination right and have free, independent exercise of their sovereignty and domestic and foreign policies.

Maria van Diepen in a book on the national question in South Africa she edited maintains incorrect position that the "1912 ANC call to give up ethnic loyalty in favour of creating an African nation is still valid."[56] It is a misunderstanding of ethnicity and its role and significance. One's loyalty to his or her ethnicity is not an obstacle towards one being a member of a particular nation. There is no need for people to give up their ethnic loyalty for them to be members of a nation. Africans are proud of their ethnic assertations. They are against imperialism, colonialism and neo-colonialism and other socio-political and economic problems. They should judiciously be used to end these problems. The ANC was formed as the proud national organisational product produced by the African people to serve as the means through which to end settler colonial and racist rule and to restructure their society in the best interests of its people regardless of race, ethnicity, languages, surnames, culture and intangible cultural heritage.

The position that the people of one country which is linguistically heterogeneous are not its members because they speak different or several languages is incorrect and ahistorical. Accordingly, the position of Neville Alexander that "Probably most people in South Africa today believe that the people who are part of the nation have got to speak the same language"[57] is incorrect and ahistorical.

His position is an integral part of his view of the national question. It is informed by the emphasis of ethnic, linguistic and cultural diversity of the South African population particularly its African section. Central to his incorrect position on the national question is his view of the issue of linguistic diversity. This is supported by his incorrect position that "Racial prejudice and racism are without any doubt reinforced and maintained by language barriers."[58] His position means incorrectly that the linguistic heterogeneity is the problem whose elimination is the solution to "racial prejudice and racism." His position can be used by racists in denying the reality that they are racists. They can use it in denying that they are racists by maintaining that those who regard them as racists confuse and equate the issue of racism with the issue of linguistic heterogeneity or "language barriers." The issue of "racial prejudice and racism" is the socio-political, ideological and economic issue, not the linguistic heterogeneity issue or the issue of "language barriers." It is the socio-political, ideological and economic issue, not linguistic issue or language issue or question. Individuals are racists, practising racism not because they speak a language or languages not spoken by those who are targets of their racism. "Racial prejudice and racism are" not "reinforced and maintained by language barriers" or linguistic heterogeneity. The issue of linguistic homogeneity is not and cannot be the solution to "racial prejudice and racism."

The position that "Racial prejudice and racism are reinforced and maintained by language barriers" cannot seriously be defended. It is incorrect. It does not make sense. A considerable number of individuals demonstrate their racism including to those who speak their language.

Alexander's position is disputed and rejected by the reality that measures of "racial prejudice" and racism are visited upon those who, among others, are English-speaking people and French-speaking people by racists who are English-speaking people and French-speaking people respectively. It absolves racists of their racist practical and theoretical position by attributing their racism to the issue of linguistic heterogeneity or "language barriers."

While it is correct that South African national liberation struggle is the process to "abolish social inequality" and that "social inequality" is "based" on the social "class" question, Alexander's position that "social inequality" is "based on colour" or race, "religious beliefs, sex" or gender and "language group"[59] diversity or linguistic heterogeneity is incorrect. Social inequality is "based," among others, on the social "class" division of the society into social classes of different and antagonistic interests. It is a class question not a question of racial, religious, gender and linguistic diversity or heterogeneity questions. His position means that "social inequality" exists in South Africa given the fact that South Africa is a racial, religious and linguistic heterogeneous social formation, that the issue of racial, religious and linguistic homogeneity is the answer or the solution to its "social inequality" in South Africa, that South African liberation struggle is the process to bring into existence racial, religious and linguistic homogeneous social formation and it cannot be eliminated or solved.

## Conclusion and Recommendations

We have produced and provided evidence that the ethnic, linguistic, cultural and intangible cultural heritage commonality of the African people of South Africa is of the strategic importance for the resolution of the national question through the nation building project.

The duration of a settler colonial and racist rule, the content and operations of race relations and the fact that racism became a cultural process in South Africa have overwhelmed the national liberation movement and the majority of its theoreticians to such an extent that relations among Africans of various ethnic and linguistic groups have not occupied their requisite strategic attention it deserved.

If the South African national liberation movement and its theoreticians correctly viewed the process of internal migration of the African people of South Africa within their country for its concrete understanding and the way it transformed their ethnicity, languages, surnames, culture and intangible cultural heritage, as they left their original places for other places in other provinces where they permanently settled, they should not have viewed the African people in terms of the emphasis of ethnic, linguistic, cultural and intangible cultural heritage diversity. They should not have viewed the national question through the nation building and its resolution on the basis of this emphasis.

Challenges the struggle for the resolution of the national question through the nation building project is confronting are not only class, race and gender questions. They are also ethnic, linguistic, cultural and intangible cultural heritage relations. They should be taken into account theoretically and practically on the political, economic and ideological fronts of the struggle. The social forces for the structural transformation of the South African society should take them seriously for tactical and strategic reasons for tribalism and narrow nationalism to be defeated as an integral part of the cause to end their continued misfortunes of capitalism and racism faced by the decisive majority of national population which survived the end of a settler colonial and racist rule. This at the same time will help to end the benefits of capitalism and racism continued being enjoyed by the decisive minority of the South African population since 1994.

There are alliances among Africans which are informed not only by political, economic and ideological loyalties, but also by ethnic, linguistic, cultural and intangible cultural heritage relations and loyalties. These relations and loyalties exist independently of political, economic and ideological manoeuvres and manipulations. While they are social resources for political, economic and ideological manoeuvres and manipulations, to reduce them to these manoeuvres and manipulations is to neglect or minimise their strategic and tactical importance as socio-historical realities. It is in this context that the strategic importance of the ethnic, linguistic, cultural and intangible cultural commonality of the African people in the service of the nation building project can be highly appreciated and treasured as the theoretical and practical proud national asset.

# Notes

### Introduction

1 Francis M. Deng, "Ethnicity: An African Predicament," *The Brookings Review*, Vol. 15, No. 3, Summer 1997, p. 28.
2 Ibid.
3 Ibid.
4 Ibid.
5 Ibid., p. 29.
6 Ibid.
7 Sam Moyo, "Policy Dialogue, Improved Governance, and the New Partnerships – Experiences from Southern Africa," in Henock Kifle, Adebayo O. Olukosi and Lennart Wohlgemuth (editors), *A New Partnership for African Development: Issues and Parameters* (Stockholm: Nordiska Afrikainstitutet, 1997), p. 65.
8 Claude Ake, "What is the Problem of Ethnicity in Africa?" *Transformation: Critical Perspectives on South Africa*, Issue 22, 1993, p. 4.
9 Ibid., pp. 4-5.
10 Ibid., pp. 13-14.
11 The task of establishing a classless society or communist social formation is the strategic objective of the communist parties. The party is communist provided it is for the dictatorship of the proletariat which is a means to end a society consisting of a capitalist class or bourgeoisie and a working class or proletariat as the two main social classes with antagonist political, economic and ideological class interests.
12 *Daily Maverick*, "Springboks Never Give Up," *Daily Maverick* (Johannesburg), 16 October 2023.

### Chapter 1

1 Paul S. Landau, *Popular Politics in the History of South Africa, 1400-1948* (New York: Cambridge University Press, 2010), p. 246.
2 Ibid., p. 56.
3 Ibid., p. 70.
4 Ibid., p. 56.
5 Ibid., p. 73.
6 Ibid., p. 64.
7 Ibid.

8   Ibid., p. 64.
9   P. Eric Louw, "Language and National Unity in a Post-Apartheid South Africa," *Critical Arts*, Vol. 6, No. 1, 1992, pp. 52-53.
10  Ibid.
11  Martin Legassick, "The Sotho-Tswana Peoples before 8000" in Leonard Monteath Thompson (editor), *African Societies in Southern Africa: Historical Studies* (New York: Praeger Publishers, 1969 p. 98.
12  Martin Chatfield Legassick, *The Politics of a South African Frontier: The Griqua, the Sotho-Tswana and the Missionaries, 1780-1840* (Basel, Switzerland: Basler Afrika Bibliographien, 2010), p. 15.
13  Legassick, "The Sotho-Tswana Peoples before 1800," in Thompson (editor), *African Societies in Southern Africa: Historical Studies*, p. 98.
14  Thato Mabolaeng Maryanne Monyakane, *The Cultural, Social and Political Similarity of the Bafokeng, Bakuena and the Bataung Lineages Amongst the Sotho*, Doctor of Literature and Philosophy, Department of African Languages, University of South Africa, Pretoria, South Africa, June 2016, p. 15.
15  Ibid., p. 193.
16  Ibid., p. 194.
17  Ibid.
18  Ibid.
19  Landau, *Popular Politics in the History of South Africa, 1400-1948*, pp. 248-49.
20  Ibid., pp. 249-50.
21  R.W. Johnson, *South Africa: The First Man, The Last Nation* (Johannesburg and Cape Town: Jonathan Ball Publishers, 2005), p. 18.
22  Sekhukhune I is referred to throughout this chapter as Sekhukhune.
23  Mampuru 11 is referred to throughout this chapter as Mampuru.
24  The Commission on Traditional Leadership Disputes and Claims is referred to throughout this chapter as the Nhlapo Commission or the Commission.
25  The Commission's members were Professor R.T. Nhlapo, chairperson, Advocate J.C. Bekker, Ms P.P. Robinson, Dr. R.M. Ndou, Professor P.P. Ntuli, Advocate S. Poswa-Lerotholi, Ms S.R. Mdluli, Professor M.A. Moleleki, Advocate S.D. Ndengezi, Mr. A.S. Hlebela, Advocate Z.P. Pungula and Professor J.B. Peires are provided in Muzamani Charles Nwaila, *Findings of the Commission on the Traditional Leadership Disputes and Claims, Presentation to the Portfolio Committee: Implementation of the Findings of the Commission on the Traditional Leadership Disputes and Claims*, Professor Muzamani Charles Nwaila, Director-General, Department of Traditional Affairs, 1 November 2011, Pretoria.
26  *South African Government, Determination on Bapedi Paramountcy, A Commission on Traditional Leadership Disputes and Claims* (Pretoria: Government Printer, no date), pp. 10-11 (https://www.gov.za<files).
27  Ibid., p. 41.
28  Ibid., p. 33.
29  Bapedi Marota Mamone v Commission on Traditional Leadership

Disputes and Claims and Others (CCT 67)/14 [2014] ZACC 36; 2015 (3) BC LR 268 (CC) (15 December 2015.

30 Ibid.

31 Mogobe B. Ramose, *African Philosophy Through Ubuntu* (Harare: Mond Books Publishers, 2005), p. 87.

32 Interviewing Mogobe Ramose on 23 August 2014 at the University of South Africa in Pretoria, South Africa, Derek Hook of Duquesne University, Pittsburgh, United States of America explains the Sotho word botho and the Nguni word ubuntu as "the concept in which philosophy, ontology and ethics are thought together in a holistic approach to humanness" and maintains that Ramose's "understanding of justice as balance and harmony demands the restoration of justice by reversing the dehumanizing consequences of colonial conquest and by eliminating racism. His work displays an unwavering commitment to questions of justice, politics, ethics, and truth," Mogobe Bernard Ramose, Derek Hook, "To whom does the land belong?" Mogobe Bernard Ramose talks to Derek Hook, *Psychology in Society* (PINS), No. 50 Stellenbosch 2016.

33 Mogobe B. Ramose, "An African Perspective on Justice and Race," *Polylog: Forum for Intercultural Philosophy*, No. 3, 2001, p. 7.

34 Ibid.

35 Mogobe Ramose emphasised this point during telephonic discussion with the author on 2 July 2023.

36 Ibid.

37 The five African members of the Constitutional Court were Dikgang Ernest Moseneke, Sisi Virginia Khampepe, Mashangu Monica Leeuw, Mbuyiseli Russel Madlanga and Raymond Mnyamezeli Mlungisi Zondo. This raises the fundamental question about the degree commitment of Africans to their African law, culture or traditions and customs. Another fundamental question is the commitment of Thabo Mbeki as the president of South Africa during the time the African Union had already in place the principle of not recognising governments which come into existence through military coups which are basically "might and bloodshed."

38 The Supreme Court of Appeal of South Africa Judgement in the matter between Bapedi Marota Mamone as appellant and The Commission of Traditional Leadership Disputes and Claims (first respondent), The President of the Republic of South Africa (second respondent), The Minister of Provincial Affairs and Local Government (third respondent), Mohlaletsi Traditional Authority (fourth respondent), and Acting Kgoshikgolo Kgaugudi Kenneth Sekhukhune (fifth respondent). The appeal before the Supreme Court of Appeal was whether the commission of traditional leadership disputes and claims ignored relevant material information placed before it when deciding that the institution of the Bapedi kingship resorts under the Sekhukhune lineage and whether such decision rationally connected to that information nor justifiable on the reasons given for it.

39 Bapedi Marota Mamone v The Commission of Traditional Leadership Disputes and Claims and Others (260/13 [2014] ZASCA 30 (28 March

2014). The judgement was read by Judge Mandisa Muriel Lindelwa Maya with Lorimer Eric Leach, Leona Valerie Theron, Nigel Willis and Baratang Constance Mocumie concurring.

40 Michael Mbikiwa, Review of Bapedi Marota Mamone v The Commission of Traditional Leadership Disputes and Claims & Others (260/13 [2014] ZASCA 30 (28 March 2014).

41 Mafori Charles Ramushu, The House of Thulare: The Problem of Succession and Split of the Bapedi Nation, 1824-1884, Master of Arts in History, Department of History and Folklore Studies, School of Social Sciences, University of Limpopo, Turfloop, South Africa, August 2007, pp. 79-106.

42 Ibid., p. 97.

43 Ibid., pp. 79-120.

44 The Volkstem, quoted in Ivor Powell, *Ndebele: A People & Their Art* (Cape Town: Struik Publishes (Pty) Ltd., 1995), p. 19

45 Ivor Powell, *Ndebele: A People & Their Art* (Cape Town: Struik Publishes, 1995), p. 17.

46 Ibid.

47 Ibid.

48 Ibid.

49 Ibid., pp. 17-19.

50 Ibid., 17.

51 Bapedi Marota Mamone was the applicant, the Commission on Traditional Leadership Disputes and Claims, the first respondent, the Minister of Provincial Affairs and Local Government, third respondent, Mohlaletsi Traditional Authority, the fourth respondent, and Acting Kgoshikgolo Kgagudi Kenneth Sekhukhune the fight respondent in this case.

52 Bapedi Marota Mamone v Commission on Traditional Leadership Disputes and Claims and Others (40404/2008) [2012] ZAGPPHC 209; [2012] 4 All SASA 544 (GNN) (21 September 2012).

53 Ibid.

54 Ibid.

55 Sir T. Shepstone to Lord Carnarvon, 11 December 1877, in Thomas Pakenham, *The Scramble for Africa, 1876-1912* (Johannesburg: Jonathan Ball Publishers, 1997), p. 52.

56 Mangosuthu Buthelezi, Address by Prince Mangosuthu Buthelezi MP, Inkosi of the Buthelezi Clan, Traditional Prime Minister to the Zulu Monarch and Nation and President of the Inkatha Freedom Party, *2017 Sekhukhune Day Commemoration On the Theme "Polelo ya Sepedi – Bohwa Bja Rena,"* Mohlaletse, Sekhukhuneland, Limpopo, South Africa, 13 August 2017.

57 *The London Times,* quoted by Mangosuthu Buthelezi, Address by Prince Mangosuthu Buthelezi MP, Inkosi of the Buthelezi Clan, Traditional Prime Minister to the Zulu Monarch and Nation and President of the Inkatha Freedom Party, *2017 Sekhukhune Day Commemoration On the Theme "Polelo ya Sepedi – Bohwa Bja Rena,"* Mohlaletse, Sekhukhuneland, Limpopo, South Africa, 13 August 2017.

58 Mangosuthu Buthelezi, Address by Prince Mangosuthu Buthelezi MP, Inkosi of the Buthelezi Clan, Traditional Prime Minister to the Zulu Monarch and Nation and President of the Inkatha Freedom Party, *2017 Sekhukhune Day Commemoration On the Theme "Polelo ya Sepedi – Bohwa Bja Rena,"* Mohlaletse, Sekhukhuneland, Limpopo, South Africa, 13 August 2017.

59 The 1899-1902 Anglo-Boer War is referred to as the 1899-1902 South African War in post-settler colonial South Africa.

60 Department of Foreign Affairs and Information, *This is South Africa* (Pretoria: Government Printer, 1980), p. 22.

61 Kate O'Regan, "Traditional and Modernity: Adjudicating a Constitutional Paradox," *Constitutional Court Review*, Vol. 6, 2014, p. 113.

62 Pius Langa, "The Fifth Bram Fischer Memorial Lecture: The Emperor's New Clothes: Bram Fischer and the Need for Dissent," *South African Journal on Human Rights*, No. 362, 2007, p. 370.

63 Mogobe B. Ramose, "An African Perspective on Justice and Race," *Polylog: Forum for Intercultural Philosophy*, No. 3, 2001, p. 7.

64 Ramose, *African Philosophy Through Ubuntu*, p. 87.

## Chapter 2

1 Theodore Nkadimeng Mahosi, *An Afrocentric Exploration of South Africa's Homeland Policy with Specific Reference to Vhavenḓa Traditional Leadership and Institutions, 1898-1994,* Doctor of Philosophy in History, Department of Cultural and Political Studies, School of Social Sciences, Faculty of Humanities, University of Limpopo, 2020, pp. 94-117.

2 Nyameko Barney Pityana, "The renewal of African moral values," in Malegapuru William Makgoba (editor), *African Renaissance: The New Struggle* (Cape Town: Mafube Publishing and Tafelberg Publishers, 1999), p. 137.

3 Ibid., pp. 170-200.

4 Edwin O.M. Hanisch, "Legends, Oral Traditions and Archaeology: A Look at Early Venda History," *Luvhone*, Vol. 3, No. 1, April 1994, pp. 71-72.

5 Mandla Darnece Mathebula, *Genealogy and Migration of the Va Ka Valoyi People of Limpopo Province, South Africa,* Philosophiae Doctor in History, Department of Cultural and Political Studies, School of Social Sciences, Faculty of Humanities, University of Limpopo, 2018, p. 3.

6 Theodore Nkadimeng Mahosi, *An Afrocentric Exploration of South Africa's Homeland Policy with Specific Reference to Vhavenḓa Traditional Leadership and Institutions, 1898-1994,* Doctor of Philosophy in History, Department of Cultural and Political Studies, School of Social Sciences, Faculty of Humanities, University of Limpopo, 2020, p. 23.

7 Mphaya Henry Nemudzivhadi, *The Conflict between Mphephu and the South African Republic, 1895-1899,* Master of Arts in History, Department of History, University of South Africa, 1977, pp. 4-8; i-iii.

8 Hermann Giliomee and Lawrence Schlemmer, *Up against the Fences of Poverty: Passes and Privilege in South Africa* (Johannesburg: David

Philip, 1985), p. vii.

9   John Donelly Fage, *A History of Africa* (London: Paperback Publishers, 1978), p. 84.

10  David Welsh, *The Rise and Fall of Apartheid* (Johannesburg: Jonathan Ball Publishers, 2010), pp. 32, 38.

11  Peter Delius, Tim Maggs, and Alex Schoeman, *Forgotten World: The Stone-walled Settlements of the Mpumalanga Escarpment* (Johannesburg: Wits University Press, 2014), pp. 22, 25, 26.

12  Matshikiri Vele Christopher Neluvhalani, *The Banguni-Bakone-Bangona and San as the Autochthones of South(ern) Africa* (Giyani, South Africa: Sasavona Publishers and Booksellers, 2018), pp. i-iii.

13  Neluvhalani, *The Banguni- Bakone-Bangona and San as the Autochthones of South(ern) Africa*, pp. iii-iv.

14  John Illife, Africans: *The History of the Continent* (New York and Cape Town: Cambridge University Press, 2007), pp. 100-101.

15  Delius, Maggs and Schoeman, *Forgotten World: The Stone-walled Settlements of the Mpumalanga Escarpment*, p. 42.

16  Illife, *Africans: The History of the Continent*, pp. 100-101.

17  Ibid.

18  McEdward Murimbika, *Sacred Powers and Rituals of Transformation: An Ethno-archaeological Study of Rainmaking Rituals and Agricultural Productivity during the Evolution of the Mapungubwe State, AD 1000 to AD 1300*, Doctor of Philosophy, Faculty of Humanities, University of the Witwatersrand, Johannesburg, 2006, pp. 1-24, 25, 28.

19  Kevin Shillington, *History of Africa* (London and New York: Palgrave Macmillan, 2012), pp. 211-212.

20  Kevin Shillington, *Encyclopaedia of African History* (London: Palgrave Macmillan, 2005), p. 325; Shillington, History of Africa, pp. 225-29.

21  Delius, Maggs and Schoeman, *Forgotten World: The Stone-walled Settlements of the Mpumalanga Escarpment*, p. 45.

22  McEdward Murimbika, *Sacred Powers and Rituals of Transformation: An Ethno-archaeological Study of Rainmaking Rituals and Agricultural Productivity during the Evolution of the Mapungubwe State, AD 1000 to AD 1300*, Doctor of Philosophy, Faculty of Humanities, University of the Witwatersrand, Johannesburg, 2006, pp. 28, 137, 150-53.

23  Shillington, *History of Africa*, p. 154.

24  Peter Balanganani Khangala, P.R. *Mphephu (1925-1988): A Study of Political Leadership in a Twentieth Century South African Society*, Master of Arts in History, Department of History, Faculty of Arts, University of the North, South Africa, 1998, pp. 7-8.

25  Neluvhalani, *The Banguni-Bakone-Bangona and San as the Autochthones of South(ern) Africa*, p. iii; Mphaya Henry Nemudzivhadi, The Conflict between Mphephu and the South African Republic, 1895-1899, Master of Arts in History, Department of History, University of South Africa, 1977, pp. 4-9.

26  Kevin Shillington, *Encyclopaedia of African History* (London, Palgrave MacMillan, 2005), p. 227.

27 Delius, Maggs and Schoeman, *Forgotten World: The Stone-walled Settlements of the Mpumalanga Escarpment*, p. 25.

28 Lufuno Jean-Pierre Mulaudzi, *Historicising the Politics of Vhuhosivhuhulu: The Venda Polity and State Formation in South Africa, c. 1800-2020*, Doctor of Philosophy in History, University of Pretoria, 2020, p. 4.

29 Hugh Arthur Stayt, *The Bavenda* (CASS Library of African Studies, General Studies, no. 58, Frank CASS and Co., 1968), p. 12.

30 Gérard Paul Lestrade, "Some Notes on the Political Organization of the Venda-speaking Tribes," *Africa*, Vol. 3, No. 3, 1930, p. 24.

31 Hanisch, "Legend. Oral Traditions and Archaeology: A Look at Early Venda History," p. 74.

32 Dowelani Edward Ndivhudzannyi Mabogo, *The Ethnobotany of the Vhavenda*, Magister Scientiae, Department of Botany, Faculty of Science, University of Pretoria, 1990, pp. 4-6.

33 Mphaya Henry Nemudzivhadi, *The Conflict between Mphephu and the South African Republic, 1895-1899*. Master of Arts in History, Department of History, University of South Africa, 1977, pp. 3-13.

34 Peter Balanganani Khangala, *P.R. Mphephu (1925-1988): A Study of Political Leadership in a Twentieth Century South African Society*, Master of Arts in History, Department of History, Faculty of Arts, University of the North, South Africa, 1998, p. 8.

35 Neluvhalani, *The Banguni- Bakone-Bangona and San as the Autochthones of South(ern) Africa*, p. 6.

36 Shillington, *Encyclopaedia of African History*, p. 227.

37 Neluvhalani, *The Banguni-Bakone-Bangona and San as the Autochthones of South(ern) Africa*, p. 6; Matodzi Rebecca Raphalalani, *U Bvulwa Maanda ha Vhuimo na Nzulele ya Musanda: Tsenguluso yo Livhanaho na Vhuhosi ha Vhavenda ho Shumiswa Thyiori ya 'Ethnopragmatics,'* Doctor of Philosophy, Department of African Studies, University of South Africa, 2015, p. 40.

38 Caroline F. Jeannerat, *An Ethnography of Faith: Personal Conception of Religiosity in the Soutpansberg, South Africa, in the 19th and 20th Centuries*, Doctor of Philosophy in Anthropology and History, University of Michigan, 2007, n.p.

39 Mathole Motshekga, interviewed on SABC 2: Sepedi News Channel, aired on Tik-tok, 2023, n.d.

40 Ibid.

41 Neluvhalani, *The Banguni- Bakone-Bangona and San as the Autochthones of South(ern) Africa*, p. 6, 10, 11.

42 Hermann Otto Mönnig, *The Pedi* (Pretoria: J.L. van Schaik (Pty) Ltd and Goodwood, National Book Printer, 1967), pp. 11; 18.

43 Neluvhalani, *The Banguni-Bakone-Bangona and San as the Autochthones of South(ern) Africa*, p. 6.

44 Mönnig, *The Pedi*, p. 81.

45 Ibid., p. 18.

46 André Chris Myburgh, *Anthropology of Southern Africa* (Pretoria: J.L. van Schaik, 1981), pp. 31-34.

47  Mönnig, *The Pedi*, p. 17.

48  Myburgh, *Anthropology of Southern Africa*, pp. 31-34.

49  Pityana, "The renewal of African Moral Values," in Makgoba (editor), *African Renaissance: The New Struggle*, pp.144-45.

50  Mahmood Mamdani, "There can be no African Renaissance without an Africa-focused Intelligentsia," in Malegapuru William Makgoba (editor), *African Renaissance: The New Struggle* (Cape Town: Mafube Publishing and Tafelberg Publishers, 1999), p. 127.

51  Moloka Kolobe Motshekga, *The Mudjadji Dynasty* (Johannesburg, Acumen Publishing Solutions, 2010), p. 163.

52  Lufuno Jean-Pierre Mulaudzi, *Historicising the Politics of Vhuhosivhuhulu: The Venda Polity and State formation in South Africa, c. 1800-2020*, Doctor of Philosophy in History, University of Pretoria, 2020, p. 5 of 1-8.

53  Moyahabo Rosina Mohale, *Khelobedu Cultural Evolution through Oral Tradition, Master of Arts in African Languages, University of South Africa*, February 2014, p. 2.

54  Caroline Jeannerat, *An Ethnography of Faith: Personal Conceptions of Religiosity in the Soutpansberg, South Africa, in the 19th and 20th Centuries*, Doctor of Philosophy, Anthropology and History, University of Michigan, 2007.

55  Moyahabo Rosina Mohale, *Khelobedu Cultural Evolution through Oral Tradition, Master of Arts in African Languages, University of South Africa*, February 2014, pp. 2-3.

56  Theodore Nkadimeng Mahosi, *An Afrocentric Exploration of South Africa's Homeland Policy with Specific Reference to Vhavenda Traditional Leadership and Institutions, 1898-1994*, Doctor of Philosophy in History, Department of Cultural and Political Studies, School of Social Sciences, Faculty of Humanities, University of Limpopo, 2020, pp. 1, 50, 67, 68-73.

57  Moyahabo Rosina Mohale, *Khelobedu Cultural Evolution through Oral Tradition, Master of Arts in African Languages, University of South Africa*, February 2014, p. 5.

58  Lufuno Jean-Pierre Mulaudzi, *Historicising the Politics of Vhuhosivhuhulu: The Venda Polity and State formation in South Africa, c. 1800-2020*, Doctor of Philosophy in History, University of Pretoria, 2020, p. 9.

59  Ibid., p. 5.

60  Lestrade, "Some Notes on the Political Organization of the Venda-speaking Tribes," p. 307.

61  Theodore Nkadimeng Mahosi, *An Afrocentric Exploration of South Africa's Homeland Policy with Specific Reference to Vhavenda Traditional Leadership and Institutions, 1898-1994*, Doctor of Philosophy in History, Department of Cultural and Political Studies, School of Social Sciences, Faculty of Humanities, University of Limpopo, 2020, pp. 74-79.

62  Matodzi Rebecca Raphalalani, *U Bvulwa Maanda ha Vhuimo na Nzulele ya Musanda: Tsenguluso yo Livhanaho na Vhuhosi ha Vhavenda ho Shumiswa Thyiori ya 'Ethnopragmatics,'* Doctor of Philosophy, Department of African Studies, University of South Africa, 2015, pp.

104-112, 126.

63  Isaac Schapera (editor), *The Bantu-speaking Tribes of South Africa* (London: Routledge and Keegan-Paul, 1962), p. 181.

64  Myburgh, *Anthropology of Southern Africa*, p. 81.

65  Lufuno Jean-Pierre Mulaudzi, *Historicising the Politics of Vhuhosivhuhulu: The Venḓa Polity and State formation in South Africa, c. 1800-2020*, Doctor of Philosophy in History, University of Pretoria, 2020, p. 9.

66  Illife, *Africans: The History of the Continent*, pp. 101-103.

67  Myburgh, *Anthropology of Southern Africa*, pp. 13-15, 19, 37.

68  Illife, *Africans: The History of the Continent*, pp. 100-106.

69  Neluvhalani, *The Banguni-Bakone-Bangona and San as the Autochthones of South(ern) Africa*, p. i.

70  Pityana, "The renewal of African Moral Values," in Makgoba (editor), *African Renaissance: The New Struggle*, pp. 140-41.

71  Anta Cheik Diop, *The African Origin of Civilization* (New York: Westport Publishers, 1974); Stephen Oppenheimer, *Out of Africa's Eden: The Peopling of the World* (Johannesburg: Jonathan Ball Publishers, 2003).

72  Pityana, "The renewal of African Moral Values," in Makgoba (editor), *African Renaissance: The New Struggle*, p. 137.

73  Myburgh, Anthropology of Southern Africa, p. 36.

74  Neluvhalani, *The Banguni-Bakone-Bangona and San as the Autochthones of South(ern) Africa*, p. i-iii.

75  Lufuno Jean-Pierre Mulaudzi, *Historicising the Politics of Vhuhosivhuhulu: The Venḓa Polity and State formation in South Africa, c. 1800-2020*, Doctor of Philosophy in History, University of Pretoria, 2020, p. 34.

76  Ibid., p. i.

77  Mönnig, *The Pedi*, preface, pp. 11, 17.

78  Neluvhalani, *The Banguni- Bakone-Bangona and San as the Autochthones of South(ern) Africa*, p. iv.

79  Myburgh, *Anthropology of Southern Africa*, pp. 24, 36.

80  Hugh Arthur Stayt, *The Bavenda* (CASS Library of African Studies, General Studies, n. o. 58 (Frank CASS and Co., Ltd, 1968), p. 9.

81  Shillington, Shillington, *History of Africa*, pp. 211-12.

82  Illife, *Africans: The History of the Continent*, p. 106; Neluvhalani, *The Banguni-Bakone-Bangona and San as the Autochthones of South(ern) Africa*, p. 28.

83  Hanisch, "Legends, Oral Traditions and Archaeology: A Look at Early Venda History," p. 68.

84  Ibid., pp. 69 and 74.

85  Moyahabo Rosina Mohale, *Khelobedu Cultural Evolution through Oral Tradition*, Master of Arts in African Languages, University of South Africa, February 2014, pp. 1-5.

86  Ibid., p. 34.

87  Ibid., pp. 31-32.

88  Myburgh, *Anthropology of Southern Africa*, pp. 36-37.

89  Neluvhalani, *The Banguni- Bakone-Bangona and San as the Autochthones*

*of South(ern) Africa*, p. 4.

90 Ibid., pp. 6 and 11.

91 Archbishop Thabo Makgoba's application submitted to the Limpopo Province Geographic Names Committee on 20 November 2020. On this see, also Thabo Makgoba, *Faith and Courage: Praying with Mandela* (Cape Town: Tafelberg Publishers, 2017).

92 Moyahabo Rosina Mohale, *Khelobedu Cultural Evolution through Oral Tradition,*" Master of Arts in African Languages, University of South Africa, February 2014, p. 1.

93 Barbara Oomen, *Chiefs in South Africa: Law, Power and Culture in the Post-Apartheid Era* (Oxford and Pietermaritzburg: James Currey and the University of KwaZulu-Natal Press, 2002), p. 29; and Barbara Oomen, "'We Must Now Go Back to Our History': Retribalisation in a Northern Province Chieftaincy," *African Studies*, Vol. 59, No. 1, 2000, pp. 71-95.

94 Eileen Jensen Krige, "Woman Marriage, with Special Reference to the Lovedu: Significance for Definition of Marriage," *Africa: Journal of the International African Institute*, Vol. 44, No. 1, 1974, pp. 11-37.

95 Nkhumeleni Matodzi Nemakhavhani Ralushai, "Further Traditions Concerning Luvhimbi and the Mbedzi," *Rhodesian History: The Journal of the Central Africa Historical Association*, Vol. 9, 1978, p. 2 of 1-8.

96 Moyahabo Rosina Mohale, *Khelobedu Cultural Evolution through Oral Tradition,*" Master of Arts in African Languages, University of South Africa, February 2014, p. 11-19.

97 Ibid., p. 21.

98 Ibid., pp. 21-22.

99 McEdward Murimbika, *Sacred Powers and Rituals of Transformation: An Ethno-Archaeological Study of Rainmaking Rituals and Agricultural Productivity during the Evolution of the Mapungubwe State, AD 1000 to AD 1300*, Doctor of Philosophy, Faculty of Humanities, University of the Witwatersrand, Johannesburg, 2006, pp. 35-36.

100 Ibid., pp. 13-14.

101 Ibid., p. 15.

102 Theodore Nkadimeng Mahosi, *An Afrocentric Exploration of South Africa's Homeland Policy with Specific Reference to Vhavenḍa Traditional Leadership and Institutions, 1898-1994*, Doctor of Philosophy in History, Department of Cultural and Political Studies, School of Social Sciences, Faculty of Humanities, University of Limpopo, 2020, pp. 101-102.

103 Lesiba Teffo, "Moral Renewal and African Experiences," Malegapuru William Makgoba (editor), *African Renaissance: The New Struggle* (Cape Town: Mafube Publishing and Tafelberg Publishers, 1999), pp. 153-54.

104 Ibid., p. 159.

105 Myburgh, *Anthropology of Southern Africa*, p. 19.

106 Ibid., p. 27.

107 Moyahabo Rosina Mohale, *Khelobedu Cultural Evolution through Oral Tradition,*" Master of Arts in African Languages, University of

South Africa, February 2014, pp. 27-32.

108 Ibid., p. 29.

109 Matodzi Rebecca Raphalalani, *U Bvulwa Maanda ha Vhuimo na Nzulele ya Musanda: Tsenguluso yo Livhanaho na Vhuhosi ha Vhavenda ho Shumiswa Thyiori ya 'Ethnopragmatics*, Doctor of Philosophy, Department of African Studies, University of South Africa, 2015, pp. 12, 37.

110 Dan Kaye, Florence Mirembe, Anna Mia Ekstrom, Grace Banteya Kyomuhendo and Annika Johansson, "Implications of Bride Price on Domestic Violence and Reproductive Health in Wakiso District, Uganda," *Africa Health Science*, 2005, December, Vol. 5, No. 4, pp. 300-303.

111 Moyahabo Rosina Mohale, *Khelobedu Cultural Evolution through Oral Tradition*, Master of Arts in African Languages, University of South Africa, February 2014, p. 30; Krige, p. 395.

112 The United Nations Educational, Scientific and Cultural Organization (UNESCO) Convention for the Safeguarding of the Intangible Cultural Heritage, 17 October 2003.

113 Neluvhalani, *The Banguni-Bakone-Bangona and San as the Autochthones of South(ern) Africa*, pp. iii-iv.

114 Hanisch, "Legends, Oral Traditions and Archaeology: A Look at Early Venda History," p. 72.

115 Ngoako Johannes Tauyatswala, *The Babirwa of Tauatswala: Aspects of the Socio-cultural and Political History of an African Community, 1930-1990*, Master of Arts, Department of History, University of Venda, Limpopo, South Africa.

116 Matodzi Rebecca Raphalalani, *U Bvulwa Maanda ha Vhuimo na Nzulele ya Musanda: Tsenguluso yo Livhanaho na Vhuhosi ha Vhavenda ho Shumiswa Thyiori ya 'Ethnopragmatics*, Doctor of Philosophy, Department of African Studies, University of South Africa, 2015, p. 10, 40.

117 Ibid.

118 Theodore Nkadimeng Mahosi, *An Afrocentric Exploration of South Africa's Homeland Policy with Specific Reference to Vhavenda Traditional Leadership and Institutions, 1898-1994*, Doctor of Philosophy in History, Department of Cultural and Political Studies, School of Social Sciences, Faculty of Humanities, University of Limpopo, 2020, pp. 81-82.

119 Wilfred Musetsho Razwimisani Daniel Phophi, "The Drum of the Dead: A Drum of Legend," *Luvhone*, Vol. 3, No. 1, 1994, pp. 78-80.

120 Ibid.

121 Caroline F. Jeannerat, *An Ethnography of Faith: Personal Conception of Religiosity in the Soutpansberg, South Africa, in the 19th and 20th Centuries*, Doctor of Philosophy in Anthropology and History, University of Michigan, 2007, n.p.

122 Krige, "Woman Marriage, with Special Reference to the Lovedu: Significance for Definition of Marriage," p. 282.

123 Moyahabo Rosina Mohale, *Khelobedu Cultural Evolution through Oral Tradition*, Master of Arts in African Languages, University of South Africa, February 2014, p. 51.

124 Ibid. p. 54.

125 Ibid.

126 Nndwakhulu Joseph Ndou, "Some Venda Dance Forms," *Luvhone*, Vol. 3, No. 1, April 1994, pp. 65-67.

127 Ibid., p. 47.

128 Ibid., pp. 66-67.

129 Caroline F. Jeannerat, *An Ethnography of Faith: Personal Conception of Religiosity in the Soutpansberg, South Africa, in the 19th and 20th Centuries*, Doctor of Philosophy in Anthropology and History, University of Michigan, 2007, n.p.

130 Moyahabo Rosina Mohale, *Khelobedu Cultural Evolution through Oral Tradition*, Master of Arts in African Languages, University of South Africa, February 2014, p. 49.

131 Ibid., p. 35.

132 Rendani Tshifhumulo, *Depicting the Vhavenda Women Initiation Schools and their Cultural Practices in Limpopo Province: Handbook of Research in Protecting and Managing Global Indigenous Knowledge Systems*. USA, IGI Global, Information Science Reference, 2022.

133 Ndou, "Some Venda Dance Forms," pp. 63-67.

134 Ibid.

135 Lydia Daphney Tshisikule, Vhonani Olive Netshandama and Pfarelo Matshidze, "The Role Played by Initiation Schools in Relation to Females among the Venda Speaking People in Thohoyandou, Thulamela Municipality in Limpopo Province," *Journal of Gender and Behaviour*, Vol. 17, No. 4.

136 Hanisch, "Legend, Oral Traditions and Archaeology: A Look at Early Venda History," p. 73.

137 Caroline Jeannerat, quoted in William Grant "Magato and his tribe," *Journal of the Anthropological Institute of Great Britain and Ireland*, Vol. 35, pp. 266-70.

138 Moyahabo Rosina Mohale, *Khelobedu Cultural Evolution through Oral Tradition*, Master of Arts in African Languages, University of South Africa, February 2014, p. 39.

139 Illife, *Africans: The History of the Continent*, p. 125.

140 McEdward Murimbika, *Sacred Powers and Rituals of Transformation: An Ethno-Archaeological Study of Rainmaking Rituals and Agricultural Productivity during the Evolution of the Mapungubwe State, AD 1000 to AD 1300*, Doctor of Philosophy, Faculty of Humanities, University of the Witwatersrand, Johannesburg, 2006, pp. 139.

141 Ibid., pp. 151-155.

142 Phophi, "The Drum of the Dead: A Drum of Legend," pp. 78-80.

143 Albert Kwadwo Adu Boahen, General History of Africa, V11: Africa Under Colonial Domination, 1880-1935 (Cape Town and Glosderry: UNESCO and New African Books, 1998) p. 217.

## Chapter 3

1 Paul S. Landau, *Popular Politics in the History of South Africa, 1400-1948* (New York: Cambridge University Press, 2010), pp. 248-49.

2 Thato Mabolaeng Maryanne Monyakane, The Cultural, Social and Political Similarity of the Bafokeng, Bakuena and the Bataung Lineages Amongst the Sotho, Doctor of Literature and Philosophy, Department of African Languages, University of South Africa, Pretoria, South Africa, June 2016, p. 15.

3 Simphiwe Sesanti, "Pan-African Linguistic and Cultural Unity: A Basic for Pan-Africanism and the African Renaissance," *Theoria*, Vol. 64, Vol. 153, 2017, pp. 10-21.

4 For a detailed study of the mainstream and dissident tradition of Afrikaner ethnology (volkekunde) from the time it was established at the Stellenbosch University in the 1920s through its development at the University of Pretoria in the 1950s to the 1970s, to its period of decline in the era of dissidence from the 1970s to the 2010s, see, Anell Stacey Daries, Visualizing Volkekunde: Photography in the mainstream and Dissent Tradition of Afrikaner Ethnology, 1920-2013, Master of Arts Thesis in History, Department of History, University of the Western Cape, Western Cape Province, South Africa, 15 November 2019.

5 Susan George, *Whose Crisis? Whose Future? Towards a Greener, Fairer, Richer World* (London: Polity Press, 2010), p. 82.

6 Maurice Zeitlin, "Corporate Ownership and Control: The Large Corporation and the Capitalist Class," *American Journal of Sociology*, Vol. 79, No. 5, March 1974, p. 1112.

7 John Kenneth Galbraith, *The Age of Uncertainty* (London: BBC, 1977), p. 44.

8 Sara Pugach, *Africa in Transition: A History of Colonial Linguists in Germany and Beyond, 1814-1945* (Ann Arbor, Michigan: University of Michigan Press, 2012), p. 4.

9 Ibid., p. 5.

10 Ibid., p. 5.

11 Dani W. Nabudere, The Epistemological and Methodological Foundations of an All-Inclusive Research Paradigm for "Field Building" and Intersubjective Accommodation: Paper presented at the "Filed Building" Workshop organised by Afrika Study Centre, Mbale, Uganda in collaboration with the Social Science Research Council, New York and the Harry Frank Guggenheim Foundation, New York, at Rida hotel, Seeta Kampala, Uganda, 22-23 June 2002, p. 16.

12 Amilcar Cabral, *Return to the Source: Selected Speeches of Amilcar Cabral* (New York: Monthly Review Press, 1973), p. 43.

13 Ibid., pp. 43-44.

14 Ibid., p. 44.

15 Amilcar Cabral, *Revolution in Guinea: Selected Texts by Amilcar Cabral* (New York: Monthly Review Press, 1969), p. 67.

16 Ibid., p. 42.

17 Ibid., p. 90.

18 Antonio Gramsci, *Selections from the Prison Notebooks* (New York: International Publishers, 1971), p. 130.

19 Ibid., p. 132.

20 Ibid., p. 133.

21 Antonio Gramsci. Quoted in Makidi-Ku-Ntima, "Class Struggle and the Making of the Revolution in Angola," in Bernard Magubane and Nzongola-Ntalaja (editors), *Proletarianization and Class Struggle in Africa, Contemporary Marxism*, No. 6, Spring 1983, p. 139.

22 Werner Welli Max Eiselen, quoted in Robert Gordon, "Apartheid's Anthropologists: The Genealogy of Afrikaner Anthropology," *American Ethnologist*, Vol. 15, No, 3, August 1988, p. 535.

23 Pieter Johannes Schoeman, quoted in Robert Gordon, "Apartheid's Anthropologists: The Genealogy of Afrikaner Anthropology," *American Ethnologist*, Vol. 15, No, 3, August 1988,p. 535.

24 Robert Gordon, "Apartheid's Anthropologists: The Genealogy of Afrikaner Anthropology," *American Ethnologist*, Vol. 15, No, 3, August 1988, pp. 535-53.

25 Ibid., p. 535

26 For Werner Welli Max Eiselen's role in the contribution towards development of volkekundige in South Africa as anthropological praxis in serving the project of the national building of the Afrikaners and their assumption and exercise of the state political power for their colonial control, domination and exploitation of the African people, see, Andrew Blank, "Broederbande [Brotherly Bonds]: Afrikaner Nationalist Masculinity and African Sexuality in the Writings of Werner Eiselen, Stellenbosch University, 1930-1936," *Anthropology Southern Africa*, Vol. 38, Nos. 3-4, 2015, pp. 180-97, Andrew Blank, "Fathering Volkekunde: Race and Culture in Ethnological Writings of Werner Eiselen, Stellenbosch University, 1926-1936," *Anthropology Southern Africa*, Vol. 38, Nos. 3-4, 2015, pp. 163-79 and Andrew Bank, "The Berlin Mission Society and German Linguistic Roots of Volkekunde: The Background, Training and Hamburg Writings of Werner Eiselen, 1899-1924," *Kronos*, Vol. 41, No. 1, 2015, pp. 166-97.

27 E.F. Dube, "Yesterday's Nazi Sympathizers, Today South African Leaders," *New York Times*, 16 August 1985, p. 28.

28 On this, see, Saul Dubow, "Afrikaner Nationalism, Apartheid and the Conceptualisation of "Race," *Journal of African History*, Vol. 33, No. 2, 1992, Cynthia Kros, "Eiselen: Idealist and Idealism Revisited," Paper presented to the Conference on Southern African History of Education in Society, Scottburgh, October 1993; Gordon, "Apartheid's Anthropologists: The Genealogy of Afrikaner Anthropology," pp. 535-53 and Robert Gordon, "Surveying the Volk with Volkekundiges," in Jonathan D. Jansen (editor), *Knowledge and Power in South Africa: Critical Perspectives Across the Disciplines* (Johannesburg: Skotaville, 1991).

29 W.D. Hammond-Tooke, N.J. Van Warmelo and the Ethnological Section: A Memoir, *African Studies*, Vol. 54, No. 1, 1995, pp. 119-28. The previous

title of the journal, *African Studies*, was *Bantu Studies*.

30  For some names of these African informants and researchers, see lists of manuscripts in Nicolaas Jacobus van Warmelo collection, Van Warmelo Collection, Department of Library Services, African Heritage Collections, Van Warmelo, N. J. (Nicolaas Jacobus) 1904-(1989), University of Pretoria.

31  Department of Bantu Administration and Development, *Ethnological and Linguistic Studies in Honour of N.J. Van Warmelo: Essays Contributed on the Occasion of His Sixty-fifth Birthday 28 January 1969* (Pretoria: Government Printer, 1969), pp. 1-242.

32  Sara Pugach, "Carl Meinhof and the German Influence on Nicholas Jacobus van Warmelo's Ethnology and Linguistic Writing, 1927-1935," *Journal of Southern African Studies*, Vol. 30, No. 4, 2004, pp. 827-28.

33  Johannes Seroto, "A Revisionist View of the Contribution of Dr Eiselen to South African Education: New Perspectives," Yesterday and Today: *Journal for History in South Africa and Abroad*, No. 9, 2013, pp. 91-105.

34  Pugach, "Carl Meinhof and the German Influence on Nicholas Jacobus van Warmelo's Ethnology and Linguistic Writing, 1927-1935," *Journal of Southern African Studies*, Vol. 30, No. 4, 2004, p. 825.

35  Ibid., pp. 425.

36  Ibid.

37  C.M. Doke, "In Memory of Carl Meinhof," *African Studies*, Vol. 5, No. 2, 1946, p. 76.

38  W.M. Eiselen, "In Memory of Carl Meinhof," *African Studies*, Vol. 5, No. 2, 1946, p. 79.

39  Adam Kuper, "Fourie and the Southern Transvaal Ndebele," *African Studies*, Vo. 31, No. 1, 2007, p. 108.

40  Ibid., p. 107.

41  G.P. Lestrade, "Meinhof's Contributions to Our Knowledge of African Languages," *African Studies*, Vol. 5, No. 2, June 1946.

42  Ibid.

43  C.M. Doke and G.P. Lestrade, " In Memory of Carl Meinhof," *African Studies*, Vol. 5, No. 2, June 1946, pp. 74-77

44  W.M. Eiselen, "In Memory of Carl Meinhof," *African Studies*, Vol. 5, No. 2, 1946, p. 79.

45  Andre Bank, The Berlin Mission Society and German Linguistic Roots of Volkekunde: The Background, Training and Hamburg Writings of Werner Eiselen, 1899-1924," *Kronos*, Vol. 41, No. 1, November 2015.

46  Ibid.

47  W.W.M. Eiselen, "Die Seksuele Leve van die Bantoe" (The Sexual Life of the Bantu) *Tydskrif vir Wetenskap en Kuns* (Journal for Science and Art) in 1923, quoted in Andre Bank, The Berlin Mission Society and German Linguistic Roots of Volkekunde: The Background, Training and Hamburg Writings of Werner Eiselen, 1899-1924," *Kronos*, Vol. 41, No. 1, November 2015.

48  T. Dunbar Moodie, *The Rise of Afrikanerdom: Power, Apartheid, and*

*the Afrikaner Civil Religion* (Berkely and Los Angelos: University of California Press, 1975, p. 277.

49  Kenneth W. Grundy, *Confrontation and Accommodation in Southern Africa: The Limits of Independence* (Berkeley: University of California Press, 1973), p. 268.

50  Patrick Harris, "The Roots of Ethnicity: Discourse and the Politics of Language Construction in South-East Africa," *African Affairs*, Vol. 87, No. 346, January 1988, p. 25.

51  Ibid., p. 37.

52  Peter Becker, *Hill of Destiny: The Life and Times of Moshesh, Founder of the Basuto* (London: Longman Group, 1969), pp. 294.

53  Julian Cobbing, "The Case Against the Mfecane," *African Studies* Seminar Paper, No. 144, African Studies Institute, University of the Witwatersrand, Johannesburg, March 1984, p. 17.

54  Ibid.

55  J.M., Nhlapo. "The Story of AmaNhalapo," *African Studies*, Vol. 4, No. 2, 1945, pp. 97-101.

56  Benjamin Pogrund, *Robert Sobukwe: How Can Man Die Better?* (Johannesburg and Cape Town: Jonathan Ball Publishers, 1990), p. 6.

57  Robert Mangaliso Sobukwe, quoted in Derek Hook, "The Lonely Prisoner was a Man of Letters," in Benjamin Pogrund (editor), *Robert Mangaliso Sobukwe: New Reflections* (Johannesburg and Cape Town: Jonathan Ball Publishers, 2019), p. 157.

58  N. Barney Pityana, "A Voice that Could Not be Silenced," in Benjamin Pogrund (editor), Robert Mangaliso *Sobukwe: New Reflections* (Johannesburg and Cape Town: Jonathan Ball Publishers, 2019), p. 28.

59  Derek Hook, "The Lonely Prisoner was a Man of Letters," in Benjamin Pogrund (editor), Robert Mangaliso Sobukwe: *New Reflections* (Johannesburg and Cape Town: Jonathan Ball Publishers, 2019), p. 153.

60  Thami ka Plaatjie, *Sobukwe: The Making of a Pan Africanist Leader*, Vol. 1 (Johannesburg: KMM Review Publishing, 2020).

61  Bernard Mbenga and Andrew Manson, *"People of the Dew": A History of the Bafokeng of Phokeng Rustenburg Region, South Africa, from Early Times to 2000* (Auckland Park, Johannesburg: Jacana Media, 2010), p. xviii.

62  James Walton, "Early Bafokeng Settlement in South Africa," *African Studies*, Vol. 15, No. 1, 1956, pp. 37-43.

63  Klaus Nurnberger, The Sotho Notion of the Supreme Being and the Impact of Christian Proclamation," *Journal of Religion in Africa*, Vol. 7, No. 3, 1975, pp. 184-85, Walton, "Early Bafokeng Settlement in South Africa," p. 38, and Manti Teboho Pitso, Stories of Origin of the Sotho People of QwaQwa: The Construction and Maintenance of Society through Narratives, Master of Philosophy in Indigenous Studies thesis, Faculty of Social Science, University of Tromsö, Norway, Spring 2009, p. 10.

64  Walton, "Early Bafokeng Settlement in South Africa," *African Studies*, p. 38.

65 Manti Teboho Pitso, Stories of Origin of the Sotho People of QwaQwa: The Construction and Maintenance of Society through Narratives, Master of Philosophy in Indigenous Studies thesis, Faculty of Social Science, University of Tromsö, Norway, Spring 2009, p. 24.

66 Patrick Harris, "The Roots of Ethnicity: Discourse and the Politics of Language Construction in South-East Africa," *African Affairs*, Vol. 87, No. 346, January 1988, p. 25.

67 Ibid., p. 37.

68 Elsabe Taljard and Sonja E. Bosch, "A Comparison of Approaches to World Class: Tagging: Disjunctively vs. Conjunctively Written Bantu Languages," *Nordic Journal of African Studies*, Vol. 15, No. 4, 2006, p. 429.

69 Ibid.

70 Richard Nordquist, "Definition and Examples of Language Contact: Glossary of Grammatical and Rhetorical Terms," *ThoughtCo.*, 2020

71 N.J. van Warmelo, *Transvaal Ndebele Texts: Ethnological Publications, Vol. 1: Union of South Africa Department of Native Affairs* (Pretoria: Government Printer, 1930), p. 28.

72 Richard Bailey, "The Bantu Languages of South Africa: Towards a Sociohistorical Perspectives," and Richard Bailey, "Sociolinguistic Evidence of Nguni, Sotho, Tsonga and Venda Origins," in Rajend Mesthrie (editor), *Language and Social History: Studies in South African Sociolinguistics* (Cape Town and Johannesburg: David Philip Publishers, 1995).

73 V.G.J. Sheddick, *The Southern Sotho: Southern Africa, Part 1* (London: International African Institute, 1953), p. 11.

### Chapter 4

1 Peter Magubane, *Vanishing Cultures of South Africa* (Cape Town: Struik Publishers, 1998).

2 Thabani Thwala, The Politics of Placing Princes in Historical and Contemporary Swaziland, Master of Arts Dissertation, Department of History, Faculty of Humanities, University of the Witwatersrand, Johannesburg, South Africa, 2013.

3 Peter Delius, The Land Belongs to Us: The Pedi Polity, the Boer and the British in the Nineteenth Century Transvaal (London: Heinmann, 1983), pp. xiv-279.

4 Ibid., p. 55

5 Philip Bonner, Kings, *Commoners and Concessionaries: The Evolution and Dissolution of the Nineteenth-Century Swazi State* (Cambridge: Cambridge University Press, 1983), p. 327

6 Ibid.

7 Joseph Mandla Maseko, *The Mighty Ngunis People* (Nelspruit, South Africa: Maseko Management Services, 2010).

8 Leroy Vail (editor), *The Creation of Tribalism in Southern Africa* (Cambridge: Cambridge University Press, 1983)

9 Peter Nicholas St. Martin Delius and Maria Hendrieka Schoeman,

Revisiting Bokoni: Populating the Stone Ruins of the Mpumalanga Escarpment, in Natalie Swanepoel, Amanda B. Esterhuysen and Philip Bonner (editors), *Five Hundred Years Rediscovered: Southern African Precedents and Prospects* (Johannesburg: Wits University Press, 2008), pp. 135-68.

10  Ibid., pp. 135-67

11  Ibid., pp. 135-168.

12  Delius, *The Land Belongs to Us: The Pedi Polity, the Boer and the British in the Nineteenth Century Transvaal*, pp. 158-180.

13  Interview with Vusi Lingwati by Rachidi Molapo, 24 July 2023.

14  Ibid.

15  Ibid.

16  Culture is a social construct and, as never natural process with natural meaning, it evolved overtime. People were born into culture and not the other way round.

17  Eric Hobsbawm and Terence Ranger (editors), *The Invention of Tradition* (London, Cambridge University Press, 1983), pp. vii-320.

18  Interview with Lingwati by Molapo, 24 July 2023.

19  Patrick Harries, Butterflies and Barbarians: Swiss Missionaries and Systems of Knowledge in South-East Africa (Oxford: James Currey, 2007), p. 264.

20  Pixley ka Isaka Seme, "Native Union," in South African History Online (SAHO), October 24, 1911.

21  Samora Machel quoted in Neville Alexander, Sow the Wind: Contemporary Speeches (Johannesburg: Skotaville Publishers, 1985), p. 151.


**Chapter 5**

1  N.J. van Warmelo, "The Classification of Cultural Groups," in W.D. Hammond-Tooke (editor), The Bantu Speaking Peoples of Southern Africa (London: Routledge & Kegan Paul, 1974), p. 67.

2  M. de Jongh and F.C. de Beer, "A Case of Ambiguous Identity – Oral Tradition and the Ba ga Seleka of Lephalala," South African Journal of Ethnology, Vol. 15, No. 4, 1992, p. 107.

3  Ibid.

4  Ibid., p. 101.

5  Ibid., p. 102

6  Ibid.

7  Gerda Lerner, The Creation of Patriarchy (Oxford: Oxford University Press, 1986), p. 220.

8  Ibid.

9  Mamphela Ramphele, quoted in Adebayo Olukoshi and Francis B. Nyamnjoh, "The African Woman," CODESRIA Bulletin, Nos. 1 and 2, 2006, p. 2.

10  Ibid.

11  Ibid.

12  Ibid.

13 Ibid.

14 Ibid.

15 Ibid.

16 Smita Tewari Jassal, "Bhojpuri Songs, Women's Work and Social Control in Northern India," Journal of Peasant Studies, Vol. 30, No. 2, January 2003, p. 202.

17 Elizabeth Spelman, quoted in Fidela Fouche, "Overcoming the Sisterhood Myth," Transformation: Critical Perspectives on Southern African Africa, Vol. 23, 1994, p. 79.

18 Cherryl Walker, Women and Resistance in South Africa (Cape Town: David Philip, 1991), p. xxi.

19 Albertina Sisulu, quoted in Diana E.H. Russell, Lives of Courage: Women for a New South Africa (New York: Basic Books, 1989), p. 114.

20 Oyeronke Oyewumi "Family Bonds/Conceptual Binds: African Notes on Feminist Epistemologies," Signs: A Journal of Women in Culture and Society, Vol. 25, No. 4, 2000, p. 1097.

21 Oyeronke Oyewumi, "Conceptualising Gender: The Eurocentric Foundations of Feminist Concepts and the Challenge of African Epistemologies," JENDA: A Journal of Cultural and African Women's Studies, Vol. 2, No. 1, 2002, p. 25.

22 Ifi Amadiume, Reinventing Africa, Matriarchy, Religion and Culture (London: Zed Books, 1997), p. 21.

23 Oyewumi, "Family Bonds/Conceptual Binds: African Notes on Feminist Epistemologies," p. 1094.

24 Meredeth Turshen, "The Political Economy of Women in Africa," in Meredeth Turshen (editor), African Women: A Political Economy (New York: Palgrave Macmillan, 2010), p. 7.

25 Robin Cohen, Pepe Roberts and Morris Szeftel, "Editorial," Review of African Political Economy, Vol. 8, Issue 21, 1981, pp. 1-6.

26 Fatima Sadiqi, "Changing Gender Dynamics in Africa," CODESRIA Bulletin, Nos. 3 and 4, 2000, p. 38

27 Ibid.

28 Melissa Leach, Rainforest Relations, Gender and Resource Use among the Mende of Gola, Sierra Leone (Edinburgh: Edinburgh University Press for the International African Studies, 1994), p. 38.

29 Ibid.

30 Judy Seidman, A Teaching Guide to: In Our Own Image (Gaborone: Foundation for Education with Production, 1995), p. 1.

## Chapter 6

1 Herman Buhr Giliomee and Bernard Mbenga, New History of South Africa (Cape Town: Tafelberg Publishers, 2007).

2 Erna Oliver and Willem Hosking Oliver, "The Colonization of South Africa: A Unique Case," HTS Theological Studies, Vol. 73, No. 3, 2017, pp. 1-8.

3 Axel-Ivar Berglund, Zulu Thought-Patterns and Symbolism (Bloomington and Indianapolis: Indiana University Press, 1976).

4   Alfred Thomas Bryant, Olden Times in Zululand, and Natal (London: Longmans, 1929)

5   Thomas Neil Huffman, "The Archaeology of the Nguni Past," Southern African Humanities, Vol. 16, No. 1, 2004, pp. 79-111.

6   Sibusiso Ngubane, "The Socio-Cultural and Linguistic Implications of Zulu Names," South African Journal of African Languages, Vol. 33, No. 2, 2013, pp. 165-72.

7   Michael Francis, "Silencing the Past: Historical and Archaeological Colonization of the Southern San in KwaZulu-Natal, South Africa," Anthropology Southern Africa, Vol. 32, Nos. 3-4, 2009, pp. 106-116.

8   Charles Tilly, "Citizenship, Identity, and Social History," International Review of Social History, Vol. 40, No. 3, 1995, pp. 1-17.

9   Eric Allina-Pisano, "Resistance and the Social History of Africa," Journal of Social History, Vol. 37, No. 1, 2003, pp. 187-98.

10  Michael Green, "Social History, Literary History, and Historical Fiction in South Africa," Journal of African Cultural Studies, Vol. 12, No. 2, 1999, pp. 121-36.

11  Patricia Jolly, "Interaction between South-Eastern San and Southern Nguni and Sotho Communities from c. 1400 to c. 1880," South African Historical Journal, Vol. 35, No. 1, 1996, pp. 30-61.

12  Monica Wilson, "The Early History of the Transkei and Ciskei," African Studies, Vol. 18, No. 4, 1959, pp. 167-79.

13  Huffman, "The Archaeology of the Nguni Past," pp. 79-111.

14  James Gump, "Origins of the Zulu Kingdom," The Historian, Vol. 50, No. 4, 1988, pp. 521-34 and Mathieu Deflem, "Warfare, Political Leadership, and State Formation: The Case of the Zulu Kingdom, 1808-1879," Ethnology, Vol. 38, No. 4, 1999, pp. 371-91.

15  John Wright, "Reconstituting Shaka Zulu for the Twenty-First Century," Southern African Humanities, Vol. 18, No. 2, 2006, pp 139-153.

16  Percy Alfred William Cook, "History and izibongo of the Swazi Chiefs," Bantu Studies, Vol. 5, No. 1, 1931, pp. 181-201.

17  Rita Astuti, "Ritual, History and the Swazi Ncwala - Sacred Kingship and the Origin of the State," Africa, Vol. 43, No. 4. 1988, pp. 603-620 and David Price Williams, "Archaeology in Swaziland," South African Archaeological Bulletin, Vol. 35, No. 131, 1980, pp 13-18.

18  Philemon Buti Skhosana, The Linguistic Relationship between Southern and Northern Ndebele, Doctor of Literature Thesis, University of Pretoria, Pretoria, 9 October 2010.

19  Deborah James, "A Question of Ethnicity: Ndzundza Ndebele in a Lebowa Village," Journal of Southern African Studies, Vol. 16, No. 1, 1990, pp. 33-54.

20  Huffman, "The Archaeology of the Nguni Past," pp. 79-111.

21  Sekibakiba Peter Lekgoathi, "Orality, Literacy, and Succession Disputes in Contemporary Ndzundza and Manala Ndebele Chieftaincies," in Christina Landman (editor), Oral History: Representing the Hidden, the Untold, and the Veiled (Pretoria: University of South Africa, 2013), p. 35.

22 Philemon Buti Skhosana, "The Literary History of isiNdebele," South African Journal of African Languages, Vol. 23, No. 2, 2003, pp. 111-119.

23 Andrew Bank, "The Great Debate and the Origins of South African Historiography," The Journal of African History, Vol. 38, No. 2, 1997, pp. 261-81.

24 James Deetz, "Archaeography, Archaeology, or Archeology?," American Journal of Archaeology, Vol. 93, No. 3, 1989, pp. 429-435 and Tanure Ojaide, "Migration, Globalization, and Recent African Literature," World Literature Today, Vol. 82, No. 2, 2008, pp. 43-47.

25 Mary Cameron Bill, "100 Years of Tsonga Publications, 1883–1983," African Studies, Vol. 43, No. 2, 1984, pp. 67-81.

26 Alan Smith, "The Peoples of Southern Mozambique: A Historical Survey," Journal of African History, Vol. 14, No. 4, 1973, pp. 565-80.

27 Fumiko Ohinata, "The Beginning of 'Tsonga 'Archaeology: Excavations at Simunye, North-Eastern Swaziland," Southern African Humanities, Vol. 14, No. 1, 2002, 23-50.

28 Mary Cameron Bill and George Poulos, "Bibliographical, Comparative and Descriptive Works," Mbita Ya Vutivi: South African Journal of African Languages, Vol. 5, No, Supplementary 1, 1985, pp. 142-49.

29 Julius Sikelela Zwangendaba Matsebula, David King Mlotshwa, Josephine Mafimi Mlotshwa and Douglas Nkomeni Ntiwane, The History of Emaswati in South Africa (Mbombela, South Africa: Mbokodo Publisher, 2016).

30 Ibid.

31 Ibid.

32 Ibid.

33 Mandla Nkosinathi Ngcobo, "On Account of a Basket:" A Socio-Historical and Ethnographic Perspective on the Development of Multilingualism in South Africa," Indilinga African Journal of Indigenous Knowledge Systems, Vol. 7, No. 1, 2008, p. 12.

34 Laketi Makalela, "Teaching Indigenous African Languages to Speakers of other African Languages: The Effects of Translanguaging for Multilingual Development," in Liesel Hibbert and Christa van der Walt (editors), Multilingual Universities in South Africa: Reflecting Society in Higher Education (Bristol: Multilingual Matters, 2014), pp. 88-104. Pp.

35 Ngcobo, "On Account of a Basket:" A Socio-Historical and Ethnographic Perspective on the Development of Multilingualism in South Africa," pp. 7-22.

36 Ibid.

37 Paul Maylam, "Explaining the Apartheid City: 20 Years of South African Urban Historiography," Journal of Southern African Studies, Vol. 21, No. 1, 1995, pp. 19-38.

38 Ngcobo, "On Account of a Basket:" Socio-Historical and Ethnographic Perspective on the Development of Multilingualism in South Africa," pp. 7-22.

39 Ibid., p. 8.

40 Meluleki Dube and Hussin Suleman, Language Identification for South

African Bantu Languages Using Rank Order Statistics (Kuala Lumpur, Malaysia: Springer International Publishing, 2019), pp. 283-89.

41 Matsebula, Mlotshwa, Mlotshwa and Ntiwane, The History of Emaswati in South Africa, p. 9.

42 Peter Joyce, Cultures of South Africa: A Celebration (Cape Town: Sunbird Publishers, 2009), p. 9.

43 Thandeka Primrose Sabela and Busile Cynthia Ndhlovu, African Transformation Agenda to Promote Inclusive Education. In Handbook of Research on Creating Spaces for African Epistemologies in the Inclusive Education Discourse (Mbombela: University of Mpumalanga, 2022), p. 229.

44 Matsebula, Mlotshwa, Mlotshwa and Ntiwane, The History of Emaswati in South Africa..

45 Ibid.

46 Ibid.

47 Ngcobo, "On Account of a Basket:" A Socio-Historical and Ethnographic Perspective on the Development of Multilingualism in South Africa," pp. 7-22.

48 Ibid.

49 Ibid., p. 8.

50 Cornelis Johannes. Coetzee, Die Strewe tot Etniese Konsolidasie en Nasionale Selfverwesenliking by die Ndebele van Transvaal, doctor Philosophiae in OntwikkelingsAdministrasie, Potchefstroomse Universiteit vir Christelike Hoër Onderwys, Potchefstroom, Suid Afrika, 1980.

51 Ibid.

52 Katjie Sponono Mahlangu, The Growth and Development of IsiNdebele Orthography and Spelling (1921-2010), Doctor of Literature Thesis, University of Pretoria, Pretoria, 6 April 2016.

53 Richards Patrick, Tibongo Netinanatelo Temaswati (Mbabane: Swaziland National Trust Commission, Natural History Society, Conversation Trust of Swaziland, Mbabane, Swaziland, 1976).

54 Viv Lifestyle Magazine, Popular Nguni Surnames of Tsonga Origin, Viv Lifestyle Magazine (vivmag.co.za), May 2, 2017.

55 Noel Casper Makhuba, A Cultural Image of South Africa: The Xitsonga-Speaking People (Randhart, South Africa: Lectio Publishers, 2006).

56 Viv Lifestyle Magazine, Popular Nguni Surnames of Tsonga Origin, Viv Lifestyle Magazine (vivmag.co.za), May 2, 2017.

57 Ibid.

58 Ibid.

59 Ibid.

60 Ibid.

61 Matsebula, Mlotshwa, Mlotshwa and Ntiwane, The History of Emaswati in South Africa.

62 Peter Joyce, Cultures of South Africa: A Celebration (Cape Town: Sunbird Publishers, 2009), p. 108.

63 Ibid.

64  Ibid.

65  Ibid.

66  Ibid.

67  Noel Casper Makhuba, *A Cultural Image of South Africa: The Xitsonga-Speaking People.*

68  Katjie Sponono Mahlangu, The Growth and Development of IsiNdebele Orthography and Spelling (1921-2010), Doctor of Literature Thesis, University of Pretoria, Pretoria, 6 April 2016.

69  Ibid.

70  Sisana Rachel Mdluli, quoted in Sibusiso.Wiseman. Ntsibande, "Culture and Tradition in Siswati Modern Literature: Lessons from Umjingi Udliwa Yinhlitiyo 'Let one follow the heart's Dictates'," *South African Journal for Folklore Studies*, Vol. 27, No. 2, 2017, p. 45.

71  Siphokazi Angelinah Dazela, *Cultural Image of South Africa: The IsiXhosa-Speaking People* (Randhart, South Africa: Lectio Publishers, 2006).

72  Ngcobo, "On Account of a Basket: A Socio-Historical and Ethnographic Perspective on the Development of Multilingualism in South Africa," pp. 7-22

73  Alfred Thomas Bryant, quoted in Mandla Nkosinathi Ngcobo, "On Account of a Basket: A Socio-Historical and Ethnographic Perspective on the Development of Multilingualism in South Africa," *Indilinga African Journal of Indigenous Knowledge Systems*, Vol. 7 No. 1, 2008, p. 13.

## Chapter 7

1  The totem of the Batau as Swazis was the sun (ilanga in Swati and letšatši in Sepedi). It was firstly changed into vulture (nong) and eventually into its current state as a lion (tau). All its transformations were as a result of migration and contact with other African ethnic groups until they become known as Batau. Migration and contacts with other Africans transformed their ethnicity, totem, language and culture. On this, see, Namanetona Joel Shai, Intervention and Resistance: The Batau of Mphanama, Limpopo Province and External Governance, Master of Arts in Anthropology, University of South Africa, Pretoria, South Africa, February 2016, p. 13.

2  Matlebjane's sons had their own separate mothers. Photo's mother was his favourite, beautiful and younger wife. He spent most of his time with her. Traditional tributes such as mahlakori and dibego were taken to her house. This caused animosity among his five wives and sons towards Matlebjane, Photo and his mother. His five sons concluded that their father was going to give leadership to Photo. They implemented a decision that their father be killed in his sleep at night with spears. Part of their plan was that their spears be bent at the tip end for them to kill him. This was not communicated to Photo who was a teenager. They entered their father's resting place and signalled that all stab him in his sleep. As planned, it was Photo's spear that pierced through and killed him. His five sons did not kill him as their spears were bent at the tip

end. Batau ba ga Masemola discovered the plan. The consequence was their division into sub-groups on the basis of the separate leadership of Matlabjane's sons who left their father's place for different places where they settled and became leaders. There are leaders who share the surname Mogashwa and those who share the surname Nchabeleng. There is a leader who adopted Marishane as his surname. There are two leaders whose surname is Phaahla and Phaahlamohlaka respectively. They are ramogolo or a senior brother of one's father and ranganwane or a junior brother of one's father. They and Kgoshi Kgaphola are originally from gaMasemola. While Kgoshi Ramphelane of ba ga Nkadimeng emanated from Kgoshi Selwane, Kgoshi Khoshi Phaahlamohlaka emanated from Kgoshi Phaahla.

The division of Batau ba gaMasemola into sub-groups on the basis of the separate leadership of Matlabjane's sons who left their father's place for different places where they settled and became leaders is referred to as fission. It took place when sons of one traditional leader leave their father's place and established their own separate meshate or chiefdoms where they became leaders on their own right. It is the product of unresolved succession disputes and claims.

3   P. Eric Louw, "Language and National Unity in a Post-South Africa," *Critical Arts*, Vol. 6, No. 1, 1992, pp. 52-53.

4   Mgwebi Lavin Snail, "Revisiting Aspects of Language in South Africa during the Apartheid Era," *Historia Actual Online*, No. 24, 2011, p. 65.

5   Ibid.

6   Neville Alexander, Language Policy and National Unity in South Africa/ Azania (Cape Town: Buch Books, 1989), p. 74.

7   Jacob Nhlapo, Bantu Babel: Will the Bantu Languages Live? (Cape Town: African Bookman, 1944), pp.1-15.

8   Ibid., p. 32.

9   Louw, "Language and National Unity in a Post-Apartheid South Africa," p. 53.

10  Ibid.

11  Ibid., p. 54.

12  Ibid.

13  Ibid.

14  Alexander Johnston, *South Africa: Inventing the Nation* (London: Bloomsbury Academic, 2014), p. 33.

15  For the church as an intangible cultural heritage see, among others, Lantz Carolina's Masters thesis, The Church as an Intangible Cultural Heritage - A Study of Liturgical Values and the Approach to them by the Conservation Field, Department of Conservation, University of Gothenburg, Gothenburg, Sweden, 2011, pp. 1-69. This work focuses on texts on liturgy and Basic Texts of the 2003 Convention for the Safeguarding of the Intangible Cultural Heritage of the General Conference of the United Nations Educational, Scientific and Cultural Organisation meeting held at its 32nd Session in Paris, from 29 September to 17 October 2003 (Paris: UNESCO, 2003).

16 Ernest Wamba-dia-Wamba, "Democracy and Multi-Partyism in Zaire," *Southern Africa Political & Economic Monthly*, Vol. 6, No. 6, 1993 p. 39.
17 Ibid.
18 Ibid.
19 Department of Foreign Affairs and Information of South Africa, *This is South Africa* (Pretoria: Government Printer, 1980), p. 10.
20 Ibid., p. 11.
21 Ibid., p. 10.
22 Ibid., p. 25.
23 Ibid.
24 Ibid, p. 10.
25 Ibid.
26 Ibid.
27 Ibid., p. 6.
28 Ibid., p. 20.
29 Ibid., p. 25.
30 Ibid., p. 28.
31 Ibid.
32 Ibid.
33 Ibid.
34 Ibid.
35 Ibid.
36 Ibid.
37 Ibid.
38 Ibid.
39 Ibid.
40 Ibid., pp. 29-30.
41 Joseph Stalin, *Marxism and the National Question* (Calcutta: Suren Dutt, 1977), p. 11.
42 Ibid., p. 8.
43 Ibid., p. 9
44 Ibid., pp. 8-9, 11.
45 Lionel Forman was a member of the South African Communist Party during the time it was called the Communist Party of South Africa.
46 Lionel Forman, in Sadie Forman and Andre Odendaal (editors), *A Trumpet from the Housetops: The Selected Writings of Lionel Forman* (Cape Town: David Philip (Pty) Ltd., 1992), p. 176.
47 Ibid.
48 Ibid., p. 183.
49 Ibid., p. 194.
50 Ibid.
51 Stalin, *Marxism and the National Question*, p. 12.
52 Forman, in Forman and Odendaal (editors), *A Trumpet from the Housetops: The Selected Writings of Lionel Forman*, p. 194.
53 Ibid., p. 195.
54 Ibid., p. 196.
55 Ibid.

56 Maria van Diepen (editor), *The National Question in South Africa* (London: Zed Press Ltd., 1988), p. 9.
57 Alexander, *Language Policy and National Unity in South Africa/Azania*, p. 8.
58 Ibid., p. 10.
59 Ibid., p. 7.